CW01464139

WYKEHAMIST
WAR SERVICE
ROLL,

manners makyth
man

Sixth and Final Edition,
Oct., 1919.

Winchester:
P. and G. Wells,
Booksellers to the College.

CONTENTS.

PREFACE TO THE FINAL EDITION.

IT is just five years since the Winchester War Service Roll came into existence. To-day the Sixth and Final Edition goes out.

Earlier Editions brought us into touch with the living Army of Wykehamists, helped us to know a little of their whereabouts, and gave some details of their service; but the knowledge was difficult to obtain and of necessity incomplete. Those volumes were read not only with pride and sorrow for the past but with hopes and fears for the future.

This Edition is a simple record of warfare accomplished. It is befitting then that it should bear a stamp of completeness lacking in the earlier volumes, and Mr. Trant Bramston, who has for five years devoted continuous thought and love to the work and won the gratitude of all Wykehamists for this his own "War Service," has added a few details of the careers of the living and the dead which will give the book the value of a complete and permanent record. It is a record which needs no commentary.

THE COLLEGE, WINCHESTER.   M. J. R.
    August, 1919.

P.S.—I have ventured to print as an Appendix four prayers which were in constant use at Winchester from May, 1916, until the close of the War. They will perhaps suggest or recall thoughts which are hardly suitable to a Preface.

EDITOR'S NOTE.

I WISH to apologize for many omissions and inaccuracies which I know must be found in this Final War Service Roll, and also to thank the many Wykehamists who have sent me material information concerning themselves and others.

It has been no easy matter to trace the careers of more than 2000 men during these five eventful years; but I have felt it a privilege to have been allowed to attempt to record the part that Wykehamists have played in the Great War.

It has been my aim to bring the record up to the date of June, 1919, and to include all who were either serving or training as Cadets before that date, and also civilians who received decorations for war services.

Under " Despatches " are included Official " Mentions " for Home Service.

J. TRANT BRAMSTON,

St. Nicholas, Winchester.

ASSISTANT MASTERS.

Besides R. H. FOWLER, H. A. JACKSON, *and* H. E. G. TYNDALE, *whose names are recorded in the body of the Roll, the following also served with His Majesty's Forces :—*

ALTHAM, H. S. ...   ... Capt., K.R.R.C., 5th Bn., 1915.
    Capt.   Brigade-Major, 1916.
                    D.A.A.G., 1917.
                    A.A.G., 1918. Temp. Major, 1918. Temp. Lieut.-Col.,
                        1918.
                    Despatches (3).
                    M.C. D.S.O.

✠ BELL, G. M.   ...   ... Capt., Hampshire Regt., 11th (Pioneer) Bn., 1914.
    Major   Major, 1915.
                    D.S.O.
                    Killed in Action near Ypres, July 31st, 1917.

CARSE, I. A.   ...   ... Pte., Wiltshire Regt., 6th Bn., 1916. Lce.-Corpl.
    Lce.-Corpl.   France, 1917. In Hospital Sept.—Feb., 1918.
                    Att. D.H.Q., 19th Division, May, 1918—Feb., 1919.

DURELL, C. V. ...   ... Lieut., R.G.A., 1916.
    Lieut.   Reconnaissance Officer, IXth Corps, 1917.
                    Orderly Officer, 45th Brigade, 1918.
                    Despatches.

GODDARD, F. W.   ... 2nd Lieut., R.F.A., 1915.
    Lieut.   Lieut., 81st Battery, 5th Brigade, 1916.
                    Retired List, 1917.
                    Wounded.

HICKS, F. M.   ...   ... Hampshire Regt., 11th Bn., 1914.
    Capt.   Temp. Capt., 10th Bn., 1915. Gallipoli, 1915.
                    R.A.F. Observer, Salonica, 1917. Pilot, Egypt and
                      Palestine. 1917--18.
                    Instructor, 44th T.D.S., Oxford, 1918. Flight Com-
                      mander.
                    Wounded.   *Despatches.*
                    Croix de Guerre.

PLATNAUER, M.   ... R.G.A., Coast Defence, 1915.
    Lieut.   94th Siege Battery, France, 1916.
                    Adjt., 45th Brigade, 1917. Acting Capt.
                    Education Officer, XVth Corps, 1918.

PYE, D. R. ... ... Experimental Officer, R.A.F., 1917.

QUIRK, REV. R. ... Chaplain to Forces, Abancourt, 1917.
C.F. IInd and VIIIth Corps, 1918. 2nd Army H.A. School, 1918. 59th Brigade, R.G.A., to Dec., 1918.

ROBERTSON, M. ... Capt., Duke of Wellington's Regt., 9th Bn., 1914.
Major Assistant Staff Capt., 52nd Infantry Brigade.
Assistant Commandant, 17th Divisional School.
Temp. Major, 1918.
Staff Capt., Comm. No. 11 Company O.C.B., Pirbright, 1917–1919.
Despatches (2).
M.C. O.B.E.

SOWERBUTTS, J. A. ... Pte., Hampshire Regt., 3rd Bn., 1916. Lce.-Corpl., 1916
Lieut. 2nd Lieut., 3/20th London Regt., 1917. Att. R.B., 7th Bn.
Lieut., 1917.
Prisoner of War, March, 1918.
Repatriated, Nov., 1918.
Wounded.
M.C.

WILSON, E. R. ... ... 2nd Lieut., R.B., 6th Bn., 1916.
Lieut. Lieut., 1917. Adjt., Depot.
School of Oriental Languages, 1917.
E.E.F., 1918. G.S.I., G.H.Q., 1918. Acting Capt.
G.S.I., Aleppo, 1919.

The following served in Winchester College O.T.C. to the end of the War :—

ARIS, H. ... ... Comm. Contingent, 1908–1918. Retired, Aug., 1918.
Major *Home Services Mention*, 1918.

DAVID, REV. F. P. ... Comm. Cadet Corps, 1901–1908.
Major Served as Capt. till 1913.
Rejoined, 1914. Commanded Contingent from Sept., 1918.

LITTLE, C. W. ... ... Resigned Cadet Corps, 1907.
Capt. Capt., in O.T.C. from 1914.

BATHER, REV. A. G. ... Resigned Cadet Corps, 1903.
Capt. Capt. in O.T.C. from 1914.

DAVIDSON, R. P. ... Joined O.T.C., 1915.
2nd Lieut.

Wykehamist War Service Roll.

ACLAND, E. F. D. ... K 05–07
Lieut.
2nd Lieut. Interpreter. Lahore, I.E.F.
Lieut., R.T.O.
1918, R.A.F. Balloon Officer, K.B.

ACLAND, T. D. ... ... B 65–69
Bt. Lieut.-Col.
Major, R.A.M.C. 2nd London Gen. Hospital.
Bt. Lieut.-Col. Consulting Physician to London
District.

·ACLAND, W. R. D. ... K 08–12
Capt.
R.N.A.S., Flight Sub-Lieut.
1918, Capt., R.A.F., Coast Patrol.
Despatches.

✠ ACWORTH, D. H. ... D 99–03
Major
(2nd Lieut., I.A., 1906.)
1914, Capt., 55th Coke's Rifles, F.F.
1915, G.S.O.₃. 1916, Staff Capt. 1917, Brigade-
Major.
1918, Major, G.S.O.₂, Palestine H.Q.
Wounded (2). *Despatches* (3).
M.C.
Died at Port Saïd, of pneumonia, Feb. 6th, 1919.

✠ ACWORTH, J. A. ... D 11–16
2nd Lieut.
1917, 2nd Lieut., Worcester Regt., 7th Bn.
Killed in action Oct. 13th, 1917, at *Dozinghem,*
near *Ypres.*

✠ ADAM, A. I. ... COLL. 07–12
Capt.
Lieut., Cambridgeshire Regt., 1st Bn.
Capt., 1916.
Killed Sept. 16th, 1916, *near Thiepval.*

ADAM, N. K. ... COLL. 05–10
Technical Assistant, R.N. Airship Factory,
Farnborough.

ADAMS, A. E. ... ... A 65–69
Major
Major, 1st Cornwall Vol. Regt.

ADAMS, C. C. ... ... D 04–09
Capt.
Lieut., R.E., 1914. 1st Signal Coy.
Capt., 1918. Instructor, R.M. Coll., Canada.
Despatches (2).
M.C.

1

ADAMS, G. COODE ... I 13–17
2nd Lieut.   2nd Lieut., R.G.A.

ADAMS, H. R. ...   ... I 94–96   (R.G.A., 1900. S. African War. Capt., 1911.)
Major   Major, R.G.A., 1914.
                                    Acting Lieut.-Col., 1918.
                                    Despatches (2).
                                    D.S.O.

✠ ADEANE, H. R. A.   ... D 95–00   (Coldstream Guards, 1902. Lieut., 1905.)
Capt.   Capt., Coldstream Guards, 1st Bn.
                                    Killed Nov. 2nd, 1914, *Veldhoeck, near Ypres.*

AGAR, Hon. F. W. A. E.   C 88–90
                                    Late Remount Officer, Sussex.

AINGER, E.   ...   ... E 07–11
Lieut.   Lieut., 3rd (King's Own) Hussars, 1914.
                                    Wounded.

AINSLIE, H. S.   COLL. 83–83   (Northumberland Fusiliers, 1890. Capt., 1896.
Lieut.-Col.   Lieut.-Col., 1912.)
                                    Temp. Brigadier-General, 1915.
                                    Comm. Worcestershire Regt., Res. Bn., 1916.
                                    Travelling Military Board, 1918.
                                    Wounded.   *Despatches.*
                                    C.M.G.
                                    Retired on half-pay, 1919.

AKENHEAD, F. ...   ... G 94–00   (New Coll., Oxford. Solicitor.)
Capt.   Lieut., Manchester Regt., 5th Bn.
                                    Capt., 1918.

ALBAN, C. F. S.   COLL. 67–72   (I.A. Lieut., 1875. Major, 1895. Retired 1891.)
Major   Recruiting Officer.

✠ ALDERSON, R. L.   ... F 94–97
Major   1914, Armoured Cars.
                                    R.N.A.S.
                                    Major, R.A.F.
                                    Died July 18th, 1918, *R.N. Hospital, Hull.*

ALDRIDGE, H. H.   ... G 83–88   (New Coll., Oxford. Trooper, Ceylon Mtd.
Capt.   Inf., 1900. Sergt., S. African War.
                                        S. African Constabulary, 1901. 2nd Lieut.,
                                        Sussex Yeomanry, 1906.)
                                    1914, Lieut., 1st Life Guards.
                                    1915, Capt., Welsh Guards. A.D.C. Staff Capt.
                                    Despatches

ALEXANDER, J. F., M.D.   I 89–95   (Trin. Coll., Camb. St. Bartholomew's Hospital.)
Lieut.   Lieut., R.A.M.C. Relinquished Commission.

2

ALFORD, V. ... COLL. 13–17
2nd Lieut.   2nd Lieut., R.G.A., 1918.

✠ ALLAN, R. G. ... COLL. 10–15
2nd Lieut.   2nd Lieut., K.O.S.B., 1916.
                              Killed April 9th, 1917, *Vimy Ridge.*

ALLEN, A. J. WHITACRE,   C 71–74   (3rd Regt., 1876. Zulu War. Soudan. Capt.,
C.B.   E. Kent Regt. Major, 1906. Tirah Expedi-
     Brig.-General   tion, A.A.G., India. Bt. Col.)
                              Brig.-General, 1914. 24th Inf. Brigade.
                              Resigned Commission.

ALLGOOD, G. H. ... D 06–09
     Capt.   Capt., Northumberland Fusiliers, 3rd Bn.
                              Wounded. *Despatches.*

✠ ALLINGHAM, H. G. ... D 01–03
                              Union Defence, S. Africa.
                              Died on active service March 28th, 1917.

✠ ALLPORT, T. C. ... ... C 96–00
     Capt.   Capt., York and Lancaster Regt., 5th Bn.
                              Killed August 1st, 1915, *Talana Farm, Boesinghe*

ALTHAM, Sir E. A., C.M.G., C 68–74   (Ch. Ch., Oxf. Lieut., Royal Scots, 1876. Staff
K.C.B.   Coll., 1889. S. Africa, 96–00. Lieut.-Col.,
     Lieut.-General   1900. Col., 1903. Brig.-General, H.Q.,
                                       S. Africa, 1906. Major-General, 1910.)
                              Lieut.-General, 1917. Inspector-General, Lines
                                   of Communication, M.E.F., 1915.
                              Q.M.G., India. Colonel, Royal Scots.
                              K.C.B. Grand Cordon, White Eagle, Serbia.
                                   Japanese Order of the Sacred Treasure.
                              Despatches (5).

ANDERSON, A. R. ... A 95–99   (To Burmah, 1903.)
     Lieut.   Lieut., 4th Rajputs, I.A. Served in Mesopo-
                                   tamia. Invalided, 1917.

ANDERSON, C. F. ... F 86–90   (2nd Lieut., R.E., 1892. Capt., 1903. Dongola
     Lieut.-Col.   Expedition.)
                              Lieut.-Col., R.E. Assistant Director, R.T.
                              Bt. Lieut.-Col.

ANDERSON, R. C. ... A 96–02   (Clare Coll., Camb. B.A., 1905.)
     Lieut.   Lieut., R.N.V.R., Motor Boat Reserves.

3

ANDERSON, R. D. ... A 92–95   (S. African Horse. 2nd Lieut., Imperial Yeo-
Capt.   manry. 1903, Civil Service, Uganda.)
                             Capt. (Act. Major), Middlesex Regt. Brigade
                                 Signalling Officer, Lake Force, German
                                 E. Africa.
                         Despatches.
                         D.S.O., O.B.E.

ANDERSON, R. J. P., D.S.O. C 86–90   (11th Hussars, 1893. S. African War. Capt.,
Lieut.-Col.   1902. India, N.W. Frontier. Uganda.)
                         Major, Instructor Cavalry School, 1909–10.
                         1917, Lieut.-Col., 11th Hussars
                         Wounded
                         C.M.G.

ANSON, E. E. ... ... A 11–15   (2nd Lieut., D. of Lancaster's Yeomanry.)
Lieut   Lieut., I.A.

ANSON, G. W. ... A 07–11
Major   Capt., Loyal N. Lancashire Regt., 7th Bn.
                         Major, 1917.
                         Wounded.
                         M.C.

ANTROBUS, M. E. COLL. 08–14
Capt.   Lieut., K.R.R.C., 6th, att. 4th Bn.
                         Capt., 1918.
                         Wounded (2).

ANTROBUS, P. R. COLL. 11–16
Lieut.   2nd Lieut., R.E. Brigade Signalling Officer,
                         101st Inf. Brigade.
                         Lieut., 1919.

ARCHDALE, A. Q. ... F 99–04
Capt.   Capt., R.H.A. Major, 1917.
                         Wounded.
                         Despatches.

ARCHER, H. G. F. ... E 93–97   (Ch. Ch., Oxford. Egyptian C.S.)
                           Divisional Assistant, Cairo City Police.

ARCHER, R. A. ... ... B 07–11   (Capt., R.F.A.)
Capt.   Temp. Major, R.A.F., to April, 1918.
                         Employed under Air Ministry.
                         Despatches.
                         M.C.

ARDEN, G. J. D. ... A 12–17
                         Cpl., Tank Corps, Equipment Branch.

4

ARKLE, B. ... ... A 05–09
    Capt.
        Capt. and Adjt., Liverpool Regt. 10th
          Scottish Bn.
        G.S.O.$_3$. Brigade-Major, 1918.
        Despatches (2).
        M.C.

ARKWRIGHT, C. H. ... I 04–08
    Lieut.
        Trooper, Hampshire Carabiniers.
        2nd Lieut., Acting Capt., R.F.A., Derby
          Battery, 232nd Brigade.
        Wounded (2).

ARKWRIGHT, H. F. ... I 96–00
    2nd Lieut.
        N.Z. Force, Wellington Regt., 2nd Bn.

ARKWRIGHT, R. H. P. ... I 02–06
    Lieut.
        (Lieut., K.A.R., late R. Irish Fusiliers.)
        Retired, ill health, Jan., 1919.

ARMITAGE, C. L. B 84–86
    Brevet Major
        (2nd Lieut., Devon Artillery, 1888. The King's
          Liverpool Regt., 1892. Capt., 1900.)
        Capt., Worcestershire Regt., 6th Bn., 1914.
        Brevet Major, 1915.
        Wounded. *Despatches.*
        D.S.O.

ARMITAGE, W. T. ... A 86–91
    Lieut.-Col.
        (Capt., R.A., 1900. Dongola Expedition.)
        Major, R.G.A., 1914. Lieut.-Col., 1917.

ARMSTRONG, C. W. ... D 12–17
    2nd Lieut.
        2nd Lieut., R.F.A., 1918.

ARMSTRONG, J. R. B. ... G 07–11
    Capt.
        2nd Lieut., 8th Hussars.
        Lieut., 1918.
        Att. Tank Corps, 1918. Capt. and Adjt.

ARTHUR, E. J. ... ... H 86–91
    Major
        (2nd Lieut., Lancs. Fusiliers, 1893. 7th Bom-
          bay Lancers, 1895. Capt., 1902.)
        Major, 46th Punjabis, I.A. Retired.

✠ ARTHUR, H. B. C. ... H 93–96
    Major
        (2nd Lieut., R.A., 1900. Lieut., 1903.)
        Major and Adjt., R.A., 5th Brigade, I.E.F.
        Wounded. *Despatches* (2).
        Killed August 10th, 1916, *near Ovillers-la-*
          Boiselle.

ASHBY, T. ... ... C 87–93
    Dr.
        (Ch. Ch., Oxford. D. Litt., 1905. Director,
          British Sch. at Rome.)
        First British Red Cross Ambulance for Italy.

✠ ASHER, R. S. ... ... F 11–16
    2nd Lieut.
                2nd Lieut., R.A.F.
                Killed Sept. 21st, 1917, *at Vitry en Artois.*

ASHTON, A. L. B. ... C 11–16
    Lieut.
                2nd Lieut., R.G.A.
                Lieut., 1918.

ASHTON, G. ... ... E 10–15
    Lieut.
                2nd Lieut., R.F.A.
                Lieut., 1917. Instructor, Army Signal School.
                Wounded.
                M.C.

ASHTON, H. ... ... E 11–16
    Lieut.
                2nd Lieut., R.F.A., 1917. Lieut., 1918.
                Intelligence Officer, H.Q., 18th Division.
                Staff Lieut., 1919.
                M.C.

ASHTON, PERCY ... ... E 08–13
    Capt.
                D.C.L.I., 1914. Lieut., 1915.
                Capt., 8th Bn., 1918.
                Wounded.   *Despatches.*
                M.C.

ASHTON, PETER ... B 02–07
    Capt.
                Capt., Herefordshire Regt., 1st Bn.
                Brigade-Major till Dec., 1918.
                Despatches (4).
                M.C.

ASHTON, S. E. ... ... C 01–06
    Capt.
                Capt., Cheshire Yeomanry.
                Posted to 10th Shropshire L.I.

ASHWELL, A. L. ... I 99–04
    Capt.
                Capt., Notts and Derby Regt., 1916.
                Temp. Lieut.-Col.
                Comm. Sch. of Instruction, Officer Cadets.
                Wounded (3).
                D.S.O.

ASQUITH, A. M. ... ... H 96–02
    Brig.-General
                (New Coll., Oxford. Soudan Civil Service.)
                Sub-Lieut., R.N.V.R., 1914, Hood Bn.
                Lieut.-Commander, 1915.
                Commander, 1916.
                Brig.-General, 1917
                Controller of Trench Warfare Dept. Min.
                    Munitions, April, 1918.
                Wounded (4).   *Despatches* (3).
                D.S.O. and 2 Bars.

6

ASQUITH, C. ... COLL. 03–09 (Ball. Coll., Oxford. Fellow, Magd. Coll.)
Capt. Capt., Q. Westminster Rifles.
Sec. for duty, Ministry of Munitions.

ASQUITH, H. ... ... H 94–00 (Ball. Coll., Oxford. Barrister.)
Lieut. 2nd Lieut., R.M.A., 1915.
Lieut., R.A.
Wounded (2).

✠ ASQUITH, R. ... COLL. 92–97 (Ball. Coll., Oxford. Fellow, All Souls.)
Lieut. 2nd Lieut., Q. Westminster Rifles.
Lieut., Grenadier Guards.
Killed Sept. 15th, 1916, *Trones Wood.*
Despatches.

✠ ATKIN, R. W. ... ... K 10–15
Lieut. 2nd Lieut., R.F.A., 1916.
Lieut., 1917.
Killed August 14th, 1917, *Pilkem Ridge, near Ypres.*

✠ AUCHINLECK, D. G. H.... A 91–95 (Trin. Coll., Oxford. 2nd Lieut., R. Inniskilling
Capt. Fusiliers. S. African War. Capt., 1904.)
Capt., R. Inniskilling Fusiliers.
Killed Oct. 21st, 1914, *Le Gheer, near Ploegstraete.*

AUDLAND, E. G. ... H 10–14
Lieut. ... 2nd Lieut., R.A., 1915.
Lieut., 1917.
(Acting Capt., 1918.)
Despatches.
M.C.

✠ AVERY, Sir W. E. T., Bart. C 03–08 (Univ. Coll., Oxford.)
Major Capt., temp. Major, R.A.S.C.
Supply Column, Guards' Division.
Died on active service, of influenza at No. 8 Gen. Hospital, Rouen, Nov. 20th, 1918.
Despatches.
M.C.

✠ AWDRY, C. S. ... ... C 90–96 (New Coll., Oxford. Served with S. African Imp.
Major Yeomanry. Capt., R. Wilts Yeomanry, 1903.)
Major, late Acting Lieut.-Col., 1914.
Posted to Wiltshire Regt., 1918.
Missing, presumed *killed,* March 25th, 1918.
Despatches.
D.S.O.

7

AWDRY, E. P. ... ... B 06–09
    Lieut.   Lieut., R. Wiltshire Yeomanry, and Adjt.
                                     Lieut., 10th Hussars.
                                     M.C.

AWDRY, J. W. ... ... E 88–92
                                     R. Fusiliers, 23rd Bn.
                                     Sergeant, 1918.

AWDRY, R. W. ... ... C 94–00   (New Coll., Oxford.)
    Capt.   Capt., R. Wiltshire Yeomanry.
                                     Posted to Wiltshire Regt., 1918.
                                     M.G.C. Temp. Major. Restored to establish-
                                         ment 1918.

AYLMER, G.   ...   ... E 00–03   (Major, K.R.R.C., 12th Bn., to Indian Army.)
                                     M.C.

BACKUS, S. E. ... ... C 04–08
    Lieut.   2nd Lieut., R.F.A.
                                     R.A.F., Lieut., K.B.

BACON, A. F. L.   ... B 92–96   (Oriel Coll., Oxford. Barrister.)
    Capt.   Lieut., Hampshire Regt., 4th Bn.
                                     Acting Capt., 1918.
                                     Despatches.

BACON, F. T.   ...   ... E 80–84   (R.M. Coll. 2nd Lieut., N. Staffs. Regt., 1887.
    Major   11th Hussars. Capt., 1893. Tirah Expedi-
                                         tion, S. African War. Retired 1902.)
                                     Capt., 11th Hussars, 1914. R.T.O. Assistant
                                         Director, R.T.
                                     Temp. Lieut.-Col.

BAILEY, J. M. ... ... K 13–17   Cadet, R.M. Coll.

BAILWARD, A. N.   ... G 08–13
    2nd Lieut.   2nd Lieut., N. Somerset Yeomanry.
                                     Wounded.
                                     Resigned Commission, 1916.

BAINES, C. S.   ...   ... C 04–08 (2nd Lieut., Oxford and Bucks L.I., 1910.)
    Acting Lieut.-Col.   Lieut., Oxford and Bucks L.I., 1915. Capt.,
                                         1916. Temp. Major, 1917.
                                     Staff Capt., Ministry of Munitions.
                                     Acting Lieut.-Col., 7th Bn. Liverpool Regt.,
                                         1917.
                                     Wounded (2).   *Despatches* (3).
                                     D.S.O. and Bar.

8

BAINES, E. R. ... ... D 12–18 (Cadet, O.C.B., Oxford.)
2nd Lieut. R.B., 1919.

✠ BAINES, F. A. F. COLL. 09–14
2nd Lieut. 2nd Lieut., K.R.R.C., 4th Bn.
Killed May 25th, 1915, *Bellewarde Wood, near Ypres.*

BAINES, J. S. ... COLL. 08–12
Capt. 2nd Lieut., R.E., 1914. Lieut. and Adjt., 1917.
Capt., Nov., 1917.
Wounded.

BAIRD, R. D. ... ... H 07–12
Capt. R.B., 1st Bn., Lieut., 1915.
Capt., 1917. A.D.C., Palestine, 1915–17,
Gen. Chetwode.
Att. London Regt., 2/24th Bn., Beersheba.
Returned to A.D.C., April, 1918.
Wounded (3).
M.C

BAIRD, W. A. ... ... A 92–96 (Lieut., Lothian and Border Horse.)
Major Major, Lothian and Border Horse, 1917

✠ BAKER, B. H. ... ... B 11–15
2nd Lieut. 2nd Lieut., R.B., 13th Bn., 1916.
Lieut., 1917.
Wounded.
Killed May 22nd, 1918, *near Mesnil Bouche.*

BAKER, E. C. A. ... G 00–05 (Oriel Coll., Oxford. Avon Rubber Works.)
Lieut. 2nd Lieut., R.B., 7th Bn.
Lieut., 1918.
Wounded.

BAKER, F. S. A. ... H 98–03 (Oriel Coll., Oxford. Barrister.)
Major Capt., Seaforth Highlanders.
Att. R.A.F., Major, S.O.$_2$.
Private Secretary, Chief of Staff, Air Ministry.
Wounded (2). *Despatches.*

BAKER, Rt. Hon. H. T. COLL. 90–96
Lieut.-Col. Q.M.G.'s Staff.
Inspector of Q.M. Services.
Despatches (2).

✠ BAKER, O. CLINTON ... C 82–87 (R. Irish Rifles, Capt., 1900. S. African War.)
Lieut.-Col. Lieut.-Col., R. Irish Rifles, 1st Bn.
Wounded.
Killed May 9th, 1915, *Fromelles.*

9

BAKER, Sir R. L., Bart. ... H 92–98 (Magd. Coll., Oxford.)
Lieut.-Col.   Lieut.-Col., Dorset Yeomanry.
Att. Midland Mounted Brigade Signal Troop.
Lieut.-Col., Tank Corps. T.F.R.
Wounded (2).   *Despatches.*
D.S.O. and Bar.

BALD, P. R. ... ... G 96–99 (R.E., 1900. Capt., 1910.)
Major   Major, late Acting Lieut.-Col., R.E., H.Q. Staff.
Despatches (4).
D.S.O., Chevalier Légion d'Honneur.

✠ BALDOCK, T. A. ... A 10–14
Capt.   Lieut., Acting Capt., R.B., 8th Bn.
Died of wounds, Dec. 3rd, 1917, *Ypres.*

✠ BALDWIN, H. R. ... C 11–15
Lieut.   Lieut., Irish Guards.
Killed August 27th, 1918, *near Ecoust.*

✠ BALFOUR, I. B. ... F 03–08
Lieut.   Lieut., Royal Scots, 14th Bn.
Killed June 28th, 1915, *Dardanelles.*

BAMPFYLDE, Hon.   G 01–06
H. de B. W.
Major   Lieut., temp. Major, K.A.R., E. African Bn.
Relinquished Commission, ill health, Jan.,
1919.

BANKIER, A. A. ... F 11–16
2nd Lieut.   2nd Lieut., R.F.A.
Orderly Officer, 56th Brigade.
Lieut., 1918.

BANKIER, A. M. ... F 08–12
Capt.   Arg. and Suth. Highlanders, 2nd Lieut., 1914.
Temp. Capt., late Adjt., 1917.
G.S.O.$_3$. Brigade-Major, 1918.
Despatches (2).
M.C., Croix de Guerre, D.S.O.

BANISTER, C. G.... ... I 03–08
Lieut.   Lieut., R.E., employed Shropshire L.I., 1915.
Att. to M.G.C.
R.A.F. Experimental Officer, 1917.

✠ BANNER, W. HARMOOD ... B 96–01
                     Capt., S.W. Borderers, 3rd, att. 1st Bn.
Killed August 29th, 1915, *near Cambrin.*

BARCHARD, A. E. ... G 82–84 (W. India Regt.)
Lieut.-Col.   Lieut.-Col. W. India Regt.
Relinquished Commission, 1917.

BARDSLEY, W. L. F. ... H 13–17
2nd Lieut.   2nd Lieut., Grenadier Guards, 1918.

BARKER, A. E. V. ... K 11–16
2nd Lieut.   2nd Lieut., 17th Lancers.
                              A.D.C.

BARKER, P. O. ... ... H 92–95
                              Capt., R. Bucks Hussars.
                              Wounded.   Despatches.

✠ BARKER, R. V. ... COLL. 93–99   (R.W. Fusiliers, 1st Bn., 1901. S. African War.)
Capt.   Capt., R. Welsh Fusiliers, 1st Bn.
                              Killed Oct. 30th, 1914, *Ypres.*

✠ BARKWORTH, K. A.   E 99–02
WILSON   Capt., E. Yorkshire Regt.
Capt.   *Killed* Oct. 25th, 1917, *between Ypres and
                                   Poperinghe.*
                              M.C.

BARLOW, E. M.   COLL. 05–10
Major   Lieut., R. Fusiliers, 9th Bn.
                              Temp. Major, Gen. List. Assistant Instructor,
                                   British Military Mission.
                              Wounded.   Despatches.

✠ BARNARD, G. R. ... A 11–15
Lieut.   Lieut., Cape Corps.
                              Served through campaign, German E. Africa.
                              Wounded.
                              *Died of malaria in Palestine, on march from
                                   Beit Nuba,* July 22nd, 1918.

BARNARD, W. L. ... A 09–14
Capt.   Oxford and Bucks L.I., 1914.
                              Lieut., 1915. Acting Capt., 1917.
                              Half-pay; ill health owing to wounds, Jan.,
                                   1919.
                              Wounded (2).

BARNES, E. C. ... ... H 11–16
Lieut.   2nd Lieut., R.G.A. 1/2nd Lancs. Heavy
                                   Battery.
                              Lieut., 1918.
                              Wounded.

BARNES, W. C. ... ... G 90–94   (Ch. Ch., Oxford.)
Lieut.   Acting Capt., 1st Devon Yeomanry.
                              Serving with Devonshire Regt.
                              Relinquished Commission, ill health, Jan., 1919.

BARNETT, E. St. J. ... c 91–95
    Lieut.   Lieut. (late Acting Capt.), Yorkshire Dragoons.
                                       Remount Service.

BARNETT, G. A. ... g 94–99
    Capt.   (Magd. Coll., Oxford.)
                                         Capt., Hertfordshire Yeomanry.
                                       A.D.C., A.P.M., Staff Capt., D.A.A.G.
                                       M.B.E.

BARNETT, R. F. ... g 96–01
    Capt.   Capt., Hertfordshire Yeomanry.
                                       Despatches.

✠ BARNETT, R. W. ... d 05–11
    Major   2nd Lieut., K.R.R.C., 11th Bn.
                                       Lieut., 1915.
                                       Capt., 1917. G.S.O.$_3$. Brigade-Major, 189th
                                           Infantry Brigade.
                                         1918, G.S.O.$_2$. Temp. Major.
                                         Wounded.   *Despatches.*
                                         M.C. and Bar.
                                       Killed August 12th, 1918, *near Hooge.*

BARRATT, A. W. ... i 01–05
    Major   Capt., The King's Shropshire L.I.
                                         Assistant Military Attaché, Jassy.
                                       G.S.O.$_2$, 1918. Temp. Major.

BARRETT, R. C. ... ... a 08–13
    Capt.   1915, 2nd Lieut., Duke of Wellington's; West
                                         Riding Regt.
                                       1917, Lieut., A.D.C.
                                       1918, Capt.

BARRY, B. J. WOLFE ... d 90–95
    Lieut.-Col.   (New Coll., Oxford. Barrister.)
                                       1915, 2nd Lieut., R.G.A.
                                       1917, Capt. Assistant Equipment Officer,
                                       R.A.F. Staff Capt.
                                       1918, temp. Lieut.-Col., R.A.F., S.O.$_1$.
                                       To unemployed list, Feb., 1919.
                                       Wounded.   *Despatches.*
                                       O.B.E.

BARRY, E. G. WOLFE ... d 99–04
    Lieut.   (Trin. Coll., Camb.)
                                         Lieut., R.N.V.R.
                                       Wounded.

BARRY, K. A. WOLFE   D 92–97   (Trin. Coll., Camb.   Civil Engineer.)
    Lieut.   2nd Lieut., R.G.A.
                                  Employed Ministry of Munitions.
                                  Temp. Capt., Oct., 1918—1919.
                                  Despatches (2).
                                  C.B.E.

✠ BARTHROPP, S. A. N. S.   E 05–09
    2nd Lieut.   2nd Lieut., R. Sussex Regt., 3rd Bn.
                                  Killed Jan. 29th, 1915, *Cuinchy.*

BARTON, P. G.   ...   D 05–08   (1911, Royal Fusiliers, 1st Bn.)
    Capt.   1915, Capt. R. Fusiliers, 1st Bn.
                                  M.G.C., Heavy, Feb.—June, 1917.
                                  Wounded.   Despatches.
                                  M.C.

BARTTELOT, G. F.   ...   H 78–81   (Lieut., R. Welsh Fusiliers.   Burmese Expedi-
    Major   tion.   S. African War.   Retired 1911.)
                                  Major, R.W. Fusiliers.
                                  London Infantry, Record Office.
                                  Despatches.

✠ BATEMAN, L. N. JONES   E 89–91   (2nd Lieut., Norfolk Regt., 1896.   S. African
    Lieut.-Col.   War.)
                                  Lieut.-Col., Norfolk Regt.
                                  Att. Dorset Regt., Brigade-Major.
                                  Died at Simla July 26th, 1917.
                                  Despatches.
                                  C.M.G.

BATES, A. G.   ...   ...   E 04–05   (R.A., 1911.)
    Capt.   1916, Capt. and Adjt., R.F.A., 127th Howitzer
                                      Brigade.
                                  1918, Capt.   Instructor in Gunnery, R.A. Sch.
                                      of Instruction.
                                  Wounded.   Despatches (2).
                                  M.C. and Bar, D.S.O.

BATES, A. S.   B 92–98   (London Rifle Vol. Brigade, 1900.)
    Lieut.-Col.   Major, London R.B., 1916.
                                  Lieut.-Col., 1917.   Comm. Lancs. Fusiliers,
                                      5th Bn.
                                  Despatches (4).
                                  D.S.O., Croix de Guerre.

BATES, C. R.   ...   ...   E 95–98   (R.A., 1900.)
    Major   Major, R.A., 1915.   Brigade-Major.
                                  Wounded.   Despatches (2).
                                  M.C., D.S.O.
                                  Relinquished Commission, ill health, 1919.

13

BATES, D. H. ... ... E 99–04
    Capt.

Capt., Duke of Lancaster's Yeomanry.
Despatches.
M.C.

BATES, F. A. ... ... E 97–03
    Major

Lieut., Denbighshire Yeomanry. A.D.C.
R.A.F., Capt., 1917. Major, 1918.
Wounded.   *Despatches* (2).
M.C., A.F.C.

BATES, Sir P. E. ... E 92–96

Director, Commercial Branch, Transport De-
    partment, Admiralty.

✠ BATES, S. G. ... ... E 98–01
    Capt.

      (7th Hussars, 1903.)
Capt., 7th Hussars.
Adjt., N. Somerset Yeomanry.
Wounded
Killed May 13th, 1915, *2nd Battle of Ypres.*

BATHER, E. J. ... ... G 02–07
    Capt.

(R.A., 1910.)
1916, Capt., R.F.A., 124th Brigade.
Acting Major, 1917.
Despatches (3).
D.S.O.

BATTCOCK, G. A. ... C 96–01
    Major

(Trin. Coll., Oxford.)
1915, Capt., R. Berkshire Regt., 4th Bn.
1916, Major.
(Employed N. Lancs. Regt., 1st Bn.)
Despatches.

BATTEN, H. C. C. ... F 99–00
    Major

(Lieut., Dorset Regt., 1903.)
Major, Dorset Regt. A.D.C.
(Comm. Squadron, R.A.F., Cadet Wing.)
D.A.A.G.
Wounded.   *Despatches* (5).
D.S.O., C.B.E.

BATTEN, J. B. ... ... F 97–99
    Lieut.-Col.

(R. Fusiliers, 1901. Capt., 1910. Retired, 1912.)
Capt., R. Fusiliers, 5th Bn.
Acting Lieut.-Col., Manchester Regt., 24th Bn.
Major, 1918. Comm. Squadron R.A.F., O.T.
    Wing.
Lieut.-Col., 1919.
Despatches.
D.S.O.

14

✠ BATTEN, J. de H.   COLL. 03–08
   CHISHOLM
    Major

                   Capt., R.F.A. Acting Major.
                   Wounded (2).
                   Killed August 6th, 1917 *near Wytschaete.*

BATTYE, J. C. A.   ... I 13–17

                   2nd Lieut., R.F.A., 1919.

BAUMANN, N. E. F.   ... H 13–18 Cadet, R.F.A.

✠ BAUMER, D. E. L. V. COLL. 10–15
    Lieut.

                   Lieut., R.F.A., T.M.B., 9th Division.
                   Wounded.
                   Killed Oct. 21st, 1917, *near Langemarck, Paschen-*
                       daele Offensive.

✠ BAYFIELD, H. L.   ... E 04–07
    Lieut.

                   Lieut., Leicestershire Regt., 1st Bn.
                   Despatches.
                   Killed March 12th, 1915, *Neuve Chapelle.*

BAYLEY, C. D. ...   ... G 09–13
    Lieut.

                   2nd Lieut., R.F.A., 1914.
                   Lieut., 1915.
                   Acting Capt., 1917.

BAYLEY, W. E. ...   ... I 82–87
    Lieut.

                   (India.)
                   R. Defence Corps, 1915–1916.
                   Foreign Office.

BAYNES E. R. ...   ... H 03–04
    Lieut.

                   Temp. Lieut., R.A.S.C.

BEADON, L. R. ...   ... B 89–93
    Lieut.-Col.

                   (W.I. Regt., 1896. Capt., 1900. Capt., A.S.C.,
                       1902.)
                   Lieut.-Col., R.A.S.C. A.Q.M.G.
                   Despatches (3).
                   D.S.O., Chevalier Légion d'Honneur, C.M.G.

BEART, C. W. ...   ... K 07–10
    Capt.

                   Durham L.I., 1914. Lieut., 1915.
                   Capt., Temp. Major, 1917. A.D.C., G.S.O.$_3$,
                       Brigade-Major.
                   Wounded.   *Despatches* (2).
                   M.C. Croce di Guerra.

BEART, R. B. ...   ... K 05–11
    Lieut.

                   Lieut., 18th Hussars.

BEATTY, C. W. ...   ... A 12–16
    Lieut.

                   2nd Lieut., R.A.F.
                   Lieut. (A.), 1918.

BEAUMONT, Sir G. A. H.,   C 95–97   (2nd Lieut., K.R.R.C., 1901.   S. African War.
Bart.   Lieut., 1904.)
    Major   Capt., K.R.R.C., 1912.
                             (Employed with 1st Garrison Bn. Oxford and
                                Bucks L.I.
                             Major, 1916.   Staff Capt.   Brigade-Major.
                             Wounded.
                             Retired on half-pay, ill health.

BEAUMONT, J. W. F.   ...   D 90–96   (Pembroke College Oxford.   Barrister.)
    Lieut.   2nd Lieut., R.G.A.
                             Lieut., 1918.

✠ BEAUSIRE, H. A. W.   ...   K 06–10
    2nd Lieut.   ...   2nd Lieut., R. Fusiliers.
                             Killed March 16th, 1915, *Chapelle d'Armentières.*

BEBB, B. J. M. ...   COLL. 05–10
    Brevet Major   2nd Lieut., R.E., 1914.   Lieut., 1915.   Capt.,
                                1916.
                             H.Q., 14th Corps Signal Coy.
                             G.S.O.$_3$, Imperial Gen. Staff Dept.
                             G.S.O.$_2$, War Office.
                             Wounded.   *Despatches* (2).

BECK, J. F. A. ...   ...   E 95–98   (Solicitor.)
    2nd Lieut.   2nd Lieut., R.A.S.C., 1918.

BECK, R. C.   ...'   ...   G 97–99   (2nd Lieut., Irish Guards.   Lieut., 1903.)
    Major   ...   Capt., Indian Army, S. and T. Corps.
                             Major, 1917.

BECKER, W. T. L.   ...   C 05–06
    Major   Capt., York and Lancaster Regt., 7th Bn.
                             Major, 1917.

BEDFORD, W. J. R.   ...   A 11–15
    Lieut.   Lieut., R.H.A., 1918, 10th Reserve Brigade.

BEEVOR, M.   ...   COLL. 12–18
                             Cadet, R.E.

✠ BEHRENS, R. P.   ...   E 07–11
    Lieut.   Lieut., S.W. Borderers.
                             Died Sept. 25th, 1915, *of wounds received during
                             landing at Gallipoli, near Eski Hissarlik
                             Point.*

BEIGHTON, T. P. D.   ...   A 10–16
    Lieut.   2nd Lieut., R.G.A.
                             Lieut., 1918.
                             Wounded.

✠ BELCHER, A. C. S.   ... H 03–07
    Capt.   Wiltshire Regt., Capt. and Adjt., 5th Bn.
                                      Killed August 13th, 1915, *Chunuk Bair.*
                                      Despatches.

BELCHER, E. B.   ... H 01–06
                                        Capt., Mysore Lancers, 5th Cavalry I.A.
                                        Special Service Officer.
                                        Served in Palestine. I.A.R.O.
                                        Despatches.
                                        M.C.

✠ BELCHER, H. G.   ... H 06–11   (To Canada.)
    Lieut.   Lieut., Wiltshire Regt, 5th Bn.
                                        Killed August 7th, 1915, *Dardanelles.*

BELL, A. H. M.   ... F 06–09   (Lieut., 3rd Hussars, 1911.)
    Capt.   Capt., 1917. Gen. Reserve of Officers.
                                        M.C.

BELL, E.   ...   ... A 98–03   (Univ. Coll. Oxford.)
    Capt.   Lieut., Surrey Yeomanry.
                                        Serving with Divisional Cavalry, 27th Division.
                                        Capt., 1915.
                                        Despatches.
                                        M.C.

BELL, F. A.   ...   ... H 02–06
    Capt.   Capt., Sherwood Rangers, Notts Yeomanry.

BELL, H. J.   ...   ... A 99–04
    Capt.   Lieut., Surrey Yeomanry.
                                        Serving with Divisional Cavalry, 27th Division.
                                        Capt., 1915.
                                        Despatches.
                                        M.C.

✠ BELL, R. de H. M.   ... F 10–14
    Capt.   Acting Capt., K.R.R.C., 10th Bn.
                                        Killed Sept. 3rd, 1916, *Guillemont.*
                                        Despatches.

✠ BELL, S. P.   ...   ... B 99–03   (R.A., 1905.)
    Capt.   Capt., R.F.A., 20th Battery.
                                        Wounded.
                                        Killed near Vermelles, Sept. 26th–27th, 1915.

✠ BENEDICT, A. E. W. J. S. C 94–99
    Lieut.   Lieut., R. Bucks Hussars.
                                        Died in England, Dec. 16th, 1915.

✠ BENNETT, A. LEIGH- ... c 99–02   (Govt. Telegraph Dept., India.)
    Capt.   Capt., Coldstream Guards, 2nd Bn.
                                      Wounded (2).   *Despatches.*
                                      Killed Oct. 3rd, 1915, *near Vermelles.*
                                      M.C.   D.S.O.

BENNETT, C. A.   ... E 90–94   (Barrister.)
    2nd Lieut.   Pte., Inns of Court, O.T.C.
                                      2nd Lieut., R.G.A., Siege Artillery.

BENNETT, E. W.   ... B 79–84   (New Coll., Oxford. Solicitor.)
    Capt.   Capt., R. Sussex Regt., T.F.R.

BENNETT, H. W. LEIGH- E 94–99   (New Coll., Oxford.)
    Lieut.   Lieut., Coldstream Guards, 4th Bn.

BENNETT, J. D.   ... H 14–17
    2nd Lieut.   2nd Lieut., Grenadier Guards, 1918.

BENSON, C. H. G.   ... I 97–98   (R.N.)
    Commander   Lieut.-Commander, H.M.S. *Essex.*
                                        Commander, 1918.
                                        D.S.O. and Bar.

✠ BENSON, E. W.   ... A 01–06   (2nd Lieut., Jersey Militia, 1906.)
    Lieut.-Col.   K.R.R.C., Capt., 1915.
                                        Temp. Lieut.-Col., 9th Bn., 1916.
                                        Wounded.   *Despatches.*
                                        Killed Sept. 15th, 1916, *Delville Wood.*
                                        M.C.

BENSON, SIR F. R.   ... A 71–77   (New Coll., Oxford. Shakespearian Actor and
                                              Manager.)
                                        Motor Lorry Driver with French Army, 1918.
                                        Croix de Guerre.

BENTINCK, B. W.   COLL. 90–96   (Exeter Coll., Oxford. Barrister.)
    Capt.   Lieut., R.B., 1915. Capt., 1916, 13th Bn.
                                        Courtmartial Officer.
                                        R.A.F., Capt., S.O., 1918.

BERKLEY, J.   ...   ... F 76–80   (Lieut., R.A., 1883. Major, 1900.)
    Lieut.-Col.   Temp. Lieut.-Col., R.A.
                                        H.Q. Embarkation Service.
                                        Reserve of Officers, 1918.
                                        Wounded (2).   *Despatches* (3).
                                        D.S.O. Brevet Lieut.-Col.

✠ BERKLEY, J. H. ...   ... F 02–02
    Capt.   Capt., W. Yorkshire Regt., 10th Bn.
                                        Killed, 1915.

✠ BERTIE, N. M. K.   ... B 10–14
   2nd Lieut.
      2nd Lieut., K.R.R.C., 4th Bn.
      Killed May 8th, 1915, *Hooge, 2nd Battle of Ypres.*

BESLEY, E. F. W.   COLL. 05–10
   Capt.
      (Ball. Coll., Oxford.)
      1914, 2nd Lieut., Seaforth Highlanders, 7th Bn.
      1917, Lieut., Acting Capt.
      Staff. Capt., 1919.
      Wounded.

BESSEMER, H. D.   ... F 08–12
   Lieut.,
      2nd Lieut., R. W. Surrey Regt., 4th Bn.
      Lieut., att. Hertfordshire Regt., T.F.R.

✠ BETHELL, E. W.   ... K 05–09
   Capt.,
      Capt., The Queen's (R. West Surrey Regt.), 2nd Bn.
      Wounded.   *Killed* Sept. 21st, 1918, *near Epéhy.*

BETHELL, L. S.   ... H 03–07
   Lieut.
      (Univ. Coll., Oxford. Columbia.)
      Lieut., Nigeria Regt., W.A.F.F.
      Relinquished Commission 1919.

BETHUNE, C. L. PATTON   I 96–00
   Capt.
      (Cameron Highlanders, 1900. Lieut., 1901. Chinese Infantry, Wei-hai-wei. S. African War.)
      Capt., Cameron Highlanders, 3rd Bn.   War Office.
      Wounded.   *Despatches.*
      M.C.

BETTINGTON, J. B.   ... E 08–13
   Capt.
      (Shropshire L.I., 1915.)
      Capt., Shropshire L.I., 1st Bn., att. 8th Bn.
      (Served with W.A.F.F., Nigeria Regt., 1915–16.)
      Education Officer.
      Wounded.
      M.C.

BEWLEY, A. G.,   COLL. 08–12
   Capt.
      Lieut., R.F.A.
      Wounded (2).   *Despatches.*
      Relinquished Commission, 1919.

BEWLEY, T. K.   COLL. 04–09
      Lieut., R.A.S.C.   Employed at Treasury.

✠ BICKERSTETH, R.   ... H 98–02
      Private, Australian Imperial Force, 52nd Regt.
      Wounded (2).
      Killed Aug. 12th, 1918, *Proyart, France.*

19

BIGGE, J. A. SELBY,   COLL. 05–09
    Lieut.

Lieut., R.A.S.C., 1915.   Att. Macedonian Mule-
    teer Corps.

BIGGS, W. H. YEATMAN,   H 92–95
    Major

(Christ Church, Oxford.)
Lieut.-Commander R.N.V.R.
Served in Russia with Locker Lampson's Motor
    Cars.
Major, R.A.F., S.O.$_{.2}$.

BINGHAM, H. F.,   ...   H 13–17
    2nd Lieut.

2nd Lieut., R.F.A.

BINGHAM, O. B. B., SMITH-   E 82–85
    Brig.-Gen., D.S.O.

(3rd D.G., 1887.   Capt. 1898.   Major, 1903.
    S. African War.)
Colonel, 1916.
Brig.-Gen., 1917.   Inspector of Cavalry.
Wounded (2).   *Despatches.*
C.M.G.

✠ BINNEY, E. H. ...   ...   E 10–14
    Lieut.

Lieut., Notts and Derby Regt.   Att. York and
    Lancaster Regt.
Wounded, 1915.
Died from effects of wound Oct. 11th, 1917.

BINNEY, W. E.   COLL. 77–82
    Major

(Lieut., R.M.L.I., 1883; Capt., 1893; Retired,
    1902.)
Major, R.M.L.I.

BIRCH, A. G.   ...   ...   D 95–00
    Major

(Trin. Coll., Camb.   Engineer.)
Temp. Major, R.E.   4th London Field Coy.
Wounded.   *Despatches* (3).
D.S.O. and Bar.

BIRKBECK, L. H. CARR-   COLL. 87–92
    (formerly BADCOCK)
    Major

(Trin. Coll., Oxford.   M.B., B.Ch.)

Major, R.A.M.C., 1918.

BIRLEY, B. L.   ...   ...   E 98–01
    Brevet Major

(Lieut., R.B., 1905.   R. Lancaster Regt., 1906.)
Capt., K.O. R. Lancaster Regt., 1915.
Major, 1916.
Acting Lieut.-Col., N. Lancs. Regt., 1917.
Acting Lieut.-Col., E. Lancs. Regt., 1917.
Despatches.
D.S.O.

BIRLEY, C. F. ...   ... G 02–08
   Lieut.

Capt., D. of Lancaster's Yeomanry.
Lieut., Grenadier Guards, 1917.
Guards, M.G. Regt.

BIRLEY, G. H. ...   ... G 07–12
   Hon. Capt.

Capt., The Queen's (R. West Surrey Regt.).
R.A.F., Capt.
Relinquished Commission, ill health, 1918.
Despatches.
Died in E. Africa, May 30th, 1917.

BIRLEY, J. L. ...   ... G 97–03
   Acting Lieut.-Col.

(Univ. Coll., Oxford. St. Thomas Hospital.)
Temp. Major, R.A.M.C.
Consultant Med. Officer to R.A.F. H.Q., France.
Acting Lieut.-Col., 1918.
Despatches (2).
O.B.E.

BIRLEY, N. A. ...   ... G 11–16
   Lieut.

2nd Lieut., 17th Lancers.
Lieut., 1919.

✠ BIRNEY, J. G. ...   ... C 11–14
   2nd Lieut.

2nd Lieut., Highland L.I.
Killed Jan. 11th, 1917, *Kut, East Mounds.*

BISCOE, H. V. ...   ... H 94–98
   Major

(Indian Staff Corps, 1901. Lieut., 1902. Employed Persian Gulf.)
Major, 1915.
I.A. Supernumerary List, 1916.
Staff Lieut., D.A.A.G.
Chevalier, Légion d'Honneur.

BLACK, C. K. ...   ... A 96–00
   Major

Capt., The Buffs. (E. Kent Regt.).
Training Reserve, 29th Bn.
Major, 1918.
Wounded (2).
M.C. and Bar.

✠ BLACK, D. M. ...   ... C 00–05
   Capt.

Capt., Essex Regt.
Killed August. 6th, 1915, *Gallipoli.*

✠ BLACK, G. B. ...   ... F 02–07
   Capt.

Temp. Capt., 17th Lancers.
Att. Tank Corps.
Despatches (2).
Montenegrin Order of Danilo.
Died of wounds August 23rd, 1918, *Warfusée
   Abancourt, near Villers Bretonneux.*

21

BLACKBURN, L. H. ... F 13–18

Gentleman Cadet, R.M. College.

✠ BLACKIE, J. S. ... H 10–15
2nd Lieut.

2nd Lieut., R.B., 5th Bn.
Killed Oct. 18th, 1916, *near Le Transloy.*

BLAIR, J. M. ... ... G 93–99
Brig.-Gen.

(Black Watch, 1901. Lieut., 1905. S. African
War. Capt., Gordon Highlanders, 1911.)
Major, Gordon Highlanders, 1917.
Temp. Lieut.-Col., 1918. Military Attaché,
Petrograd.
G.S.O.$_1$, 1918. Temp. Brig.-Gen. Brevet
Lieut.-Col.
Despatches.
D.S.O., C.M.G., Orders of St. Stanislas and
St. Vladimir, Officier Légion d'Honneur.

BLAKE, A. E. ... ... D 88–94
Capt.

(Univ. Coll., Oxford. Barrister.)
Capt., P.A. Somerset L.I.
Retired, 1918.

BLAKE, G. ... ... B 95–96

Commander, R.N., H.M.S. *Iron Duke.*
D.S.O.

BLAKE, J. ... ... B 94–98
Capt.

Capt., Remount Service.
Dep. Assistant Director, Southern Command.

BLAKE, T. R. H. ... I 93–98
Capt.

(Pembroke Coll., Cambridge.)
Capt., R.A.M.C.
Despatches.
M.C.

BLAMEY, J. N. L. ... E 05–10
Capt.

Capt., R.A.M.C.

BLAXLAND, Rev. E. C. COLL. 03–08

Chaplain to Forces.

BLOMFIELD, A. ... A 09–10
Lieut.

Lieut., R. Sussex Regt., 5th Bn.
R.A.F., Lieut., Observer.

✠ BLUNDELL, C. B. MOSS COLL. 04–10
Lieut.

Lieut., Durham L.I.
Wounded.
Killed Sept. 26th, 1915, *Loos.*

22

BLUNT, E. H. ... ... c 79–82 (Ch. Ch., Oxford. R.M. Coll. R. Berks. Regt.
Capt.   Capt., 1899. S. African War. Retired,
                                   1907.)
                               Assistant Embarkation Staff Officer.

BLUNT, H. P. ... COLL. 13–18
                               Cadet, R.F.A.

BOEVEY, M. CRAWLEY-... c 96–01 (Trin. Coll., Oxford. D.C.L.I., 1904. Capt.,
Bt. Major   1914. Served with K.A.R., 1909–14.)
                               Capt., D.C.L.I.
                               Staff Capt. Brigade-Major. Brevet Major,
                                   1917.
                               G.S.O.$_2$, 1918.
                               Despatches (4).
                               M.C., D.S.O.

BOGER, A. J. ... ... c 85–90 (Magd. Coll., Oxford. Barrister.)
Lieut.   Motor Ambulance Driver, 1914.
                               Lieut., R.N.V.R.

BOOTH, L. C. G. ... B 95–00 (New Coll., Oxford.)
Major   Major, W. Yorkshire Regt.
                               Wounded.
                               Relinquished Commission, 1919.

✠ BOOTH, L. E. ... ... K 05–10
Major
                               R.F.A., 2nd Lieut., 1914. Capt., 1915. Major,
                                   1917.
                               Wounded.   *Despatches.*
                               M.C. and Bar.
                               Killed April 13th, 1918, *near Neuve Eglise.*

BORTHWICK, A. S. ... A 93–97
Lieut.
                               Lieut., R.F.A.
                               Wounded.
                               Relinquished Commission 1919.

BORTHWICK, R. G. P. ... B 95–00 (10th Hussars, 2nd Lieut. Reserve of Officers.)
Capt.   Interpreter, A.D.C.
                               Capt., 3rd Co. of London Yeomanry.
                               Camp Commandant.

BOSTOCK, S. C. ... ... I 07–11
Lieut.
                               2nd Lieut., 1st Life Guards.
                               Resigned Commission, ill health, 1916.
                               Hon. Lieut.
                               Wounded.

23

BOSVILE, T. J. B. ... G 10–14
    Capt.
                              Lieut., R.B., 11th Bn.
                              Acting Capt., Adjutant, 1918.
                              Employed with London Regt, 33rd Bn.
                              Wounded.
                              M.C.

✠ BOUCHER, A. G. COLL. 11–16
    2nd Lieut.
                              2nd Lieut., K.R.R.C., 6th, att. 2nd Bn., 1917.
                              Killed July 10th, 1917, *Nieuport.*

BOULT, P. S. ... ... H 03–07
    Lieut.
                                Lieut., Lancs. and Cheshire R.G.A.
                              Sec. for Anti-Aircraft duties.

BOWEN, J. B. ... ... H 96–02
    Lieut.-Col
                                (Trin. Coll., Camb.)
                              Capt., Temp. Major, Pembroke Yeomanry.
                              Comm. S.W. Brigade Signal Troop.
                              R.A.F., Temp. Lieut.-Col.
                              Comm. No. 1 Wireless School, Winchester.
                              O.B.E.

✠ BOWERS, W. A. ... ... G 00–06
    Lieut.
                                Lieut., N. Staffs. Regt.
                              Died of wounds July 2nd, 1916, *near Warlincourt.*

BOWLY, W. A. T. ... F 94–97
    (Lieut.-Col.)
    Brevet Major
                              (B.N.C. Oxford.   R. Warwickshire Regt., 1902.
                              S. African War.   Capt. Dorset Regt., 1912.)
                              Temp. Lieut.-Col.
                              A.D.C., G.S.O.$_2$, G.S.O.$_1$, 1918.
                              (Personal Military Secretary to Secretary of
                                  State.)
                              Despatches (4).
                              M.C.   Chevalier Order of Leopold.   Croix de
                                Guerre.

✠ BOWMAN, A. H. ... B 05–10
    2nd Lieut.
                                (Brevet Major, 1st Cumberland Howitzer
                              Battery.)
                              2nd Lieut., R.F.A., 1915.
                              Died May 20th, 1916, *of wounds received at
                              Arras,* May 19th.

✠ BOYD, N. J. L. ... ... I 08–12
    2nd Lieut.
                                2nd Lieut., Black Watch (R. Highlanders),
                              1st Bn.
                              Died at Rouen, Oct. 12th, 1914, *of wounds
                              received in Battle of the Aisne,* Sept. 14th,
                              1914.

BOYLE, C. R. C. ... D 99–03 (Oxford Militia, 1905. 2nd Lieut., Oxford and
Major   Bucks L.I., 1907.)
Capt., Oxford and Bucks L.I., 1916.
Major (Temp. Lieut.-Col.), 1917.
Acting Lieut.-Col., Berkshire Regt., 1918.
Wounded. Despatches (2).
D.S.O. and Bar.

BOYLE, HON. J. D. ... F 98–00 (Lieut., R.B., 1905.)
Lieut.-Col.   Capt., R.B., 1914.
Temp. Lieut.-Col., 1916.
R.A.F., Major, Balloons.
R.A.F., S.O.$_1$. Employed under Air Ministry,
1918.
Despatches (2).
D.S.O., C.B.E.

BRABANT, F. H. ... K 05–11 (Ball. Coll., Oxford.)
Lance-Cpl., Warwickshire Regt., 4th Bn.

BRACE, A. G. ... ... A 99–03
Capt.   Capt., Acting Major, R.E.
Wounded.
M.C.

BRAIN, J. H. P.... ... F 09–14
Capt.   Capt., Welsh Regt., 3rd Bn.
(Att. Highland L.I.)
War Office.
R.A.F., Administrative Officer, 1918.

✠ BRAITHWAITE, F. J. ... D 86–89 (Loyal N. Lancs. Regt., 1893. Capt., 1895.
Major   S. African War.)
Major, Loyal N. Lancs. Regt.
Killed Nov. 4th, 1914, *Tanga, E. Africa.*

✠ BRAITHWAITE, V. A. ... E 10–12
Lieut.   Lieut., P.A. Somerset L.I., 1st Bn.
A.D.C.
Despatches (2).
M.C.
Killed July 1st, 1916, *Serre.*

BRAITHWAITE, W. J. ... D 88–90 (New Coll., Oxford. Home C.S.)
Capt.   Capt., London Vol. Regt., 6th Bn.

BRAMLY, A. W. JENNINGS   B 88–92   (20th Hussars, 1905.   S. African War.   Egyp-
Col.   tian Army.   Governor of Sinai, 1912.)
                                     Col., 1914.
                                     Intelligence Staff Officer.   Suez Canal Defence.
                                     G.S.O.₁
                                     Director, Police School, Cairo, 1918.
                                     Despatches (3).
                                     D.S.O., Order of White Eagle (Serbia).

BRAMLY B. JENNINGS ...   B 02–05
                                     Lieut., R.A.   A.D.C.
                                     Capt., 1918.   Staff Capt. till 1919.
                                     Despatches (2).
                                     M.C.

BRAY, Sir C. A., C.B.   COLL. 71–77   (30th Regt.   Afghan War.   S. African War.
Major-General   Major, 1899.   Col., 1906.)
                                     Major-General.   Paymaster-in-Chief, 1914.
                                     Retired Jan. 1st, 1919.
                                     Despatches (8).
                                     Commandeur Légion d'Honneur.   K.C.M.G.

BREITMEYER, G. C. A.   B 06–10   (7th Hussars, 1911.)
Capt.   Capt. and Adjt., 7th Hussars, 1914.
                                     Despatches.

BREITMEYER, G. W.   ...   A 11–16
Lieut.   2nd Lieut., 9th Lancers, 1917.
                                     Lieut., 1918.

BRERETON, A. S.   ...   I 12–17
2nd Lieut.   2nd Lieut., R.E., 1918.

BRETT, S.   ...   ...   B 94–97   (Business in London.)
Capt.   Capt., Inns of Court O.T.C., 1916.
                                     Employed, Guards M.G.C.

BREWIN, C. N. ...   COLL. 09–12
Capt.   R.A., 1914.
                                     Lieut., R.G.A.   Capt., 1917.
                                     Acting Major, 1918.
                                     Despatches.
                                     M.C.

BRICKDALE, M. FORTESCUE   A 04–09   (Ch. Ch., Oxford.)
Capt.   Capt. London Regt., 8th Bn.
                                     Wounded.

BRIDGES, A. H. ...   ...   H 93–96   (R.A., 1898.   Lieut., R.H.A., 1901.   Capt.,
Major   1907.)
                                     Major, R.A., 1914 (Acting Lieut.-Col.).
                                     Brigade-Major, H.Q., 1918.

BRIDGES, E. J. ...   ... H 95-00   (14th Hussars, 1902. Lieut., 1905. S. African
    Brevet Lieut.-Col.   War.)
                                      Major, 14th Hussars.   Acting Lieut.-Col., 1917.
                                      Despatches (3).
                                      M.C.

BRIDGES, G. H. ...   ... H 06-11   (Oriel Coll., Oxford.)
    Lieut.   Pte., Public School Brigade, 1915.
                                      2nd Lieut., E. Surrey Regt.
                                      Lieut., 1918.
                                      Wounded.

BRIDGES, J. V. ...   ... H 01-06
    Major   Capt., Worcestershire Regt., 1915.
                                      Acting Lieut.-Col. Northumberland Fusiliers.
                                      Temp. Lieut.-Col., Leicestershire Regt.
                                      Acting Lieut.-Col., Wiltshire Regt., 1918.
                                      Despatches (2).
                                      D.S.O.

BRIDGES, R. F.   ... H 97-02   (Univ. Coll., Oxford.)
                                      Capt., R.A.M.C.

BRIGHT, R. A. ...   ... A 83-86   (R.F.A., 1892.   On Staff, S. African War.
    Brig.-General   G.S.O.$_2$, 1909.)
                       .   Major, R.F.A., 1914.
                                      G.S.O.$_1$. Temp. Brig.-General, 1915.
                                      Inspector of Artillery, India.

                                      Brevet Col., Order SS. Maurizio e Lazzaro, C.B.
BRINTON, R. S.   COLL. 82-88   (New Coll., Oxford.)
                                      Capt., Worcestershire Vol. Regt., 1st Bn.

BRISE, SIR H. G. RUGGLES-, H 76-82 (Ball. Coll., Oxford.   Gren. Guards, 1885.
  M.V.O.   Major, 1902.   S. African War.   Temp.
    Major-General   Major-General, 1911.)
                                      Comm. Brigade, Gren. Guards, 1914-15.
                                      Gen. Staff.
                                      Military Secretary, G.H.Q., 1918.
                                      Wounded. Despatches (6).
                                      C.B., K.C.M.G.

BRISE, H. R. RUGGLES- ... H 04-09   (School of Mines.)
    Capt.   Lieut., S. African Citizen Defence Force.
                       .   A.D.C. to Governor-General, S. Africa.
                                      2nd Lieut., R.E.
                                      Acting Capt. and Adjt. A.D.C.   G.S.O.$_3$.
                                      Wounded.·
                                      M.C., Croix de Guerre.

27

BROADHURST, A. F. B. ... c 04–09
Capt.
                                         Capt., Highland L.I., 1st Bn.
                                         Military Accounts Dept., Mesopotamia.
                                         Capt., R.A.F., A. and S., 1918.
                                         Despatches.

✠ BROADHURST, G. H. ... e 05–10
2nd Lieut.
                                         2nd Lieut., R.F.A., 52nd Battery.
                                         Wounded.
                                         Killed May 8th, 1915, *2nd Battle of Ypres.*

BROADHURST, W. R. ... e 10–15
Lieut.
                                         Lieut., Gordon Highlanders, 1st Bn.
                                         Wounded (3).

BROCKMAN, G. P. L. c 09–13
DRAKE
Capt.
                                         Capt., Border Regt.
                                         G.S.O.$_3$. Brigade-Major.
                                         Despatches (3).
                                         M.C.

✠ BRODIE, D. E. ... ... i 87–92
Capt.
                                         (British S. African Co.)
                                         Capt., Cameron Highlanders.
                                         Killed August 17th, 1916. *Place unknown.*

BRODIE, H. C. ... ... h 89–93
Major
                                         Major, Middlesex Hussars.

BRODIE, L. C. ... ... i 90–93
Major
                                         (4th Hussars, 1900. Capt., 1902. W.A.F.F.,
                                                   1908–12.)
                                         Major, Essex Regt., 1916.

BROOKE, A. C. ... h 00–05
Major
                                         (R.A., 1907. Capt., 1914.)
                                         Capt., R.A.
                                         Major, 1917. Brigade-Major. D.A.A.G.
                                         Despatches (2).
                                         D.S.O., Chevalier, Légion d'Honneur.

BROOKE, A. H. ... ... h 97–00
Major
                                         (4th D.G., 1903. 18th Lancers, I.A., 1905.
                                                   Capt., 1912.)
                                         Capt. (temp. Major), 18th Lancers, I.A.
                                         M.G.C. Cavalry, 1916.
                                         M.C.

BROOKE, B. G. ... ... h 08–11
Lieut.
                                         2nd Lieut., S. Irish Horse, 1914.
                                         17th Lancers, 1915.
                                         Lieut., 1917. Reserve of Officers, 1919.

28

BROOKE, Sir B. S., Bart.... D 01–05 (R. Fusiliers, 1908. 10th Hussars, 1911.)
    Capt.   Lieut., 10th Hussars. A.D.C.
                                 Capt., 1917.
                                 Relinquished Commission, 1919.
                                 M.C., Croix de Guerre.

BROOKE, B. W. D.   ... D 89–92 (Trin. Coll., Camb. R.F.A., 1901.)
                                 Capt., R.H.A.
                                 Relinquished Commission, Tuan Muda of
                                    Sarawak.

BROOKE, C. R. I.   ... D 83–86 (Yorkshire L.I., 1890. Capt., 1899. S. African
    Lieut.-Col.   War. Major, 1908.)
                                   Lieut.-Col., Yorkshire L.I., Comm. 6th Bn.,
                                 1916.
                                 Temp. Brig.-General, April—Nov., 1916.
                                 Retired.
                                 Wounded.
                                 Despatches (2).
                                 D.S.O., C.M.G.

BROOKE, F. H. ...   ... H 96–99 (2nd Lieut., K.R.R.C., 1903. S. African War.)
    Capt.   Capt., S. Irish Horse.

BROOKE, G. T. ...   ... H 10–13
    Lieut.   Lieut., 16th Lancers.
                                   Croix de Guerre.

✠ BROOKS, A. B. CLOSE ... I 98–03 (Trin. Coll., Camb.)
                                 Lieut., Manchester Regt.
                                 Despatches.
                                 M.C.
                                 Died of wounds Jan. 10th, 1917, *Mesopotamia.*

BROOME, G. S. F.   ... E 84–86 (R.A., 1889. Major, 1906.)
    Major   Major, Reserve of Officers.

BROWN, D. S. GORDON ... E 09–14
    Capt.   2nd Lieut., K.O.S.B.
                                   R.M. Coll.
                                 Lieut., Black Watch (R. Highlanders), 1916.
                                 Temp. Capt., Instructor, School of Musketry,
                                 1918.
                                 Wounded.

✠ BROWN, D. HURST   ... F 11–14
    2nd Lieut.   2nd Lieut., R.F.A.
                                   Killed June 15th, 1915, *Dickebusch.*

✠ Brown, J. C. Forster   I 06–08
    Capt.

    Capt., R.B.
    Killed August 27th, 1916, *France.* *Exact*
    locality unknown.

Brown, J. L. Crommelin   I 01–07
    Lieut.

    (Trin. Coll., Camb. Repton School.)
    Lieut., R.G.A.
    Officer Cadet Bn., Trowbridge, 1917–18.
    Wounded.

Browne, P. A. ...   ... H 11–16
    Lieut.

    2nd Lieut., Black Watch (R. Highlanders), 1st Bn.
    Lieut., 1918.
    Wounded.

Browne, W. L. F.   ... H 07–12
    Capt.

    Lieut., R.F.A., 162nd Battery.
    Capt., 1917.
    Wounded.

Bruce, Hon. C. N.   ... D 99–04
    Capt.

    (New Coll., Oxford.)
    Capt., Glamorgan Yeomanry.
    Lieut., 2nd Life Guards, Reserve Regt.
    A.D.C.
    Guards M.G.C., 1918.

✠ Bruce, G. J.   ...   ... G 94–99
    Capt.

    (New Coll., Oxford.)
    Capt., R. Irish Rifles.
    General List. G.S.O.$_3$. Brigade-Major.
    Despatches (2).
    M.C. and Bar. D.S.O.
    Killed Oct. 2nd, 1918, *Molenhoek, Flanders.*

✠ Bruce, Hon. H. L.   ... D 94–99

    Capt., Royal Scots, 3rd Bn.
    Despatches.
    Killed December 14th, 1914, *Kemmel Nieustraet.*

✠ Bruce, J. F.   ...   ... I 11–16
    2nd Lieut.

    2nd Lieut., Arg. and Suth. Highlanders.
    Died of wounds Feb. 28th, 1918, *Poperinghe.*

Bruce, Hon. J. H.   ... D 03–08
    Lieut.

    Lieut., Glamorgan Yeomanry.
    Resigned Commission, ill health, 1916.

✠ Bruce, N. M.   ...   ... I 03–08
    Lieut.

    2nd Lieut., Yorkshire Regt., 1914.
    Lieut., 1915.
    Killed at landing at Suvla Bay, August 7th, 1915.

BRUNSKILL, W. H. F.   c 15–18

Corporal, R.M. College.

BRUTTON, C. P. ...   ... F 12–17
    2nd Lieut.

2nd Lieut., Grenadier Guards.
Lieut., 1919.
Wounded.

BUBB, H. J.   ...   ... A 86–89
    Capt.

(London University.)
Capt., R.F.A., 3rd Highland Howitzer Brigade.
Employed Ministry of Munitions.

BUCHANNAN, G. H.   ... B 91–95
    Capt.

(Solicitor, 1900.)
Lieut., S. Wales Borderers.
Capt., 1917.
Employed Ministry of National Service.

✠ BUCK, C. M.   ...   ... H 08–10
    Lieut.

Lieut., I.A.R.O.
Lieut., R.A.F.
Killed Jan. 27th, 1917, near *Wytschaete.*

✠ BUCK, G. S.   ...   ... H 10–14
    Capt.

Capt., London Regt., 1st Bn.
R.A.F., Flight Commander.
Att. Independent Air Force.
Despatches.
M.C., D.F.C.
Killed Sept. 3rd, 1918, at *Rambervillers, near
    Nancy.*

BUCKLAND, F. J.   ... H 11–16
    Lieut.

R.A.F., Lieut. (A.).
Wounded.

BUCKLE, G. W.   ... c 99–04
    Capt.

(Trin. Coll., Camb.)
Capt., York and Lancaster Regt.
17th N. Div. Cyclist Coy.
M.G.C., Infantry, 1918.
Relinquished Commission, 1918.
Despatches.

✠ BUCKLE, M. P., D.S.O. ... H 83–86
    Major

(R.W. Kent Regt., 1889. Capt., 1898. S.
    African War. Staff. Capt. War Office,
    1904. Brigade-Major, 1906.)
Major, R.W. Kent Regt., Comm. 1st Bn.
Despatches (2).
Killed Oct. 27th, 1914, *Neuve Chapelle.*

31

BUCKLEY, B. T. ... c 87–93 (Northumberland Fusiliers, 1895. Soudan.
   Brig.-Gen.   S. African War.)
                                    Brevet Major, Northumberland Fusiliers, 1915.
                                      Brevet Lieut.-Col., 1917.
                                      G.S.O.$_3$, G.S.O.$_2$, G.S.O.$_1$, Sub-Director, Military
                                        Intelligence.
                                      Temp. Brig.-Gen., 1918, War Office.
                                      Despatches.
                                      Officier Légion d'Honneur, Corona d'Italia,
                                      Commander, Star Roumania, Order Crown
                                      of Siam, C.M.G., C.B.

BUCKMASTER, HON. O. S. F 04–09
   Capt. ... ...   Capt., D.C.L.I.
                                        Officer Cadet Bn.
                                        Wounded.

BUDD, Sir C. L. ... H 77–83
                                        Ministry of Munitions.
                                        C.B.E., K.B.E.

✠ BUDD, E. ... ... H 07–11
   Capt.   2nd Lieut., R.A.S.C.
                                          Lieut., Irish Guards.
                                        Capt., 1917.
                                        M.C. and 2 Bars.
                                        Killed May 3rd, 1918, *Ayette, near Bapaume.*

BUDD, J. C. ... COLL. 13–16
   Lieut.   2nd Lieut., R.G.A.
                                          Lieut., 1919.

BUDD, N. A. H. ... H 77–81 (Lieut., Oxford L.I., 1885. I.A. 1st Brahmans,
   Lieut.-Col.   Major, 1903).
                                        Lieut.-Col., Comm. 1st Brahmans I.A.

BURGE, M. R. K. COLL. 07–13
   Capt.   Lieut., The Buffs (E. Kent Regt.).
                                        Temp. Capt., War Office.
                                        G.S.O.$_3$, 1918.
                                        Wounded.   *Despatches.*
                                        Croix de Guerre.

BURGE, S. F. M. ... D 13–18
   2nd Lieut.   2nd Lieut., Scots Guards, 1918.

BURGES, D. ... ... B 87–91 (Gloucester Regt., 1893. S. African War).
Bt.-Lieut.-Col. Major, Acting Lieut.-Col., Gloucestershire Regt.
Temp. Lieut.-Col., Comm. S. Wales Borderers,
7th Bn., 1917.
Wounded (2).   *Despatches* (2).
𝔙.𝕮.
D.S.O., Croix de Guerre, Greek Military Cross.

✠ BURGES, E. ... ... B 90–96 (Cape Mounted Rifles, 1897. S. African War.)
Major Major, 1st S. African Infantry.
West F.F., Egypt.
France.
·*Despatches.*
Killed, July 18th, 1916, *Delville Wood*.

BURGES, F. ... ... I 81–86 (Gloucester Regt., 1889. Khartoum.)
Capt. Capt., Gloucestershire Regt. Retired, 1908.
Employed in Soudan.
Order of the Nile.

BURGES, G. H. ... ... C 77–80 (Merton Coll., Oxford.)
Lieut.-Col. Lieut.-Col., Gloucestershire Regt. Relinquished
Commission, 1918.
Despatches.

BURLTON, E. R. J. ... I 02–04
Lieut. Lieut., R.A.S.C.
Lieut., R.F.A., 1917.
Acting Capt., 1918.
Acting Major, 1919.
M.C. Croix de Guerre.

BURLTON, F. A. ... I 97–02
Lieut. Lieut., Hertfordshire Yeomanry.
M.G.C. Cavalry.
Wounded.

✠ BURMESTER, M. G. ... H 87–90 (California, 1903. With Gloucestershire Yeo-
Lieut. manry, S. African War.)
Lieut., Essex Regt.
Killed, Aug. 25th, 1915, *Suvla Bay.*

✠ BURN, H. H. ... ... H 09–13
Capt. Lieut., Coldstream Guards, 1915.
Capt., 1916.
M.C.
Killed, Sept. 16th, 1916, *Guinchy.*

BURN, R. C. W. ... F 96–01 (Oriel Coll., Oxford.)
Major Capt., Sussex Yeomanry.
Temp. Major, M.G.C. Cavalry.
Wounded.

BURNE, A. H. ... ... E 00–04   (R.A., 1906.   Capt., 1914.)
     Major   Major, R.H.A., 1917.
                                Brigade-Major, 1918.
                                Despatches (3).
                                D.S.O. and Bar.

BURNE, C. H. ... ... E 03–07
     Lieut.   Lieut., R.A.S.C.
                                Royal Defence Corps.
                                Lieut., Gen. Staff, Intelligence Officer.

BURNE, S. F. ... ... G 99–03   (R.A., 1904.)
     Major   Capt., R.F.A., 1914.
                                Major (Acting Lieut.-Col.), 1918.
                                Br'gade Major, 1918.
                                Despatches (2).
                                D.S.O.

✠ BURNELL, A. COKE ... G 08–12
     Capt.   Capt., R.B.
                                Wounded.
                                Killed March 18th, 1916, *Fleurbaix*, near
                                     Armentières.

BURNETT, R. E. S. F. ... D 09–11
     Lieut.   Lieut., R. West Kent Regt.
                                General List, Army Signal Service.
                                Wounded.

BURNEY, G. T. ... ... H 03–07   (Gordon Highlanders, 1909.)
     Capt.   Lieut., Gordon Highlanders, 1914.
                                Capt., 1915.
                                Served with Nigeria Regt., W.A.F.F., 1912–18.
                                Despatches.
                                M.C.

BURRA, L. T. ... ... G 87–
     M.D.   Temp. Capt., R.A.M.C.
                                Relinquished Commission, Jan., 1918.

BURRELL, G. P. ... A 95–98
     Major   Major, Hampshire Regt.
                                R.A.F. Equ'pment Officer.
                                Relinquished Commission, May, 1918.
                                M.C.

BURRELL, H. A. ... A 96–00
     Capt.   Capt., Hampshire Regt.
                                Relinquished Commission, 1918, ill health.

✠ BURROUGHES, R.   ... C 10–13
    2nd Lieut.   2nd Lieut., Norfolk Regt., 5th Bn.
                            Killed August 13th, 1915, *Anafarta, Gallipoli.*

✠ BURROUGHES, S.   ... C 12–14
    2rd Lieut.   Pte., Inns of Court. O.T.C. R.M. Coll.
                            2nd Lieut., K.R.R.C., 2nd Bn.
                            Killed Nov. 4th, 1918, *on the Sambre Canal.*

BURTON, M. G. W.   ... C 07–10
    Capt.   Temp. Capt., R.A.S.C. M.T.

✠ BURTON, R. C. ...   ... C 96–01   (R.B.)
    Capt.   Capt., R.B.
                            Died March 16th, 1915, *of wounds received,*
                                   Neuve Chapelle.

✠ BURTON, S. J. ...   ... C 96–00   (Coldstream Guards.)
    Major   Major, Coldstream Guards.
                            Wounded (2).
                            Killed July 20th, 1917, *Elverdinghe, Flanders.*

BUSHELL, C. W....   COLL. 96–00   (R.E., 1901. Capt., 1912.)
    Major   Major, R.E., 1916 (late Sappers and Miners,
                               I.A.)
                            Staff Officer to Engineer-in-Chief.
                            Despatches.

✠ BUSK, H. A.   ...   ... C 07–08   (King's Coll., Camb.)
    Capt.   R.N.A.S., Flight Commander, 1914.
                            Missing, presumed killed over Gallipoli, Jan. 6th,
                               1916.

BUTLER, J. F. ARADECKNE   H 83–86   (2nd Lieut., E. Surrey Regt., 1890. Capt.,
    Capt.   1899. Retired, 1908.)
                            Reserve of Officers.

BUTLER, Hon. L. J. P.   ... B 89–92   (D.L.I., 1900. Lieut., Irish Guards, 1902.
    Brig.-Gen.   S. African War. Capt., 1909.)
                            Col., Irish Guards, 1915.
                            Brigade-Major, 1914. G.S.O.$_2$, 1915.
                            Temp. Brig.-Gen., 8th Infantry Brigade, 1916.
                            Wounded.   *Despatches* (5).
                            D.S.O., C.M.G.

BUTLER, Hon. R. T. R. P.   B 96–00   (Civil Engineer. P.W.D., India.)
    Capt.   Temp. Capt. (Acting Major), R.E.
                            Tank Corps.
                            Wounded (2).   *Despatches* (2).
                            M.C., D.S.O.

BUTLER, S. S. ... ... E 94–97   (Warwickshire Regt., 1899. S. African War.
   Col.   K.A.R., 1905–08. Capt., S. Staffs Regt.,
                                  1908. Egyptian Army, 1909–15.)
Major, S. Staffs Regt.
G.S.O.$_3$, 1915. G.S.O.$_2$, 1915. G.S.O.$_1$, 1918.
Temp. Col., att. Egyptian Army.
Wounded (2).   *Despatches* (3).
D.S.O., C.M.G., Croix de Guerre, Order of Nile.

BUTLER, Hon. T. P. P. ... B 98–00   (R.F.A., 1903. Capt., 1914.)
   Major   Major, R.F.A., 1916.
Serving with Egyptian Army.
D.S.O., Order of Nile.

BUTTON, G. T.   ... I 00–04   (New Coll., Oxford.)
   Capt.   Capt., Oxford and Bucks L.I.
Prisoner of War.
Wounded.

BYASS, G. R. S. ... ... F 09–14
   Capt.   Lieut., Glamorgan Yeomanry.
Posted to Welsh Regt.
Capt., 1918.
Wounded.

✠ CAIGER, F. H. S.   ... H 10–14   (Caius Coll., Camb.)
   2nd Lieut.   2nd Lieut., R.F.A.
Killed Nov. 11th, 1916, near *Flers on the Somme.*

CAILLARD, W. M. C. du Q. D 87–89   (7th D.G., 1894. Capt., 1903. S. African War.
   Major   Retired, 1908.)
Hon. Major, 7th Dragoon Guards.
Ministry of Munitions.
Despatches.

✠ CAMERON, C. H.   ... G 05–10
   2nd Lieut.   2nd Lieut., R.H.A.
Despatches.
Killed March 12th, 1918, *Neuve Chapelle.*

CAMERON, D.   ... G 00–06   (2nd Lieut., 1908.)
   Capt.   Capt., Cameron Highlanders, 1915.
M.G.C. Instructor, 1916.
G.S.O.$_3$, 1917. D.A.A.G., 1918.
Wounded.   *Despatches* (2).
M.C.

CAMERON, E.   ... G 09–10
    Capt.
                            2nd Lieut., Staffs Yeomanry.
                            R.A.F., Capt., 1917.

CAMERON, N. O. M.   ... A 10–14
    Lieut.
                            Lieut., Cameron Highlanders, 1915.
                            (Comm. Sch. of Technical Instruction, R.A.F.,
                                1917.)
                            Wounded.

CAMPBELL, H.   ... F 88–93
    Capt.
                            Lieut., R. Welsh Fusiliers.
                            Capt., 1915.
                            General List, Staff Capt., 1918.
                            M.C.·

CAMPBELL, J. H.   ... B 02–06
    Capt.
                            Capt., Black Watch (Royal Highlanders).
                            War Office, Permit Dept.
                            A.D.C., Governor of Newfoundland.

CAMPBELL, J. M. H.   COLL. 04–10
    Capt.
                            Capt., R.A.M.C.
                            Despatches.
                            O.B.E.

✠ CAMPBELL, K. G.   ... B 08–14
    Lieut.
                            Lieut. and Adjt., H.L.I.
                            Killed Sept. 25th, 1915, *Loos.*

CAMPBELL, M. F. MACIVER   E 81–84
    Capt.
                            (Clare Coll., Camb.   Vancouver.)
                            Capt., Canadian Army Pay Corps.

CAMPBELL, P. J.   COLL. 11–16
    Lieut.
                            2nd Lieut., R.F.A.
                            Lieut., 1918.
                            M.C.

CAMPBELL, W. M.   ... B 92–95
    Lieut.-Col.
                            (Suffolk Regt., 1902.   S. African War.)
                            Capt., Suffolk Regt., 1914.
                            Major, 1916.
                            Prisoner of War, escaped from Germany, 1917.
                            Att. K.O.S.B., 5th Bn.
                            Acting Lieut.-Col., Suffolk Regt., 1919.
                            Wounded.   *Despatches.*
                            D.S.O.

CAMPBELL, W. O.   ... F 91–93
    Major
                            (Lieut., Remington's Guides.   S. African War.)
                            Capt., R.A.S.C.
                            H.Q. Intelligence Dept. Motor Service.
                            Major, 1918.
                            M.C.

CAMPION, W. S. ... E 09–14
    Lieut.   Lieut., Seaforth Highlanders.

CAPES, G. W. ... C 07–10
    Capt.   2nd Lieut., Hampshire Regt., 1914.
                         Capt., 1917.

CARDINALL, A. W. ... F 00–01
                         District Political Officer.
                         British Force of Occupation, Togoland.

✠ CAREW, F. L. ... G 08–12
    2nd Lieut.   2nd Lieut., 20th Hussars.
                         Killed Oct. 30th, 1914, *Oostaverne, near Ypres.*

CAREW, P. G. ... G 07–12
    Capt.   (Lieut., R. 1st Devon Yeomanry.)
                         Remount Dept.
                         1918, Capt., First Assistant Superintendent.
                         Restored to establishment, 1919.
                         Wounded.

CAREY, G. G. S. COLL. 79–83
    Major-General   (R.A., 1886. Major, 1901. S. African War.)
                         Lieut.-Col., R.F.A., 1913. Brevet Col.
                         Brigadier-General, 1915.
                         Major-General, 1918.
                         Despatches (7).
                         C.B.,C.M.G.,Commandeur Order of La Couronne.

CARMICHAEL, W. B. G. G 12–17
    2nd Lieut.   2nd Lieut., I.A.

CAROE, O. K. K. ... E 06–11
    Capt.   2nd Lieut., R.W. Surrey Regt., 1914.
                         Capt., 1916.

✠ CARPENTER, E. B. ... H 99–05
    Capt.   (Univ. Coll., Oxford. Home C.S.)
                         Capt., R.M.L.I., Plymouth Bn.
                         Died at Sea August 18th, 1915, *of wounds*
                                 received Gallipoli.

CARR, P. COMYNS ... H 88–92
    Capt.   (B.N.C. Journalist.)
                         Temp. Capt. Staff Capt., Intelligence Dept. B.
                         Education Officer, R.A.F.
                         Resigned Commission, 1919.
                         Despatches.

CARR, P. W. K. ... F 97–99
    Capt.   (Seaforth Highlanders, 1905.)
                         Capt., Seaforth Highlanders, 1914. G.S.O.$_3$,
                               1916. War Office, Staff Capt., 1917.
                         Temp. Major.

✠ CARRICK, J.   F 10–13
    Lieut.

Lieut., Cameron Highlanders.
Despatches.
Killed July 31st, 1917, *near Frezenberg, E. of Ypres.*

CARRICK, R. B.   F 06–10
    Lieut.

Lieut., R.F.A.
Madras Artillery Volunteers.
Acting Capt., 1918.
Despatches.

CARRINGTON, R. H.   ...   B 96–00
    Brevet Lieut.-Col.

(R.F.A., Lieut., 1904. S. African War. Capt., 1914.)
Major, R.H.A., 1915.
Brigade-Major, 1916. G.S.O.$_2$.
Despatches (4).
D.S.O.

CARTE, R. D'OYLY   H 89–94

Temp. Lieut., R.N.V.R.

CARTER, A. L. BONHAM-   F 01–06
    Capt.

(K.R.R.C., 1907.)
Capt., K.R.R.C., 1915.
G.S.O.$_3$, 1916. Brigade-Major, 1917.
Wounded (2).   *Despatches* (4).
D.S.O.

✠ CARTER, A. T. BONHAM-   H 83–87
    Capt.

(Trin. Coll. Camb. Lieut, Vol. Hants Coy. S. African War. Judge at Mombasa, 1907.)
Director of Military Supplies, E.A.F.
Capt. Hampshire Regt.
Killed July 1st, 1916, *Battle of the Somme, near Beaumont Hamel.*

CARTER, F. G. BONHAM-   H 91–96
    Capt.

Temp. Capt., Grenadier Guards.
T. M. Battery.
Chief Instructor, School of Instruction.
Wounded.

✠ CARTER, G. BONHAM-   H 97–01
    Capt.

(Magd. Coll., Oxford. 19th Hussars.)
Capt., 19th Hussars.
Despatches.
Killed May 15th, 1915, *near Ypres.*

✠ CARTER, G. F.   D 10–13
    2nd Lieut.

2nd Lieut., K.R.R.C., 7th Bn.
Died in Sanctuary Wood July 31st, 1915, *of wounds received* July 30th, *at Hooge.*

39

CARTER, H. BONHAM- Lieut.-Col.	H 75–80	(R.E., 1883. Major, 1900. Soudan Expedition.) Lieut.-Col., R.E., retired 1910. Assistant Director, R.T.
CARTER, P. H. Major	A 80–84	Major, R. Warwickshire Regt, 5th Bn., 1914– 1916. Att. H.Q., Vth Army. War Office. T.D. *Despatches.*
✠ CARTLAND, G. T. Capt.	F 06–11	Capt and Adjt., R.B. G.S.O.$_3$. *Despatches.* *Killed* July 1st. 1916, *Battle of the Somme.*
CARVER, F. E. Capt.	D 10–14	Lieut., Dorset Regt. Capt., 1916.
✠ CASSON, R. A. 2nd Lieut.	B 07–11	2nd Lieut., R. Welsh Fusiliers. *Killed* Sept. 26th, 1917, *Polygon Wood, Zonnebeke.*
CAVE, K. McC. Bt. Major	A 07–11	(R.E., 1913.) Capt., R.E., 1917. Brevet Major, 1919. *Wounded.* *Despatches.* M.C.
CECIL, A. W. J. Capt.	E 89–91	(Trin. Coll. Camb. Grenadier Guards, 1900. S. African War.) Capt., Grenadier Guards. Reserve of Officers.
✠ CECIL, G. E. 2nd Lieut.	B 09–12	2nd Lieut., Grenadier Guards. *Killed* Sept. 1st, 1914, *Villers Cotteret.*
CECIL, R. E. Major	E 92–97	(8th Hussars. 21st Lancers. Capt, 1901.) Major, 21st Lancers. Brigade-Major, 1914. Att. 9th Lancers. G.S.O.$_2$, 1917. G.S.O.$_1$, 1918.
CHADWICK, E. W. Capt.	C 98–01	(R.G.A., 1903. Capt., 1911.) Capt., R.G.A. Acting Major, 1918. M.C.
✠ CHAMBERLAYNE, T. E. O. Lieut.	A 07–10	Lieut., R.F.A. *Wounded.* *Killed* August 18th, 1916, *Battle of the Somme.*

CHAPLIN, R. E.   E 80–83   (Leicester Regt., 1887.   Ind. Staff Corps, 1888.
     Lieut.-Col.   Major, 1905.)
                                  Lieut.-Col., Bengal Lancers, 8th Bn.

✠ CHAPLIN, R. E. E.   COLL. 08–13
     Lieut.   2nd Lieut., R.E., 1914.
                                  Killed April 22nd, 1917. *Neuville Vitasse.*

✠ CHARLES, A. A. M.   COLL. 01–06
     Capt.   Capt., R.F.A.
                                  Killed Dec. 20th, 1914, *Cuinchy.*

CHARLES, E. M. S.   COLL. 91–95   (R.E., 1897.   S. African War.   Capt., 1907.)
     Lieut.-Col.   Major, R.E., 1914.
                                  Ordnance Survey.
                                  Brevet Lieut.-Col., 1918.
                             .   *Despatches* (2.)
                                  D.S.O., C.M.G.

CHARLES, F. R. S.   COLL. 86–91   (Merchant, Calcutta.)
                                  Veterans' Corps, Calcutta.

CHARLES, J. R. E.   COLL. 89–92   (R.E., Lieut., 1897.   Capt., 1901.   S. African
     D.S.O.   War.)
          Brigadier-General   Brevet Major, R.E., 1908.
                                  Brigadier-General, H.Q. General Staff, I.E.F.
                                  Brevet Lieut.-Col., 1915.   Brevet Col., 1916.
                                  Temp. Major-General, 25th Div., 1918.
                                  Brigadier-General, Staff College.
                                  Despatches (5).
                                  C.B., C.M.G.   Officier Légion d'Honneur.

CHARNWOOD, Lord   ... A 77–83
                                  Late Major, London Vol. Regt.

CHARRINGTON, G. N. ... E 03–06
     Capt.   2nd Lieut., Hertfordshire Yeomanry.
                                  Lieut.
                                  Capt., 1918.

CHARTERIS, N. K.   ... E 92–95   (2nd Lieut., Royal Scots, 1899.   S. African
     Lieut.-Col.   War.   Capt., 1907.)
                                  Temp. Lieut.-Col., Royal Scots, 1916.
                                  M.G.C.   School Commandant.
                                  Brevet Lieut.-Col., 1918.
                                  Temp. Col. Army M.G. Officer, 1918.
                                  Despatches (2).
                                  D.S.O., C.M.G.

CHAWNER, L. C. ... F 92–97 (Hants Regt., Lieut., 1901. Retired 1910.)
    Capt.   Capt., Dorset Regt., 3rd Bn.
                             Brigade-Major. Temp. Major.
                             Despatches.

✠ CHEESMAN, G. L. COLL. 97–03 (New Coll., Oxford.)
    Lieut.   Lieut., Hampshire Regt.
                             Killed August 10th, 1915, *Chunuk Bair, Gallipoli.*

CHELMSFORD, Lord ... B 81–87 (Magd. Coll., All Souls, Oxford. Governor
                                 Queensland, Governor N.S. Wales.)
                             Capt., Dorset Regt., 1914.
                             Viceroy of India. G.C.M.G., G.C.S.I., G.C.I.E.,
                                 G.C.B.E.

CHESNEY, G. L. ... D 07–11
    Lieut.   1916, Lieut., King's Own R. Lancaster Regt.
                             Wounded.

CHEYNE, W. H. ... C 03–07
                             R.N. Surgeon, R. Naval Hospital, Chatham.

CHICHESTER, C. F. S. F 07–10
    Lieut.   2nd Lieut, 4th Hussars.
                             Lieut., 1918.

CHINNOCK, H. S. ... A 87–88
    Lieut.   Lieut., Assistant Superintendent, Remount
                                 Service.

CHIPPENDALE, F. W. C. ... E 04–07
    Capt.   Capt., Oxford and Bucks L.I.
                             A.D.C., 1917.
                             Wounded.

CHITTY, J. H. ... COLL. 11–17
    2nd Lieut.   2nd Lieut., K.R.R.C., 6th Bn.
                             Wounded.

CHITTY, J. T. ... ... C 07–08
    Capt.   Sub-Lieut., R.N.A.S.
                             R.A.F., Capt., Technical Branch.

CHITTY, T. H. W. ... D 04–10
    Capt.   Capt., R.F.A., 6th London Brigade.
                             T.F.R. War Office, Ministry National Service.
                             Relinquished Commission, ill health, May, 1918.

CHRISTIAN, R. E. E. ... C 02–05
    Lieut.   2nd Lieut., R. West Surrey Regt., 4th Bn.
                             Lieut., 1917.

42

CHRISTIE, A. H. ... I 05–08
Lieut., 4th Hussars. Adjt., Special Reserve.
Assistant Commandant, School of Instruction.
M.C.

CHRISTIE, J. T. COLL. 13–18 (Cadet Household Brigade, O.C.B.)

CHRISTOPHERSON, N. ... I 07–13
Lieut.
Acting Capt. and Adjt., R.F.A., 5th London
Brigade.
Acting Major, 1918.
Despatches.
M.C.

CHRISTY, H. A. ... E 90–94 (Christ Church, Oxford.)
Capt.
Lieut., Glamorgan Yeomanry.
Att. Welsh Regt., 7th Bn.
Capt., 1918.

CHURCH, E. F. R. ... A 89–90 (Farming, S. Africa. With Imp. Yeomanry,
Capt.
S. African War.)
Lieut., London Regt., 25th Bn.
Capt., 1917. T.F.R.

CHURCH, G. S. ... ... C 00–05 (Univ. Coll., Oxford.)
Capt.
Capt., R.F.A., 1917.
Acting Major, 1918.
M.C.

CHURSTON, Lord, M.V.O. E 87–90 (Scots Guards, 1896. Capt., 1902. S. African
Lieut.-Col.
War.)
Capt., Scots Guards.
Temp. Major, 1918.
Staff Capt. D.A.Q.M.G.
Inspector of Q.M.G.'s Service, London District.
Lieut.-Col., 1919.
Reserve of Officers.
C.B.E.

CHUTE, Rev. A. W. COLL. 98–03 (Magd. Coll., Oxford.)
Chaplain to the Forces.
Despatches (2). O.B.E.

CLARK, C. A. GORDON ... D 77–82 (K.R.R.C., 1884. Major, 1901. S. African War.)
Lieut.-Col.
Lieut.-Col., Comm. Q. Westminster Rifles.
Retired, T.F.R.
D.S.O., C.M.G.

CLARK, H. G. ... ... I 95–99 (New Coll., Oxford. Stock Exchange.)
Lieut.
Lieut., R.A.S.C.

CLARK, H. M. GORDON ... G 09–14
    Lieut.
                      2nd Lieut., R.A.S.C.
                      Lieut., M.T.
                      Wounded.

CLARK, J. E ... ... c 04–07
    Capt.
                      Capt., R.A.S.C.
                      Att. Essex Regt.
                      M.C.

CLARK, J. G. W. ... E 06–10
    Major
                      Lieut., 16th Lancers.
                      Temp. Capt., 1916.
                      Temp. Major, General Staff. Brigade-Major,.
                        1917.
                      G.S.O.$_2$, 1918.
                      Wounded. *Despatches* (2).
                      M.C. and Bar.

CLARK, L. ... ... G 97–00
                      Pay Sergt., 30th Bn., C.E.F.

CLARK, L. C. E. ... ... c 05–10
    Capt.
                      2nd Lieut., Scots Greys.
                      Att. Berks Yeomanry.
                      Capt., 1916.

CLARK, N. J. GORDON ... G 11–15
    Lieut.
                      2nd Lieut., Devonshire Regt.
                      Lieut., 1917.

CLARKE, A. C. L. STANLEY B 00–05
    Lieut.-Col.
                      (Univ. Coll., Oxford. Scottish Rifles, 1909.)
                      Capt., Cameronians (Scottish Rifles), 1914.
                      Temp. Lieut.-Col., Comm. 10th Bn., 1916.
                      Wounded. *Despatches* (4).
                      D.S.O. and Bar, Chevalier Légion d'Honneur,.
                        Croix de Guerre.

✠ CLARKE, A. G. ... COLL. 96–02
    2nd Lieut.
                      (New Coll., Oxford.)
                      2nd Lieut., R.B.
                      Killed July 2nd, 1916.

CLARKE, A. L. C. ... E 91–92
    Capt.
                      (Christ Church, Oxford.)
                      Lieut., Cheshire Regt., 1915.
                      Acting Capt., 1918.

CLARKE, G. V., D.S.O. ... E 89–94
    Lieut.-Col.
                      (4th D.G. 18th Hussars. Capt., 1904. S.
                        African War.)
                      Lieut.-Col.
                      Temp. Brig.-Gen., City of London, Rough-riders..
                      Despatches (2).
                      C.M.G.

✠ CLARKE, J. G. ... ... E 85–89
    Capt.

    Capt., R. Sussex Regt., 9th Bn.
    Killed Sept. 27th, 1915.

CLAY, J. C. ... ... H 11–16
    Lieut.

    2nd Lieut., R.F.A.
    Lieut., 1918.

CLAYPON, J. C. LANE COLL. 95–00
    Lieut.

    (Pemb. Coll., Camb. Solicitor.)
    Lieut., Lincolnshire Regt.
    Staff. Lieut. Gen. List. Sp. Appointment.
    Wounded.

CLEGG, W. G. ... ... B 83–88
    Lieut.

    (Magd. Coll., Oxford.)
    Lieut., Manchester Regt., 1916.
    Acting Capt., 1917, 53rd, Y.S. Bn.

CLELAND, M. W. D'A. ... C 08–11

    2nd Lieut., K.R.R.C.
    Relinquished Comm., ill health.

CLEMENTS, E. F. ... A 98–03
    Capt.

    (New Coll., Oxford.)
    2nd Lieut., Lincolnshire Regt.
    Capt., M.G.C., Tank Corps.

CLERK, A. G. ... ... D 01–05
    Major

    Major, Hertfordshire Regt.
    Wounded (4).   *Despatches* (2).
    M.C., D.S.O.

CLIFFORD, A. W. ... D 91–92
    Capt.

    (Trin. Hall, Camb. Glos. Regt., 1900. Lieut.,
        1904. S. African War.)
    Capt., Gen. List, 1914.
    Officer, Cadet Bn., Gloucestershire Regt.

CLOVER, H. ... COLL. 88–92
    Capt.

    (King's Coll., Camb. S. Staffs Regt., 1900.
        S. African War. Retired, 1903.)
    Barrister.
    Capt., S. Staffs Regt. Retired.

CLOWES, G. C. K. ... A 95–00
    Lieut.-Col.

    (Magd. Coll., Oxford.)
    Major, London Scottish.
    D.A.Q.M.G.
    Lieut.-Col., 1918.
    Despatches (2).
    D.S.O.

✠ CLUTTERBUCK, D. COLL. 04–09
    Lieut.

    Lieut., R.F.A.
    Despatches.
    Killed May 6th, 1917, *Vimy Ridge.*

CLUTTON, B. ... ... F 98–02
    Lieut.   Lieut., Bedfordshire Regt., 5th Bn., 1918.
                                     Wounded.

COBB, B. C. ... ... B 90–94 (Land Agent.)
    Capt.   Capt., R.F.A. T.F.
                                       Acting Major, R.G.A., 1917.

COBB, C. H. ... ... D 81–86 (New Coll., Oxford. Solicitor.)
    Lieut.-Col.   Lieut.-Col., Oxford and Bucks L.I., 5th Bn.,
                                       Retired.
                                       Despatches.

COBB, E. H. ... ... C 13–17
                                       Indian Cadet, Quetta.

✠ COBB, F. C. ... ... D 03–07
    Capt.   Capt., K.O.S.B.
                                       Killed Sept. 26th, 1915, *Loos.*

COBB, R. S. ... ... E 03–07
    Capt.   Capt., Middlesex Regt.
                                       To S. Staffs Regt., 1918.

COCKERELL, F. W. P. COLL. 90–95 (New Coll., Oxford. Rhodesian F.F., S. African
    Capt.   War. District Commissioner, N.W.
                                       Rhodesia.)
                                     Capt., Intelligence Officer H.Q.
                                     Camp Commandant, A.P.M.
                                     Administrative Commandant.
                                     Acting Lieut.-Col., Allied Commissioner of
                                     Police, Baku, 1918.
                                     Despatches (3).
                                     M.C. O.B.E.

COCKROFT, E. T. ... I 83–87 (B.N.C., Oxford.)
    Capt.   Capt., S.W. Borderers.

COLBORNE, Hon. F. L. L. E 69–71 (New Inn Hall, Oxford. R. Irish Rifles, 1878.
    M.V.O.   Major, 1885. Kandahar, Soudan, S.African
    Col.   War. Comm. 24th Middlesex Rifles, 1901.)
                                     Col. Administrative Commandant.
                                     Retired.

✠ COLE, N. W. WELLS ... G 05–10 (R.H.A.)
    Major   2nd Lieut., R.H.A., 1914.
                                     Capt., 1915.
                                     Major, R.F.A.
                                     Despatches.
                                     Killed Jan. 6th, 1918, *Langemarck.*

COLE, V. H. WELLS ... G 09–14
Lieut.   Lieut., Yorkshire L.I., 9th Bn.
                                    Brigade Intelligence Officer.
                                    Labour Corps, 1918.
                                    Wounded (2).
                                    M.C.

COLES, A. H., c.m.g., d.s.o. A 70–73   (E. Kent Regt., 1876.   Egyptian Army, Soudan,
Lieut.-Col.   K.A.R., Uganda.)
                                    Lieut.-Col. Northumberland Fusiliers.
                                    Retired, 1918.
                                    Despatches (2).

✠ COLES, G. H. ... ... A 84–89   (Engineer.)
                                    Private, R. Fusiliers, 24th Bn.
                                    Killed Jan. 27th, 1916, *Festubert*.

✠ COLGATE, R. ... ... F 95–97
                                    R.N.V.R., Armoured Car Division.
                                    Wounded.
                                    Killed July 12th, 1916, *Mametz Wood*.

COLLARD, A. W.... COLL. 66–72   (1st Comm., 1872.   Soudan.   Col., 1898.)
Col.   Director Supplies, Woolwich Dockyard.
                                    Colonel, Director S. and T. Irish Command.
                                    District Barracks Officer.

COLLINS, Hon. R. H. ... I 86–90   (Berks Regt., 1892.   Capt., 1902.   S. African
d.s.o.   War.)
Lieut.-Col.   Major R. Berkshire Regt., 1914 (A.A.Q.M.G.)
                                    Brevet Lieut.-Col., 1916.   A.A.Q.M.G., 1918.
                                    Temp. Brigadier-General.
                                    Despatches (2).
                                    C.M.G.   Cav. SS. Maurizio e Lazaro.

COLLIS, W. E. R. ... F 77–81   (5th Lancers, 1884.   Major, 1901.   S. African
Major   War.)
                                    Major, 5th Lancers.   Comm. Depot.
                                    Retired.

COLMAN, J. ... ... A 00–05   (Trin. Coll., Camb.)
Capt.   2nd Lieut., London Regt, 3/23rd Bn.
                                    Capt. and Adjt., 1917.

COLVILL, D. C. ... ... G 12–15
Lieut.   2nd Lieut., Oxford and Bucks L.I., 1916.
                                    Lieut., 1918.
                                    Wounded.
                                    M.C.

47

✠ COLVILL, G. C. ... G 07–12
    Capt. .

        Capt., S. Irish Horse.
        Killed Nov. 30th, 1917, *Fontaine les Croiselles,*
           near Bapaume.

COLVILLE, Hon. J. G. ... I 06–10
    Lieut.
        Lieut., R.N.V.R.

COLVILLE, R. A. ... H 00–05
    Capt.
        (Grenadier Guards, 1906–08.)
        Capt., Cameron Highlanders.
        Sec. for Service with Egyptian Army.
        Despatches.

✠ COLVIN, R. A. ... ... G 02–08
    Capt.
        Capt., W. Yorkshire Regt.
        Adjt., 2nd Bn.
        Despatches.
        Killed March 10th, 1915, *Neuve Chapelle.*

COMBER, J. O. ... ... B 12–16
    Lieut.
        2nd Lieut, R.A.F.
        Lieut., 1918.

CONDER, E. ... ... A 02–07
    Capt.
        Capt., Gloucestershire Regt.
        M.G.C., Infantry.
        Employed under Admiralty.
        Despatches.
        M.C.

CONYNGHAM, Marquess ... G 05–06
    2nd Lieut.
        2nd Lieut., N. Irish Horse.
        Resigned Commission, ill health.

✠ COOK, A. B. K. COLL. 98–04
    2nd Lieut.
        (New Coll., Oxford. Architect.)
        2nd Lieut., R. Fusiliers.
        Killed July 7th, 1916, *Ovillers Wood.*

COOPER, O. ... ... D 08–13
    Capt.
        Lieut., Lancashire Fusiliers.
        Capt., 1916, 6th Bn.
        Wounded.

COOPER, W. B. ... ... D 04–09
    Major
        Major, R.F.A., 6th London Brigade.
        Wounded.   *Despatches* (3).
        M.C.

COOTE, E. O. ... COLL. 07–13
    Lieut. ...
        (Civilian prisoner in Germany to June, 1916.)
        Pte., Devonshire Regt.
        2nd Lieut., Gen. List.
        Lieut., 1917.
        War Office, Intelligence Dept.
        Despatches.

COSENS, C. R. G. ... K 06–08
    Capt.
                  Lieut., R.E. Signal Service, T.F.
                  Capt., R.E., 1918.
                  Employed at Admiralty.

✠ COTTON, R. C. F. ... D 96–02
    Lieut.
                  (New Coll., Oxford.)
                  Lieut. and Adjt., Hampshire Carabiniers.
                  Att. M.G.C. Cavalry.
                  Despatches.
                  Croix de Guerre.
                  Died at Evreux March 28th, 1918, of wounds
                        received Bois des Essarts, Noyon.

COTESWORTH, R. ... C 79–82
    Major
                  (Ceylon. Mounted Infantry. S. African War.)
                  Capt., R.M. Artillery.
                  Major, 1918.

✠ COUCH, B. B. QUILLER- ... B 04–09
    Capt.
                  Capt., Acting Major, R.F.A., 41st Brigade.
                  Wounded.   *Despatches* (2).
                  M.C., D.S.O.
                  Died, Feb. 8th, 1919, of pneumonia, at Durren.

COUPER, J. D. C. ... D 89–94
    Col.
                  (Trin. Coll. Camb. A.M.I.C.E.)
                  Temp. Col., R.E.
                  C.B.E.

COURTENAY, Rev. Hon.   A 89–
    F. L.
                  (Exeter Coll., Oxford.)
                  2nd Lieut., Devon Vol. Regt., 1st Bn.

COURTHOPE, E. A. C. ... D 93–98
    Lieut.
                  (R.I.E., Coopers Hill. Lieut., Garwhali Rifles.)
                  Att. W. Yorkshire Regt.
                  Wounded.
                  Relinquished Commission.

COURTNEY, G. B., M.D. ... A 77–80
                  (Pemb. Coll., Camb.)
                  Temp. Capt., R.A.M.C.
                  Despatches.

COVENTRY, F. C. A. ... H 88–92
                  Ministry of Munitions.
                  O.B.E.

✠ COWAN, H. V., C.B., C.V.O.   B 68–72
    Col.
                  (R.A., 1873. Major, 1890. Afghan War.
                      Tel-el-Kebir. S. African War. Governor,
                      R.M. Academy, 1904.)
                  Col., A.A.G., Irish Command.
                  Despatches.
                  Died in England, Jan. 25th, 1918.

COWAN, J. I. ... ... B 76–79
Lieut.   2nd Lieut., R.A.S.C., 1915, Suvla Bay.
Lieut., 1917.
Transport Officer, S.W. Mounted Brigade,
Egypt.

COWAN, W. W. ... COLL. 10–15 (R.A., 1916.)
Capt.   Lieut., R.A., 1917.
Acting Capt. and Adjt., 1919.

COWLAND, W. S.... ... D 01–07 (Schoolmaster, Twyford.)
Major   Hampshire Regt., 1914.
Capt., 1915.
Major, 1917.
Despatches (2).
D.S.O.

Cox, R. F. de L. ... ... G 97–03 (St. John's Coll., Oxford.)
Lieut.   Lieut., R.F.A., 1st Home Counties Brigade,.
1916.
Staff. Lieut.

✠ CRABBE, C. T. EYRE ... H 10–12
Lieut.   Lieut., Grenadier Guards, 3rd Bn.
Reported Missing. No further information.
Killed Sept. 27th, 1915.

✠ CRAGGS, J. J. ... ... G 01–05
2nd Lieut.   2nd Lieut., K.R.R.C., 6th, att. 1st Bn.
Killed Feb. 17th, 1917.

CRAIES, C. ... ... A 95–96 (To Westminster School. Business. Inner
Lieut.   Temple, 1905.)
Lieut., Interpreter.
Intelligence Dept., Salonica.
Despatches.

CRANE, M. E. ... ... D 03–07 (I.A., 1913.)
Capt.   Duke of Wellington's W. Riding Regt., 1914..
Lieut., 1914.
Capt., 1917.

CRAWFORD, A. J. D. ... D 13–16
2nd Lieut.   2nd Lieut., 6th Inniskilling Dragoons, 1918.

✠ CRAWHALL, F. P. COLL. 08–14
Lieut.   Lieut., K.R.R.C., 6th Bn.
Killed March 10th, 1915, *Givenchy, Lez-la-*
Bassee.

CRAWLEY, C. W....   COLL. 11–17
     2nd Lieut.   2nd Lieut., K.R.R.C., 6th Bn., 1918.

CRAWLEY, R. P., M.V.O.   I 89–95   (S.W. Borderers, 1897.   Capt., A.S.C., 1903.
     Lieut.-Col.   S. African War.)
                                        Major, R.A.S.C., 1914.
                                        Temp. Lieut.-Col., Dep. Director Transport.
                                        Asst. Director S. & T., 1918.
                                        Brevet Lieut.-Col.
                                        Despatches (5).
                                        D.S.O., O.B.E.

✠ CREAGH, H. J. P.   ... A 06–11
     Capt.   Lieut., Suffolk Regt.
                                        Acting Capt., 1918.
                                        Wounded (3).
                                        M.C.
                                        Died of wounds, Nov. 23rd, 1918, *Le Treport.*

CREASY, R.   ...   ... B 01–05
                                        Surgeon, R.N.
                                        Wounded.

CRESSWELL, H. G. BAKER   D 91–96   (B.N.C., Oxford.)
     Capt.   .   Capt., R.E., London Signal Coy.

✠ CRICHTON, C. J. M. M. ... H 94–99   (Hants. Imp. Yeomanry.   S. African War.)
                                        Major, Gordon Highlanders.
                                        Killed, Sept. 25th, 1915.

CRICK, REV. P. C. T.   COLL. 95–01   (Pemb. Coll., Camb.   Fellow, Clare Coll.)
                                        Senior Chaplain to Forces, 3rd Division.

CRIPPS, HON. A. H. S. ... A 95–01   (New Coll., Oxford.)
     Lieut.   Lieut., Lincolnshire Yeomanry.
                                        A.D.C.
                                        Temp. Capt., Court-Martial Officer, 1918.

CRIPPS, HON. F. H.   ... A 99–03   (New Coll., Oxford.)
     Major   Major, Acting Lieut.-Col., Bucks Hussars.
                                        M.G.C. Infantry, 1917.
                                        Wounded.   *Despatches* (2).
                                        D.S.O. and Bar.

CRIPPS, H. R.   ...   ... I 85–   (Solicitor.)
     Major   Lieut., Gen. List.
                                        A.D.C., H.Q. Eastern Command.
                                        Staff Capt.
                                        Temp. Major, D.A.Q.M.G., 1919.

51

CRIPPS, HON. R. S. ... A 01–07

Red Cross Service, Boulogne.
1915, Ministry of Munitions, Dept. of Explosives.
1916, Asst. Superintendent, H.M. Factory, Queensferry.

CROFT, P. R. ... ... B 97–02
Capt.

(Ch. Ch., Oxford.)
Capt., R.F.A., 4th E. Anglian Brigade.
Invalided, 1918.

CROFTON, M. R. H. ... D 94–99
Major

(R.A., 1900. Lieut., 1903. Capt.,1911.)
Major, R.F.A., 1914, 5A Res. Brigade.
Temp. Lieut.-Col., 1916.
Wounded (3). *Despatches* (6).
D.S.O. and Bar.

CROFTS, E. S. ... ... E 72–77
Lieut.-Col.

(Keble Coll., Oxford. 37th Regt., 1880. Major, 1897. S. African War. Retired, 1907.)
Lieut.-Col., Hampshire Regt., 13th Bn.
Recruiting Duties.

✠ CROMBIE, J. E. ... ... C 09–14
Capt.

Capt., Gordon Highlanders.
Wounded.
Killed, April 23rd, 1917, *Roeux, near Arras.*

CROOK, A. H. ... ... C 11–15
Capt.

Capt., London Regt., 1st Bn.
Major, R.A.F., 1918.
M.C.

CROOK, E. A. ... ... B 07–12
Lieut.

Pte., Middlesex Regt., Public Sch. Bn.
Surgeon-Lieut., R.N., 1918.

✠ CROOK, P. J. ... ... B 05–10
Lieut.

Lieut., D. of Lancaster's Yeomanry.
Killed, Nov. 7th, 1917, *Wadi Hesi, near Gaza.*

CROSBIE, D. S. K. ... I 99–01
Capt.

(Arg. and Suth. Highlanders, 1907. W.A.F.F., 1912–14.)
Capt., Arg. and Suth. Highlanders, 1914.
R.A.F., Capt. A.
Prisoner of War. Repatriated Nov., 1918.
Despatches.

CROSS, A. R. ... ... F 08–13
Capt.

Capt., Gordon Highlanders.
Acting Capt., R.A.F., 1918.
Wounded (3).
M.C. and Bar.

CROSS, D. ... ... F 14–18
Sergt., R.M. College.

CROSS, M. R. ... ... E 12–17
2nd Lieut.
2nd Lieut., R.F.A., 1918.

CROSS, P. K. ... ... E 11–15
Capt.
2nd Lieut., R.F.A.
Lieut., 1918.
Acting Capt. and Adjt., 1918.

CROSTHWAITE, A. T. ... G 93–99
Capt.
(New Coll., Oxford. Barrister.)
2nd Lieut., R.A.S.C., 6th London Brigade.
Temp. Capt., 1918. Court Martial Officer.
Staff Capt.
Despatches.

CRUDDAS, B. ... ... D 95–99
Lieut.-Col.
(Northumberland Fusiliers, 1900. Capt., 1909.)
Major, Northumberland Fusiliers, 1915.
Temp. Lieut.-Col., Oxford and Bucks L.I.
Acting Lieut.-Col., R. Scots Fusiliers, 1918.
Despatches (2).
D.S.O.

CRUMP, N. E. ... COLL. 09–14
Lieut.
Lieut., Middlesex Regt., 9th Bn.
Egyptian E.F.
Att. R.E. for Army Signal Service, 1917.

CULLINAN, F. J. F. ... E 09–14
Capt.
(Trin. Coll., Dublin.)
2nd Lieut., The King's Liverpool Regt., 1914.
Temp. Lieut., Duke of Wellington's W. Riding
        Regt., 9th Bn.
Temp. Capt., 1915.
Acting Major, 1915.
(Employed at Admiralty, 1918.)
Capt. and Adjt., Dec., 1918.
Wounded.
M.C.

CULLINAN, M. W. F. ... E 06–12
Capt.
(Magd. Coll., Camb.)
Lieut. and Adjt., K.R.R.C., 1915.
Officer, Cadet Bn.
Capt., Education Officer, 1919.
Despatches.
M.C.

CUMMINS, W. A. ... I 00–03
Capt.
Capt., Oxford and Bucks L.I.
G.S.O.$_3$.

✠ Cunliffe, J. L. ... H 01–07 (Univ. Coll., Oxford.)
  Capt.   Capt., Manchester Regt.
      Killed Sept. 4th, 1916, *Delville Wood.*

Cure, G. E. Capel ... c 66–70 (Lancs. Fusiliers, 1875. Major, 1893. Reserve
  Major   of Officers.)
      Major R.F.A., 3rd N. Midland Brigade.
      Retired.

Curtis, J. D. C. ... G 06–10
  Lieut.   2nd Lieut., R. Lancaster Regt.
      Lieut., R.A.F. (Technical Branch).
      Wounded.
      M.C.

Curtis, W. P. S. ... F 12–17
  2nd Lieut.   2nd Lieut., R.B., 1918.

Cuthbertson, M. coll. 07–11
  Major   Major, R. Fusiliers.
      Staff Capt.
      Despatches (2).
      M.C.

✠ Daffarn, M. ... ... F 01–06
  Lieut.   Lieut., 2nd Mobile Column, Rhodesia.
      Killed April 14th, 1915, *N.E. Rhodesia.*

Dalbiac, P. H., c.b. ... H 70–72 (70th Regt., 1875. 45th Regt. Retired, Major,
  Lieut.-Col.   1890.)
      Lieut.-Col., A.S.C., 2nd London Divisional
      Train.

Dalton, E. G. T. Tuite... F 98–01 (3rd Gurkha Rifles, 1905.)
  Capt.   Capt., 3rd Gurkha Rifles.
      Brigade-Major, 1916.
      Despatches.
      M.C.

Dalton, L. Grant ... I 02–07 (Dorset Regt., 1912.)
  Capt.   Capt., Dorset Regt., 1915.
      Prisoner of War.
      Interned Holland, 1918.

Daly, A. C. ... ... D 84–88 (W. Yorkshire Regt., 1890. Brevet Major, 1902.
  Bt.-Col.   S. African War.)
      Temp. Major-Gen., 24th Division.
      Despatches (7).
      C.B., C.M.G.

✠ DAMER, Hon. G. S.   G 05–10   (New Coll., Oxford.)
   DAWSON   2nd Lieut., 10th Hussars.
    2nd Lieut.   *Killed* April 12th, 1917, *Monchy-le-Prieux,*
                                     near Arras.

DANCKWERTS, H. O. ... C 01–06
    Lieut.   Acting Capt., E. Riding Yorkshire Yeomanry.
                               (With M.G.C., 1918.)

✠ DANCKWERTS, R. W. ... C 06–12   (Univ. Coll., Oxford.)
    Lieut.   Lieut., Gloucestershire Regt.
                               Died of wounds Dec. 22nd, 1914, *Festubert.*

DANCKWERTS, V. H. ... C 02–04   (R.N. Midshipman, 1906.)
   Lieut.-Commander   R.N. Gunnery Lieut., H.M.S. " Kent."
                               Lieut.-Commander, 1918.
                               Despatches.

✠ DANIELL, A. S. L. ... B 09–13
    2nd Lieut.   2nd Lieut., R.B.
                               Despatches.
                               Killed Dec. 19th, 1914, *Ploegsteert Wood.*

DANIELL, R. A. ... ... D 86–91
    Lieut.   Lieut., Worcestershire Regt., Transport Workers
                               Bn.

DARBY, W. S. ... ... A 87–93   (Trin. Coll., Camb. S. Bartholomew's Hospital).
                               Lieut., R.A.M.C.
                               Relinquished Commission, 1917.

DARLEY, R. ... ... I 10–14
    Lieut.   R.F.A., 1915. Lieut., 1917.
                               Acting Capt., 1918.
                               Acting Major, 1919.
                               Wounded.   *Despatches.*
                               M.C.

DARLING, P. STORMONTH   C 99–05   (New Coll., Oxford.)
    Major   Capt., Black Watch (Royal Highlanders).
                               Acting Lieut.-Col., 1918.
                               Despatches.

DARLING, R. STORMONTH   C 94–99   (Oriel Coll., Oxford.)
    Capt.   Capt., Lothian and Border Horse.
                               A.D.C. to G.O.C., 51st Division, till 1919.
                               Temp. Major.

DARWIN, C. J. W. ... C 08–11
    Capt.   Coldstream Guards, 1914.
                               Capt., 1916.
                               R.A.F., Temp. Major, A., 1918.
                               Wounded.
                               D.S.O.

DARWIN, G. W. L. ... c 13–18
Cadet, R.A.F.

DARWIN, R. H., D.S.O. ... B 88–88 (Yorkshire L.I., 1897. S. African War. Capt.,
Capt. 1904.)
Capt., Reserve of Officers.

DARWIN, W. R. ... B 08–13
Lieut. Lieut., Durham L.I.
Temp. Capt., R.E.

DAUBENY, C. W. ... A 73–78 (Keble Coll., Oxford. Sarawak Government
Capt. Service.)
Capt., Somerset L.I., 1914.
48th Bn. Training Reserve.
Capt., Shropshire L.I.

DAVENPORT, S. ... ... G 90–92 (R.B., 4th Bn., 1896. Capt.)
Lieut.-Col. Lieut.-Col., Gloucestershire Regt., 4th Bn.
Despatches (4).
D.S.O.

DAVEY, F. G. G. ... A 12–16
2nd Lieut. 2nd Lieut., R.E., 1918.

DAVIDSON, G. ... ... H 89–92 (Stock Exchange.)
Lieut.-Col. Major, R.A.S.C.
Temp. Lieut.-Col., 1918.
Despatches (2).
D.S.O.

DAVIES, J. C. ... ... E 11–14
Lieut. 2nd Lieut., W. Yorkshire Regt., 1915.
Lieut. 1916.
A.D.C., 1918.

DAVISON, J. A. ... ... B 10–15
Capt. 2nd Lieut., R.B., 5th Bn., 1915.
Lieut., 1916. Adjt., 1917.
Acting Capt., 1918.
Despatches.
M.C.

DAVY, R. M. M. ... H 83–86 (2nd Lieut., W.I. Regt. Capt., Gloucestershire
Lieut.-Col. Regt., 1900. S. African War.)
Major, Gloucestershire Regt.
Temp. Lieut.-Col., 1917. Comm. Bn.] E.
Lancs. Regt.
Commandant, H.Q.
Despatches (2).

✠ DAWSON, A. ... ... I 09–14
    2nd Lieut.
        2nd Lieut., R.B.
        Killed July 12th, 1916, *near Vermelles.*

DEANE, J. B. L. ... H 90–92
    Capt.
        (2nd Lieut., Scots Guards, 1896. S. African
            War.)
        Capt., Scots Guards, 1914.
        Brigade-Major.
        Reserve of Officers.

DEANE, M. W. B. ... I 10–13
    Lieut.
        Lancs. Fusiliers, 1915.
        Lieut., 1915.
        Wounded.   *Despatches.*

DE BATHE, P. W. ... H 90–93
    Capt.
        (Diplomatic Service.)
        Capt., Gen. List.
        Staff Capt.
        Train Conducting Officer.

DEBENHAM, H. G. W. ... I 11–16
    Capt.
        Lieut., R.A.F.
        Temp. Capt. A., 1918

✠ DE BLAQUIERE, Hon. J.   E 03–07
    Lieut.
        Lieut., Cameronians, Scottish Rifles.
        Killed March 10th, 1915, *Neuve Chapelle.*

DE BRETT, E. A.   COLL. 80–86
    Lieut.
        (New Coll., Oxford. I.C.S.)
        Lieut., Royal Defence Corps.

DE BOSDARI, A. H.   COLL. 12–18
        Cadet, O.C. Bn., Oxford.

DE CRESPIGNY, T. O. W.   A 73–75
    CHAMPION
    Brig.-Gen.
        (15th Hussars, 1879. Candahar. Transvaal,
            Tel-el-Kebir. Major, 1896. Lieut.-Col.,
            1902. Col. Comm. Brigade, 1907. Retired,
            1909.)
        Hon. Brigadier-General, 1917.
        Despatches.
        C.B.

DEEDES, C. P., D.S.O. ... G 93–97
    Brig.-Gen. ...
        (K.O.Y.L.I., 1899. Capt., 1903. S. African
            War.)
        G.S.O.$_3$, 1914, G.S.O.$_2$, 1916, G.S.O.$_1$, 1917.
            Dep. Director Staff Duties.
        Temp. Brig.-Gen. War Office, Dep. Director.
        Despatches. (4)
        C.M.G. C.B. Chevalier Légion d'Honneur.
            Croix de Guerre.

DEEDES, H. G. ... ... c 92–96 (E. Kent Regt., 1898.)
Major   Major, 2nd Pioneers, Can. E.F.
     Western Ontario Regt.

DENMAN, J. F. ... ... k 10–14
Lieut.   Sub-Lieut , R.N. H.M.S. " *Indomitable.*"
     Acting Lieut., 1918.

DENNISTON, J. D. COLL. 99–06 (New Coll., Oxford.)
Major   Capt., K.O.S.B.
     Employed War Office.
     Temp. Major, 1918. G.S.O.$_2$.
     Wounded (2).
     Croix de Guerre.

✠ DENNYS, R. M. ... f 98–00
Capt.   Capt., N. Lancashire Regt.
     Died in Hospital, Rouen, July 24th, 1916, *of*
         wounds received July 12th.

DENT, J. A. G. ... a 12–17
2nd Lieut.   2nd Lieut., Scots Guards, 1918.

D'ERLANGER, H. R. ... b 09–10
Lieut.   Lieut., Motor M.G.C.
     Gen. List., A.D.C.
     M.G.C.

DE SAUSMAREZ, C. COLL. 83–88 (R.A., 1889. Capt., R.G.A., 1899. S. African
D.S.O.   War. Brevet Lieut.-Col. D.A.A.G., India,
Brevet Col.   1909–13.)
     Brevet Col., R.A. H.Q. Staff, War Office.
     A.A.G., 1915.
     Temp. Brigadier-Gen., 1917.
     Inspector of Demobilization, 1919.
     Despatches (3).
     C.M.G.

DE SELINCOURT, O. COLL. 12–16
2nd Lieut.   2nd Lieut, R.F.A.
     Wounded.

DEWEY, H. G. ... ... d 08–13 (R.A., 1915.)
Lieut.   Lieut., R.F.A., 1916. Acting Capt., 1917.
         Acting Major, 1918.
     Wounded (3).   *Despatches.*
     M.C.

DEWEY, N. S. ... ... D 10–13
    Lieut.
                           2nd Lieut., R.F.A., 1916.
                           Lieut., 1918.
                           R.A.F., Lieut., A. and S., 1918.
                           M.C.

✠ DICKENSON, A. G. N. ... D 10–13
    Lieut.
                           Lieut., K.R.R.C.
                           Wounded.
                           Killed June 30th, 1916, *Loos.*

DICKENSON, E. N. ... D 09–14
    Capt.
                           Lieut., K.R.R.C.
                           Capt. and Adjt., 1918.
                           M.C.

✠ DICKINS, G. ... COLL. 95–00
    Capt.
                           (New Coll., Oxford. British School, Athens.)
                           Capt., K.R.R.C.
                           Killed July 17th, 1916.

DIMOND, C. F. W. ... E 91–95
    Lieut.-Col.
                           (Solicitor.)
                           Lieut.-Col., Comm. Middlesex Regt., 10th Bn.
                           T.D.

DIMOND, P. W. ... E 94–97
                           2nd Lieut., H.A.C.
                           Lieut., 1918.
                           Wounded.

DIXON, F. H. Mc N. ... G 07–10
    2nd Lieut.
                           2nd Lieut., R.A.S.C., relinquished Commission.

DIXON, G. H. S. ... E 05–06
    Lieut.
                           2nd Lieut., R.H.A., Warwickshire.
                           Lieut., 1916.
                           M.C.

DOBBS, H. R. C., C.I.E. COLL. 85–90
                         (B.N.C., Oxford. I.C.S., 1892.)
                         Despatches.

DOBBS, S. P. ... COLL. 13–14
                         (Gentleman Cadet, R.M. Academy, 1918.)

✠ DOBBS, W. C. ... ... I 84–89
    Capt.
                         (Trin. Coll., Camb. Partner in Broadwoods.)
                         Capt., Middlesex Regt., 2nd Bn.
                         Wounded (2).
                       Killed July 31st, 1917, *Ypres.*

DODGSON, A. D.... ... B 98–03
                         (Christ Church, Oxford.)
                         Lieut., R.A.S.C.
                         Capt., 1918.

✠ DODGSON, G. ... ... B 08–13
    Capt., Hertfordshire Regt.
    Wounded (2).
    Died of wounds Nov. 14th, 1918, *Caudry.*

DODGSON, H. B., D.S.O. ... B 77–81
    Major
    (R.H.A., 1893. Major, 1901. S. African War.
        Retired, 1903.)
    Major, R.G.A. Reserve of Officers.

DODGSON, P. H.... ... B 05–10
    (Lieut., R.F.A., 7th London Brigade).
    Acting Capt., 1918.
    Wounded.
    M.C.

✠ DON, A. W. R. ... F 04–09
    Lieut.
    (Trin. Coll., Camb.)
    2nd Lieut., Black Watch (Royal Highlanders),.
        1914.
    Lieut., 1915.
    Died at Salonica on active service Sept. 11th,.
        1916.

DON, J. A. ... ... F 96–00
    Major
    (R.F.A., 1902.)
    Capt., R.F.A., 1914.
    A.D.C., 1915.
    Major. G.S.O.$_3$. Brigade-Major, 1916.
    Despatches (3).
    D.S.O.

✠ DON, R. M. ... COLL. 07–12
    Lieut.
    (New Coll., Oxford.)
    Lieut., Black Watch (Royal Highlanders`,.
        10th Bn.
    Killed May 8th, 1917, *W. of L. Doiran, Salonica.*

✠ DON, V. G. ... ... F 09–14
    2nd Lieut.
    2nd Lieut., West Kent Regt., 8th Bn.
    Wounded.   *Despatches.*
    Killed Sept. 26th, 1915, *2nd Battle of Loos,.*
      between Loos and Halluch.

✠ DONALD, A. J. I. ... K 07–12
    2nd Lieut.
    2nd Lieut., Manchester Regt.
    Killed June 4th, 1915, *Gallipoli.*

✠ DOUGLAS, B. C. O. ... A 08–12
    Capt.
    Lieut., Connaught Rangers.
    Capt., R.A.F.
    Killed Oct. 21st, 1918, *in accident, flying at*
      Hounslow.

DOWDING, H. C. T. ... G 95–99 (R.A., 1900. Lieut., R.G.A., 1902. Capt.,
    Brig.-Gen.   1913.)
                               Temp. Lieut.-Col. R.G.A., 1916.
                               Temp. Brig.-Gen., 1917.
                               R.A.F., Brig.-Gen., 1918.
                               Wounded.   *Despatches* (2).
                               C.M.G.

DOWELL, G. W. ... G 74–78   (N. Lancs. Regt., 1880. Major, 1901. S.
    Brevet Col.   African War.   Retired, 1908.)
                               Temp. Brig.-Gen.
                               Assistant Director, Remount Service.
                               Despatches (6).
                               C.M.G., C.B.E.   Serbian Order " White Eagle."
                                  Greek Order " The Redeemer."

DOWLING, B. B. ... H 10–10
                               2nd Lieut., Manchester Regt.
                               Lieut.
                               Acting Capt., 1918.
                               Wounded.

DOWLING, W. E. B. C. ... H 05–10   (E. Lancs. Regt., 1911.)
    Capt.   Capt., E. Lancs. Regt., 1915.
                               Officer Cadet Bn.
                               Capt., R.A.F., 1918.
                               Wounded (2).

✠ DOWNES, A. C. ... ... A 06–11
    Lieut.   Lieut., Cheshire Regt.
                               Died of wounds Nov. 20th, 1914, *Poperinghe.*

✠ DOWNES, V. C. ... ... A 05–09
    Lieut.   Lieut., Bedfordshire Regt.
                               Died of wounds Oct. 18th, 1914, *St. Omer.*

DOWNING, H. C. ... B 96–00   (Keble Coll., Oxford.   Solicitor.)
    Capt.   Capt. and Adjt., Welsh Regt., 1916.
                               Wounded.

DOYLE, J. B. H. ... B 06–11   (R.E., 1913.)
    Capt.   Lieut., R.E.
                               Capt., 1917.   Staff Officer to Engineer-in-chief.
                               Temp. Major.
                               D.A.A.G., 1918.
                               Wounded.   *Despatches.*
                               O.B.E.

DOYNE, H. C. ... ... G 03–07
    Capt.   Capt., A.S.C., M.T.
                               Despatches.

DOYNE, P. G. ... ... G 00–04 (Trin. Coll., Oxford.)
Capt. Capt., R.A.M.C.

DRAGE, Rev. E. ... C 80–86 (Christ Church, Oxford.)
Capt. Capt., 2nd Vol. Bn., Yorkshire Regt.

DRAGE, R. L. ... ... C 02–07
Capt. Temp. Capt., att R.E. Assistant Director, R.T.

DRAKE, A. W. C. ... F 95–00 (Pemb. Coll., Camb.)
Capt. Capt., R.A.M.C.

✠ DRAKE, F. A. ... ... I 97–10 (Solicitor.)
Capt. Capt., Warwickshire Yeomanry.
*Drowned in Mediterranean by the sinking of the
Leasowe Castle,* May 27th, 1918.

✠ DRAPER, D. ... ... C 10–15
Lieut. Lieut., R.F.A.
*Died Feb. 21st, 1918, in London from illness
contracted on active service.*

DRAPER, G. N. ... ... C 12–17
2nd Lieut., R.F.A., 1918.

DREW, F. G. ... ... G 06–10 (R.E., 1911.)
Capt. Lieut., R.E., 1914.
Capt., 1917.
Acting Major, 1918.
Wounded.   Despatches.

DRIVER, G. R. ... COLL. 05–11 (New Coll., Oxford.)
Capt. British Red Cross, Serbia, 1914–15.
Censorship, French, German, and Greek mails,
1915.
Acting Capt., Graves Registration Commission,
France, 1916.
Dep. Asst. Director, 1917.
Lieut., Gen. List.
Capt., Intelligence, Eastern Armies, 1919.
Wounded.   Despatches.
M.C.

DROUGHT, J. B. A. ... I 98–01 (R. Irish Rifles, 1905.)
Capt. Capt., R. Irish Rifles.
Retired, 1917.

DRUMMOND, A. B. ... D 83–87 (Northumberland Fusiliers, 1889. **Indian Staff
Lieut.-Col. Corps.**)
1916, Lieut.-Col., I.A., Supernumerary List.

Du Boulay, N. W. H. ... c 74–78   (R.A., 1880.   Soudan.   China Expedition.
    Brig.-Gen.   Capt.,   1898.   Brigade-Major,   1911.
                                     D.A.Q.M.G., 1904.   Col., 1911.)
                                 A.Q.M.G., 1914.   D.A. and Q.M.G., 1915.
                                 Temp. Brig.-Gen.
                                 Retired, 1919.   Hon. Brig.-Gen.
                                 Despatches (2).
                                 C.M.G.

Du Boulay, P. H.   ... c 94–
    Lieut.   Lieut., Acting Major, Egyptian Labour Corps.
                                 Capt., 1919.

Du Boulay, R. F.   ... c 90–95
    2nd Lieut.   2nd Lieut., R.A.S.C., 1918.

Du Cane, C. G. ...   ... h 92–98   (Trin. Coll., Camb.   Civil Engineer.)
    Major   Temp. Major, R.E.
                                 Despatches (3).
                                 O.B.E.

Ducat, J. K.   ...   ... d 04–07
    Capt.   Capt., Leinster Regt.

Dudgeon, A. F.   ... a 92–97   (Trin. Coll., Camb.   Guinness Brewery.)
    Capt.   Capt., E.A. Rifles.
                                 Asst. Director, M.T.

Duff, A. Gordon   ... f 97–02   (Trin. Coll., Camb.   Solicitor.)
                                 Private, R. Fusiliers, Public Schools Bn.

Duff, J. B. Gordon   ... g 12–16
    2nd Lieut.   2nd Lieut., R.B., 2nd Bn.

Duff, J. F.   ...   coll. 10–16
    2nd Lieut.   2nd Lieut., R.A.F.

Dufferin and Ava,   · h 89–91   (2nd Lieut., 9th Lancers, 1897.   Capt., 1904.
    Marquis of, d.s.o.   S. African War.   Retired, 1912.)
    Capt.   Capt., Grenadier Guards, 5th Bn.
                                 Instructor, M.G.C., 1918.
                                 Wounded (2).

Dugdale, A.   ...   ... e 83–87   (Christ Church, Oxford.   Oxford Hussars,
    Lieut.-Col.   1892.   Major, 1905.)
                                 Lieut.-Col., Oxford Yeomanry.
                                 Despatches.
                                 D.S.O., C.M.G.

DUGDALE, T. G.   ... I 93–99   (Cotton Manufacturer.)
    Capt.   Capt., E. Lancs. Regt.
                                     Musketry Instructor, Adjutant.
                                     M.C.

DUMAS, B. J. M.   ... A 01–07
    2nd Lieut.   R.A.F., 2nd Lieut., Adj., 1918.

DUMAS, H. R. M.   ... A 00–04
    Lieut.   2nd Lieut., R.A.S.C.
                                     Lieut., 1917.

DUNDAS, R. W.   COLL. 94–00   (New Coll., Oxford.)
    Major   Lieut., Royal Scots.
                                     Temp. Capt., 1917. Staff Capt.
                                     Temp. Major. D.A.Q.M.G.
                                     M.C.

DUNLOP, C.   ...   ... D 06–11
    Capt.   Seaforth Highlanders, 1915.
                                       Temp. Major, Gen. List.
                                     R.A.F., Capt., A. 1917.
                                     Despatches.

✠ DUNLOP, C. D. H.   ... A 94–97   (Turner, Morrison & Co., Calcutta.)
    2nd Lieut.   2nd Lieut., The King's Liverpool Regt., Scottish
                                       Bn.
                                   Killed June 16th, 1915, *Hooge.*

DUNN, W. S.   ...   ... C 83–86   (B.N.C., Oxford.)
    Capt.   British Red Cross, Interpreter.
                                       Capt., Remounts Service.
                                     2nd Assistant Superintendent.

DU PRE, W. B. ...   ... G 88–93   (K.R.R.C., 1895. S. African War. T.F.R.,
    Lieut.-Col.   1900.)
                                       Lieut.-Col., Leicestershire R.H.A.

EARLE, F. W. ...   ... D 94–98   (Hants Regt., 1901. S. African War. Capt.
    Brevet Lieut.-Col.   1909.)
                                       Măjor, Hampshire Regt., 1916.
                                     Brigade-Major, Allahabad Brigade, 1916.
                                     Acting Lieut.-Col. E. Lancs. Regt., 1918.
                                       Despatches (3).
                                     D.S.O.

EARLE, G. H. ...   ... D 91–94   (Inniskilling Dragoons, 1899. S. African War.
    Major   Capt., 1903. Retired 1916.)
                                       Major, Hampshire Regt., Record Office.

EARLE, H. A. ... ... D 00–02
    2nd Lieut.
        2nd Lieut., A.S.C.
        Relinquished Commission, 1918, ill health.
        Despatches.

EARLE, J. W. A. ... A 04–08
    Lieut.
        Lieut., Irish Guards.
        Acting Capt., 1917. Household Brigade, O.C.B.,
           Bushey, till 1919.

EAST, C. F. T. ... COLL. 08–12
    Lieut.
        2nd Lieut., Northamptonshire Regt., 3rd Bn.,
           1915.
        Lieut., Pioneer Bn., 1917.
        Wounded (2).

✠ ECCLES, J. DENNISON ... H 09–14
    Capt.
        Capt., London Regt., Q.V. Rifles.
        Wounded (2).
        M.C.
        Died of wounds Sept. 27th, 1916, *in England.*

ECKERSLEY, N. ff. ... E 71–75
    Col.
        (B.N.C., Oxford. S. Lancs. Regt. Capt., 1883.
           S. African War. Retired 1908.)
        Hon. Col., Manchester Regt., 5th Bn.
        Lieut., Shropshire Vol. Rgt.

EDELSTEN M. ... ... I 02–07
        Late Capt., R.A.S.C.

EDEN, C. H. ... ... C 96–98
    Capt.
        (Engineer.)
        Capt., Acting Major, R.A.S.C.

EDEN, G. B. ... ... D 09–14
    Capt.
        2nd Lieut., K.R.R.C., 1914.
        Capt., 1918. Reserve of Officers, 1919.
        Wounded.

EDEN, J. R. ... ... D 05–11
    Lieut.
        Lieut., S. Wales Borderers, 1916.
        Acting Captain, 1918.

EDGCUMBE, O. PEARCE ... C 05–10
    Capt.
        (D.C.L.I., 1911.)
        Capt., Duke of Cornwall's L.I., 1916.
        Acting Major, 1917.
        Att. R.E. Signalling Service.
        Wounded.   *Despatches* (4).
        M.C.

EDMONDES, C. T. ... H 12–17
        Cadet, R.E.

EDMONDSON, F. ... ... C 86–91
    Lieut.
        (Banker, Liverpool.)
        Lieut., Liverpool Vol. Regt.

EDMONDSON, H. C. ... H 97–02
    Lieut.
        (Turner, Morrison & Co., Calcutta.)
        Calcutta Light Horse.
        Lieut., I.A.R.O. Cavalry.

✠ EDMONDSON, K. J. ... H 94–99 (Guayakil and Quito Railway, Ecuador.)
    Capt.   Capt., Lincolnshire Regt.
                                  Killed June 4th, 1916, *Fricourt.*

EDMONDSON, N. G. ... H 00–05 Business in Liverpool.
    Lieut.   Lieut., Lincolnshire Regt.
                                  Wounded (2).
                                  Invalided.

EDMUNDS, M. W. ... I 00–05 (Exeter Coll., Oxford.)
    Lieut.   Lieut., Oxford and Bucks L.I., Bucks Bn.

EDWARDS, H. B. R. GREY H 04–09 (Ball. Coll., Oxford.)
    Major   Lieut., R.F.A., 1914.
                                  R.A.F. Capt.
                                  Major, 1917.
                                  Retired 1919.
                                  Wounded.   *Despatches.*
                                  M.C.

EDWARDS, H. I. POWELL E 98–02 (Oriel Coll., Oxford.)
    Major   Major, Acting Lieut.-Col., Sussex Yeomanry.
                                  Despatches.
                                  D.S.O.

EDWARDS, J. B. ... F 02–07
                                  Lieut., Monmouth Regt., 1916.
                                  Att. S. Wales Borderers.

EDWARDS, J. C. LLOYD ... C 10–15
    Lieut.   2nd Lieut., R. Welsh Fusiliers, 1916.
                                  Lieut., 1918.

✠ EDWARDS, J. S. ... E 06–09
    Capt.   Lieut., Lancashire Hussars.
                                  Acting Capt., Liverpool Regt., 18th Bn.
                                  Despatches.
                                  M.C.
                                  Died of wounds, April 24th, 1918, *No. 62 C.C.S*
                                        France.

EDWARDS, W. G. H. E 04–09 (Oriel Coll., Oxford.)
    POWELL   Capt., Sussex Yeomanry.
        Major   R. Sussex Regt., 16th Bn.
                                  Major, 1918.
                                  M.C.

EGERTON, B. S. ... E 99–03
    Lieut.   Lieut., R.A.S.C.
                                  2nd Lieut., R.F.A.
                                  Lieut., 1918.

✠ Egerton, J. F. ... ɪ 10–14
2nd Lieut.   2nd Lieut., K.R.R.C.
                               A.D.C.
                               Killed April 3rd, 1916, *Doullens.*

✠ Egerton, P. J. ... ᴇ 95–00
Lieut.   (Border Regt., 1903.)
                               Lieut., Border Regt.
                               Killed October 17th, 1914, near *Ypres.*

Ellenberger, G. F.   ᴄᴏʟʟ. 09–14
Capt.   Lieut., Yorkshire L.I.
                               Capt., 1917.
                               Prisoner of War, 1918.
                               Repatriated Jan., 1919.
                               Wounded.
                               M.C. and Bar.

Elles, E. H. ... ꜰ 80–86
2nd Lieut.   (New Coll., Oxford.   India.)
                               2nd Lieut., General List.   Interpreter.

Ellis, C. M. J. ... ᴇ 08–12
Capt.   Capt., Hampshire Regt.
                               Despatches.

Ellis, F. H. B.   ᴄᴏʟʟ. 78–83
Corporal   (B.N.C., Oxford.   Schoolmaster.)
                               Corporal, Middlesex Regt.

Ellis, H. L. ... ꜰ 08–13
Lieut.   Lieut., Notts and Derby Regt., 11th Bn.
                               General List.
                               Labour Corps, 1917.
                               Wounded.

Ellis, J. B.   ᴄᴏʟʟ. 09–14
Capt.   2nd Lieut., K.R.R.C., 1915, 6th Bn.
                               Capt., 1917, Garrison Bn.
                               A.D.C., Sec. for duty with Labour Corps.
                               Wounded.

Emmons, R. V. B. ... ꜰ 09–13
                               (New Coll., Oxford.)
                               American Hospital, Neuilly.
                               Automobiles Américains, Section Militaire.

✠ Erle, C. ... ... ᴄ 87–90
Capt.   (2nd Dragoons, 1895. Capt., Hants Regt., 1901.
                                    S. African War.   Barrister, 1902.)
                               Capt., Northamptonshire Regt.
                               Died of wounds Feb. 10th, 1917, *Alexandria.*

Erskine, I. D. ... ... ꜰ 11–16
Lieut.   2nd Lieut., Scots Guards, 1917.
                               Lieut., 1918.
                               Wounded.

EVANS, A. J. ... ... F 02–08   (Oriel Coll., Oxford.)
    Major   Lieut., R.A.F., 3rd Squadron, 1914.
                                  Prisoner of War, 1916. Escaped from Germany, 1917.
                                  Temp. Major, 142nd Squadron, E.E.F.
                                  Prisoner of War, Turkey, 1918. Repatriated, 1918.
                                  Despatches.
                                  M.C.

EVANS, A. S. ... ... B 99–02
    2nd Lieut.   Late 2nd Lieut., R.F.A.

EVANS, C. ... ... I 85–89   (R.A., 1891. Capt., 1900. S. African War.
    Brig.-Gen.   G.S.O.$_3$, 1909. G.S.O.$_2$, 1911.)
                                    Lieut.-Col., R.F.A., 1915.
                                  G.S.O.$_1$, War Office.
                                  Brig.-Gen., 1918.
                                  Despatches.
                                  C.M.G.

EVANS, C. T., TASKER ... G 90–93
                                    Late 2nd Lieut., R. Defence Corps.

EVANS, D. Mc. N. ... C 00–04   (I.A., 1906.)
    Capt.   Capt., 1915, and Adjt. 55th Coke's Rifles, I.A.
                                  Wounded.   *Despatches.*
                                  M.C.

EVANS, E. C. C. ... C 04–07
    Lieut.   Lieut., R.A.S.C.

EVANS, H. K. D. ... H 99–04   (4th Hussars, 1907.)
    Major   Capt. and Adjt., 4th Hussars, 1914.
                                      Acting Major, H.Q., 1917.
                                    Despatches (2).
                                    M.C.

EVANS, J. D. D. ... H 95–00   (Magd. Coll., Oxford. S.W. Borderers, 1904.)
                                    Capt., Montgomeryshire Yeomanry.
                                    Relinquished Commission, 1918, ill-heath.

EVANS, J. W. D. ... H 98–00   (Trin. Coll., Camb. 21st Lancers, 1908.)
    Capt.   Capt., 21st Lancers, 1914.
                                    G.S.O.$_3$, H.Q., M.E.F.
                                    Wounded.

EVANS, R. DU B. ... F 05–09   (Trin. Coll., Camb.)
    Lieut.   Lieut., Shropshire L.I.
                                    Prisoner of War. Interned, Switzerland.
                                  Repatriated, 1918.
                                  Wounded.
                                  Retired List, 1919.

EVE, A. M. TRUSTRAM ... K 07–13
  Capt.   Capt. and Adjt., R. Welsh Fusiliers.
                                 G.S.O.₃.
                                 Brigade-Major, 1918.
                                 M.C.

EVE, J. D. TRUSTRAM ... K 11–15
  Lieut.   2nd Lieut., Hertfordshire Regt.
                                 Lieut., 1918.
                                 Wounded.

EVE, R. A. TRUSTRAM ... K 15–16

                                 Gentleman Cadet, R.M. College.

✠ EVERITT, R. E. ...   COLL. 89–94 (Worc. Coll., Oxford. Schoolmaster.)
                                 2nd Lieut., R.G.A.
                                 Killed June 24th, 1917, *Poperinghe.*

✠ EWART, C. F. K.   ... B 01–03   (Belfast.)
  Capt.   Capt., R. Irish Rifles.
                                 Killed July 1st, 1916, *Thiepval, Battle of the
                                     Somme.*

EWART, G. V. ...   ... B 97–01   (Trin. Coll., Dublin. Belfast.)
  Major   Capt., A.S.C.
                                 Acting Major, 1918.

EYRE, J.   ...   ... F 72–78   (Christ Church, Oxford.)
                                 Hon. Sec., Red Cross Society.
                                 O.B.E.

FAGAN, A. W. ...   COLL. 04–09   I.C.S.
  Capt.   2nd Lieut., I.A., 92nd Punjabis.
                                 Capt., 1918, I.A.R.O.

FAIRFAX, B. C. ...   ... C 87–89   (Durham L.I., 1893. Capt., 1900. China E.F.
  Brevet Lieut.-Col.   S. African War. Retired, 1914.)
                                 Lieut.-Col., Liverpool Regt.
                                 Temp. Col., A.A.G.
                                 Wounded.   *Despatches* (3).
                                 C.M.G.

FAIRFAX, J. G. ...   ... D 00–05   (New Coll., Oxford.)
  Capt.   Lieut., R.A.S.C.
                                 Capt., 1918.
                                 Despatches (3).

✠ FALCONER, J. K. ... K 11–15
   Lieut.   2nd Lieut., Hampshire Carabiniers.
                                   Lieut., Hampshire Regt.
                                   Killed July 31st, 1917, *St. Julien.*

FANNING, F. W. BURTON,   E 78–81 (Univ. Coll. Hospital.)
   M.D.   Lieut.-Col., R.A.M.C.
                                   1st Eastern Hospital.

FANSHAWE, Sir E. A.   ... B 72–77 (R.A., 1878.   Afghan War, Soudan. Capt.,
   Lieut.-Gen.   1886. Lieut.-Col., 1903.)
                                   Brig.-Gen., 1914.
                                   Lieut.-Gen., 5th Army Corps, 1916–18.
                                   Major-Gen.
                                   Despatches (8).
                                   K.C.B., Comm. SS. Maurizio e Lazzaro, Gd.
                                      Officier La Couronne, Croix de Guerre.

FANSHAWE, Sir H. D., C.B. B 74–79 (19th Hussars, 1880.   Capt, 1890.   Egypt,
   Major-Gen.   Soudan, Nile Exp., S. African War. Lieut.-
                                      Col., 2nd D.G., 1903.   Col., 1904–07.
                                      1913, Major-General, 58th Division.)
                                   Despatches (3).
                                   K.C.B.   K.C.M.G.

FAUSSETT, E. G. GODFREY   G 82–85 (R.E., 1888.   S. African War.   Major, 1906.)
   Col.   Lieut.-Col., R.E., 1914.
                                   Brevet Col., 1917.
                                   Col. Dep. Director Army Signals, 1916–18.
                                   Despatches (4).
                                   C.M.G., C.B., Officier SS. Maurizio e Lazzaro.

FAWCUS, G. E. ...   COLL. 98–04   (New Coll., Oxford.)
   Capt.   Capt., Cycle Corps.   Chota Nagpur Horse.

FELL, M. A. H.   COLL. 97–03   (Univ. Coll., Oxford.)
   Lieut.   Lieut., N. Zealand R.B.
                                   R.A.F., Assistant Instructor in Gunnery.
                                   Lieut., T., Overseas Contingent.

FELLOWES, C. ...   ... G 12–16
   2nd Lieut.   2nd Lieut., Scots Guards.
                                   Lieut., 1918.
                                   Wounded.

✠ FELLOWES, R. ...   ... G 10–13
   2nd Lieut.   2nd Lieut., K.R.R.C., 1st Bn.
                                   Killed March 10th, 1915, *Givenchy.*

FELLOWES, W. A.   ... G 13–18
                                   Household Brigade, O.C. Bn.

FENTON, R. J. K. ... H 09–12
  Lieut.
                                2nd Lieut., E. Lancs. Regt., 1914.
                                R.M. College, 1915.
                                2nd Lieut., R. Fusiliers.
                                Instructor, Army Signal School.
                                Lieut., 1918.
                                Wounded.

FENWICK, C. H. ... C 75–79   (D.C.L.I., 1884. Lieut., K.R.R.C. Retired
                                  1893.)
                                Superintendent, Remount Dept.
                                Resigned Commission, 1917.

FERARD, C. L. ... ... E 08–13
  Lieut.
                                Lieut., R.F.A., 1914.
                                R.A.F.
                                Lieut., R.F.A., 1917.
                                Despatches.
                                M.C.

✠ FERARD, G. D. ... ... E 10–14
  Lieut.
                                2nd Lieut., Acting Capt., K.R.R.C.
                                Att. Devonshire Regt.
                                Wounded.
                                Killed Feb. 21st, 1918, *Passchendaele.*

✠ FERGUSON, A. ... ... G 10–14
  Lieut.
                                Lieut., Duke of Wellington's, W. Riding Regt.
                                Killed July 4th, 1916, *Fricourt.*

✠ FERGUSON, J. ... ... K 13–16
  2nd Lieut.
                                2nd Lieut., R.A.F.
                                Killed March 12th, 1917, *accidentally, while
                                  flying, Catterick, Yorkshire.*

FERGUSON, R. ... ... G 11–16
  2nd Lieut.
                                2nd Lieut., Duke of Wellington's, W. Riding
                                  Regt. 2nd., att. 10th Bn.

FERGUSSON, C. H. ... C 08–13
  2nd Lieut.
                                2nd Lieut., Northamptonshire Regt.
                                Lieut., 1917, 3rd Bn.
                                Wounded (2).

✠ FERGUSSON, J. A. H. ... C 05–09
  Lieut.
                                Lieut., Highland L.I.
                                Killed Sept. 14th, 1914, *Battle of the Aisne.*

71

FESTING, F. L. ...   ... D 90–94 (Northumberland Fusiliers, 1896. Capt., 1901.
    Temp. Brig.-Gen.   Soudan. S. African War.)
                         Major, Northumberland Fusiliers.
                         Temp. Lieut.-Col., 1916. D.A. and Q.M.G.'
                             1915. A.A. and Q.M.G., 1916. D.A.G.,
                             1917.
                         Bt. Col. Temp. Brig.-Gen., R.A.F.
                         Despatches (3).
                         C.M.G., C.B.

✠ FESTING, H. W.   ... H 96–98 (Durham L.I., 1901. S. African War.)
    Lieut.-Col.   Major, Durham L.I.
                         Temp. Lieut.-Col., Comm. Bn. Yorkshire L.I.
                         Despatches.
                         D.S.O.
                         Killed, Mar. 21st, 1918, *Epehy.*

FESTING, M. C. ...   ... H 93–96 (R.M.L.I., 1898. Capt., 1909.
    Lieut.-Col   Major, R.M.L.I., 1917.
                         Brigade-Major, 1915. D.A.A.G. G.S.O.$_2$, 1916.
                         Temp. Lieut.-Col., G.S.O.$_1$, 1918.
                         Despatches (4)
                         D.S.O. Croix de Guerre.

FIENNES, H. E. T.,   ... D 80–80 (9th Lancers, 1887. Capt., 1894. S. African
    WYKEHAM   War. Ret., 1902.)
    Major   Capt., 9th Lancers.
                         Capt., R.E. Kent Yeomanry.
                         Major, Hertfordshire Yeomanry. R.O.

✠ FINCH, H. M. ...   ... A 80–84 (Berks Regt., 1886. S. African War, Major,
    Lieut.-Col   1906.)
                         Lieut.-Col., R. Berkshire Regt.
                         Wounded.   *Despatches.*
                         D.S.O.
                         Killed, May 9th, 1915, *Fromelles.*

FINLAY, G. L. K.   ... F 86–90 (Trin. Coll., Camb. Edinburgh Univ.)
    Capt.   Capt., R.A.M.C. Retired.
                         Wounded.

FINNEY, A. D.   COLL. 06–12
    Capt.   2nd Lieut., R.F.A.
                         R.A.F. Capt., S.O.$_3$.

FIRTH, J. D'E. E.   COLL. 12–18
                         Cadet, Household Brigade O.C.B.
                         2nd Lieut., Grenadier Guards, Special Reserve.

FISHER, G. A. ...   ... A 06–09
   Lieut.   Lieut., K.R.R.C.
                             Resumed Medical Studies.
                             Wounded (2).   *Despatches.*
                             M.C.

✠ FISHER, H. B. ...   ... A 09–12
   Lieut.   Lieut., Northumberland Fusiliers.
                             M.G.C.
                             Killed, July 24th, 1916, *Delville Wood.*

FITZHUGH, A. E. L.   ... E 86–89 (Trin. Hall., Camb.)
   Lieut.   Lieut., R. Sussex Regt., retired.

FLEMING, A. L. ...   ... F 05–10 (Trin. Coll., Camb.)
   Capt.   Lieut., D.C.L.I.
                             Capt., R.A.F. (A).
                             Wounded (2).
                             M.C.

FLEMING, C. M.   ... F 12–16
   2nd Lieut.   2nd Lieut., Welsh Guards, 1917.
                             Wounded.

FLEMING, J. B. WILLIS ... E 09–13
   Lieut.   Lieut., Hampshire Carabiniers.
                             Capt., Hampshire Regt.
                             Lieut., 6th Inniskilling Dragoons, 1918.

✠ FLEMING, R. T. C. WILLIS E 10–13
   2nd Lieut.   2nd Lieut., Hampshire R.H.A.
                             Killed Aug. 4th, 1916, *Romani, E. of Suez Canal.*

FLINT, A. L. A. ...   ... I 96–98 (2nd Lieut., I.A., 1902. Capt., 1910.)
   Major   Capt., 7th Rajputs, I.A., S. and T. Corps.
                             Major, 1916.

FLOWER, C. H. ...   ... H 95–01 (Magd. Coll., Oxford. Engineer.)
   Major   Capt., Q. Westminster Rifles.
                             Major, 1918.
                           M.C.

✠ FLOWER, H. J. ...   ... H 96–01 (2nd Lieut., K.R.R.C., 1902.)
   Major   Major, K.R.R.C. Adjt., Q.W. Rifles.
                             Staff Capt., 1917. Assistant to Q.M.G.
                           Wounded.
                           Relinquished Commission, ill health, 1918.
                           Despatches (2).
                           Died Jan. 31st, 1919, *from wounds received*, 1915.
                           M.C., D.S.O.

✠ FLOWER, V. A. ... ... E 89–93 (Architect.)
    Lieut.-Col. Lieut.-Col., London Regt., 22nd Bn.
    Despatches (2).
    D.S.O.
    Killed August 15th, 1917, near *Ypres*.

FOOT, C. J. ... ... A 01–05
    Capt. Capt., R.F.A.
    R.A.F., Capt., S.O.
    Wounded.
    Retired, 1918.
    M.C.

FOOT, R. C. ... ... B 06–10
    Capt. Capt., R.F.A., 310th Brigade.
    M.C.

FOOT, R. W. ... ... A 03–07
    Capt. Lieut., R.F.A.
    Staff Capt., H.Q., 1st Army Corps.
    Capt., 1916.
    Despatches.
    M.C.

FORBES, A. ... ... E 83–86 (R.A., 1889. Capt., R.G.A., 1899. Major,
    Col. 1906.)
    Chief Ordnance Officer.
    Lieut.-Col., Army Ordnance Dept.
    Col., 1918. Dep. Director, Ordnance Service.
    Despatches (2).
    C.M.G.

FORBES, C. F. O. G. ... B 12–14
    Lieut. 2nd Lieut., Cameron Highlanders.
    Lieut., Coldstream Guards, 1917.

✠ FORBES, K. ... ... F 06–12
    Lieut. Lieut., London Rifle Brigade.
    Killed Feb. 10th, 1915, *Ploegsteert*.

FORBES, Lord ... ... B 96–00 (Christ Church, Oxford, 1902. Grenadier
    Major Guards, 1907. Capt., 1914.)
    Capt. and Adjt., Grenadier Guards.
    D.A.A.G.
    Major, 1919.

FORBES, T. L. ... ... F 03–08
    Capt. Capt., London Rifle Brigade, 1916.

FORD, J. A. ... ... E 83–88 (B.N.C., Oxford. Land Agent. S. African
    Major War with D. of C.'s Spec. Corps.
    Major, R.E. Cornwall Fortress Engineers.

✠ FORSTER, A. H.   ... F 11–15
      Lieut.   2nd Lieut., Scots Greys, 1916.
                                 Lieut., 1918.
                                 Wounded.   *Despatches.*
                                 Died in Hospital March 10th, 1919, *of wounds*
                                       received Oct. 17th, 1918.

✠ FORSTER, J. G. ...   ... F 90–93
      Major   (Cheshire Yeomanry. S. African War.)
                                 Enlisted 1914 P.P. Canadian L.I.
                                 2nd Lieut., R. Fusiliers, 5th Bn.
                                 Major, 1918.
                                 Wounded (2).
                                 M.C. and Bar.
                                 Died of wounds Oct. 2nd, 1918, *Boisleux St. Marc.*

FORSTER, S. A. ...   ... E 13–17
      2nd Lieut.   2nd Lieut., Coldstream Guards, 1918.

FORSTER, T. G. B.   ... H 00–03
      Capt.   Capt., R.E. R. Monmouthshire.
                                 (Staff Capt).
                                 Despatches.

FORSTER, T. H. B.   COMM. 63–68
      Lieut.-Col.   (93rd Highlanders, 1872. Capt., 1880. Lieut.-
                                 Col., 1902. S. African War.)
                                 Lieut.-Col.
                                 A.A. and Q.M.G.
                                 Retired 1917.

FORSTER, W. E. ARNOLD   H 99–01
      Lieut.-Comdr.   Lieut. Commander, R.N.V.R.

FORSYTH, B.   ...   ... B 96–00   (Ch. Ch., Oxford. Actor.)
                                 Private, Q. Victoria's Rifles.
                                 Wounded.

FORSYTH, G.   ...   ... B 94–00   (Caius Coll., Camb. Architect.)
      Lieut.   Lieut., Q. Victoria's Rifles.
                                 A.D.C. to G.O.C. Vth Division.
                                 M.C.

FORSYTH, L. W....   ... B 89–92   (Caius Coll., Camb. Dentist.)
                                 Capt., R.A.M.C.

✠ FORTESCUE, G.   ... G 00–04   (R.B., 1906.)
                                 Capt., R.B.
                                 Killed Sept. 4th, 1915.

FORTUNE, V. M. ... D 97–01 (Black Watch, 1903. Capt., 1914.)
    Brig.-Gen.   Capt., Black Watch (Royal Highlanders), 1914.
                                  Brigade-Major, 1915.
                                  Lieut.-Col., 1916.
                                  Brigadier-General, 45th Brigade, 1918.
                                  Despatches (4).
                                  D.S.O., Chevalier Légion d'Honneur, Officier
                                      Légion d'Honneur.

FOSTER, B. A. LE NEVE   K 07–10
                                  Pte., R. Fusiliers. Public Schools Bn.

FOSTER, R. M.   COLL. 12–15
    Capt.   2nd Lieut., Royal Fusiliers, 1916.
                                    Lieut., 1918.
                                    R.A.F., Capt., A. Comm. 20th Squadron.
                                    D.F.C.
                                    Despatches.

✠ FOWLER, C. G. ...   COLL. 08–14
    Lieut.   2nd Lieut., Norfolk Regt., 1915.
                                    Lieut., 6th Cycle Bn.
                                    Wounded.
                                  Killed April 6th, 1917, *Ecourt St. Mein, near*
                                      Bullecourt.

FOWLER, R. H.   COLL. 02–08
    Capt.   Capt., R. Marine Artillery.
                                    Ministry of Munitions.
                                    Wounded.
                                    O.B.E.

FOX, A. B.   ... ... G 78–80 (Middlesex Regt., 1882. Somerset L. I.,
    Major   1884. Major, 1904. Burmese Expedition.
                                    Retired 1906.)
                                    Major, late Somerset L.I.
                                    R.T.O. till Sept., 1918.

FOX, E. T.   ... ... D 05–08
                                  Lieut., Gloucestershire Regt.
                                    Resigned Commission, 1915.
                                  R.A.S.C., Motor Driver, M.T.

FOX, F. E.   ... ... H 09–13
    Capt.   Lieut., Somerset L.I., Mesopotamia.
                                    Capt., 1917, Lines of Communication, Kerman-
                                      shah.
                                  Despatches.

FRANCE, A. H. HAYHURST   B 07–12
    Lieut.   Lieut., 4th Hussars, 1914.
                                  M.C.

FRANCE, G. F. HAYHURST   B 09–13
     Capt.   2nd Lieut., K.R.R.C., 1914.
                                    Capt., 1917.
                                    Wounded (3).   *Despatches.*
                                    M.C. and Bar.

FRANCIS, H. K. ...   ... K 11–16
                                    R.A.F., 3rd Air Mechanic.

✠ FRASER, A. K.   COLL. 06–11
      Capt.   Capt., Seaforth Highlanders.
                                    Wounded.
                                    M.C.
                                    Killed Nov. 22nd, 1917, *Village of Fontaine.*

FREELAND, A. ...   ... H 05–09
      Capt.   Capt., Middlesex Regt.
                                    A.D.C.
                                    Adjt., Field Survey Coy., R.E., G.H.Q.

FREEMAN, A. F.   ... A 03–07
      Capt.   Lieut., Montgomeryshire Yeomanry.
                                    Capt., R. Welsh Fusiliers, 25th Bn.
                                    Wounded.
                                    M.C.

FREEMAN, A. G.   ... C 11–16
     2nd Lieut.   2nd Lieut., R.F.A.
                                    Labour Corps, 1915.

✠ FREEMAN, R. H.   ... C 07–12
      Major   Capt., Worcestershire Regt.
                                    Temp. Major.
                                    R.A.F., Major.   Instructor, Central Flying
                                      School.
                                    Despatches.
                                    M.C., Croix de Guerre.
                                    Killed July 21st, 1918, *flying near Belleau.*

✠ FREEMAN, T.   ...   ... D 05–10
                                    Lieut., Worcestershire Regt.
                                    Killed March 12th, 1915, *Wytschaete, Flanders.*

FRENCH, M. KING   ... F 00–05   New Coll., Oxford.
      Capt.   Lieut. and Adjt., R.F.A.
                                    Temp. Capt., 1917.

✠ FRENCH, V. J. S.   ...   ... E 12–17
     2nd Lieut.   2nd Lieut., Irish Guards, 1918.
                                    Killed Oct. 10th, 1918, *Beauvois, near Cambrai.*

FREUDENTHAL, N. F. H.   B 11–16
Lieut.

Pte., Q. Westminster Rifles, 1916.
2nd Lieut., R.B., 1917.
2nd Lieut., Grenadier Guards, 1918.
Lieut., 1918.
Wounded.

FREWEN, L.   ...   ...   I 00–03
Lieut.-Col.

(2nd Lieut., R.B., 1906.)
Lieut.-Col., K.R.R.C., 8th Bn.
Retired, 1917.
Despatches (2).
D.S.O.

FREWEN, T.   ...   ...   B 88–91
Capt.

(Leicestershire Regt., 1899. S. African War.
    Capt., 1905.)
Capt., R. Fusiliers.
Retired, 1917.

FRIPP, A. T.   ...   ...   I 11–17

2nd Lieut., Household Cavalry, Res. Regt.
Guards M.G. Regt.

FROST, R.   ...   ...   H 06–10
Major

(Ch. Ch., Oxford.)
Capt., Cheshire Regt.
Temp. Major, 1918.
Gen. List. Instructor, Officers' Convalescent
    Hospital.
Wounded.   *Despatches.*

FRY, T. P.   ...   ...   C 05–09
Lieut.

2nd Lieut., Durham L.I.
(Northumberland Fusiliers, Garrison Bn.)
Lieut., 1916.
Wounded.

FULLER, D. H. F.   ...   H 09–14
Lieut.

Lieut., R.B., 1915.
Officer, Cadet Bn.
Employed at Admiralty.

✠ FULLER, E. F. ...   ...   H 91–95
2nd Lieut.

(Tea Planter, Ceylon.)
Acting 2nd Lieut., R. Wilts Yeomanry.
    Died in England, 1914.

✠ FULLER, Sir J. M. F.,   A 78–82
Bart.
Major

(Ch. Ch., Oxford. Governor-General, Victoria.)
Major, R. Wilts Yeomanry.
Died in England, Sept., 1915.

FULLER, R. F. ...   ...   H 89–95
Major

(Avon Rubber Works Co.)
Major, R. Wilts Yeomanry.
T.F.R., 1918.
T.D.

✠ Fuller, W. B. ...   ... D 97–01   (R.W. Surrey Regt., 1903.)
    Capt.   Capt., R.W. Surrey Regt.
                                     Killed May 16th, 1915, *Festubert.*
                                     Despatches.

Fuller, W. F. ...   ... A 79–81
    Major   Major, R. Wiltshire Yeomanry.
                                     To Wiltshire Regt.
                                     Spec. Appt.
                                     Despatches (2).
                                     D.S.O., T.D.

Furneaux, C. H.   ... D 88–92   (Cheshire Regt.,1901. R.A.S.C. S. African War.)
    Lieut.-Col.   Major, R.A.S.C., 1914.
                                     D.A.Q.M.G., 1915. Temp. Lieut.-Col., 1915.
                                     A.Q.M.G., 1917–1919.
                                     Despatches.
                                     D.S.O., Order " White Eagle," Serbia ;
                                         " Redeemer," Greece.

Fyers, E. W. H.   ... H 78–81   (Ch. Ch., Oxford. Lieut., Middlesex Regt.
    Major   Capt., 1897. Retired, 1913.)
                                     Major, Reserve of Officers.
                                     Recruiting Officer, Carlisle.

Fyffe, A. H. ...   ... E 98–03   (Univ. Coll., Oxford.)
    Lieut.   Lieut., R.G.A., 1917.

Gadban, V. J.   ... D 92–98   (New Coll., Oxford. Solicitor.)
    Capt.   2nd Lieut., R. West Kent Regt.
                                     Lieut., 1917.
                                     Acting Capt., Adjt., Labour Corps, 1918.
                                     Temp. Capt., 1919.
                                     Wounded.   *Despatches.*
                                     O.B.E

Gairdner, C. D.   ... F 11–16
    2nd Lieut.   Glasgow University Cadet Corps.
                                     2nd Lieut., Arg. and Suth. Highlanders, 4th
                                         Bn., 1917.

Gallie, J. B. ...   ... K 11–15
    Lieut.   Lieut., Arg. and Suth. Highlanders.
                                     Att. Cameron Highlanders, 5th Bn.

Gallwey, J. Payne- ...   F 03–08
    Brevet Lieut.-Col.   Major, Northumberland Fusiliers.
                                     Assist. Superintendent, Experimental Gunnery.
                                     Major, R.E.
                                     Brevet Lieut.-Col.
                                     Despatches (2).

79

✠ GALLWEY, P. F. PAYNE-   F 06–11
    Lieut.   Lieut., 21st Lancers, att. 9th Lancers
                                   Killed Oct. 31st, 1914, *Messines.*

GAMMELL, J. A. H.   ...   G 05–11   (Trin. Coll., Camb.)
    Capt.   R.F.A., 1914.   Capt., 1915.
                                   G.S.O.$_3$, 1915.   A.D.C.
                                   G.S.O.$_2$, 1916.
                                   (Temp. Lieut.-Col., R.A.F., S.O.$_1$.)
                                   War Office.
                                   Wounded (2).   *Despatches* (5).
                                   M.C., D.S.O., Order Karageorge, Cav. Corona
                                       d'Italia.

GAMON, G. P.   ...   COLL. 90–96   (Ch. Ch., Oxford.   Bombay-Burmah Trading
    Capt.   Co.)
                                   Capt., R.A.S.C.
                                   Temp. Major.   Assist. Controller of Labour.
                                   Despatches.

GARDINER, F.   ...   ...   E 03–05
    Capt.   Capt., R.E.
                                   5th Corps Signalling Coy.
                                   M.C.

GARDINER, J.   ...   ...   E 01–05
    Capt.   Lieut., R.N.A.S.
                                   Capt., R.A.F., T., 1918.

GARNER, C. W.   ...   H 02–06
    Major   R. Irish Rifles.
                                   Major, 1917.
                                   Wounded.

GARNIER, G. W.   E 91–95   (Land Agent.)
    CARPENTER-   Lieut., R.G.A., Wessex Brigade.
    Lieut.   Relinquished Comm. April, 1919, ill health.

GARNIER, Rev. M. R.   E 95–99   (Oriel Coll., Oxford.   All Saints, Margaret St.)
    CARPENTER-   Chaplain to Forces, 1918.
    C.F.

GARNIER, Rev. T. V.   ...   C 89–94
                                   Chaplain to Forces, 1916.
                                   Despatches (2).
                                   O.B.E.

GARRARD, A. G. B.   D 99–04   (Ch. Ch., Oxford.   Antarctic Expedition.)
        CHARRY   R.N.A.S.

GARRATT, SIR F. S., C.B., D.S.O. Brig.-Gen.	D 73–77	(6th D.G., 1878. Afghan War, Capt., 1888; Major, 1897. S. African War. Lieut.-Col., 6th D.G., 1904. Col., 1906. Retired, 1911. Brigadier-General, Director of Remounts, 1914. *Despatches* (6). C.M.G. Officier Legion d'Honneur. K.C.M.G. Croix de Guerre. Order Couronne.
GARRETT, A. B.	... H 15–18	Gentleman Cadet, R.M. College.
GARROD, H. G. ... Lieut.	COLL. 00–05	(New Coll., Oxford.) Lieut., City of London Sch., O.T.C.
✠ GASELEE, A. M. 2nd Lieut.	... K 07–12	(King's Coll., Camb.) 2nd Lieut., 15th Hussars. *Killed*, May 24th, 1915, *near Hooge.*
GATER, G. H. ... Brig.-Gen.	... E 00–05	(New Coll., Oxford.) Capt., Notts and Derby Regt., 1914. Major, 1915. Lieut.-Col., 1916. Brigadier-General, 1917. *Wounded* (2). *Despatches* (4). D.S.O. and Bar. Croix de Guerre. C.M.G.
✠ GAY, E. ... ... Capt.	... F 97–01	(New Coll., Oxford.) Capt., Norfolk Regt. *Killed*, Aug., 1915, *Dardanelles.*
GELDART, N. ... Major	... B 03–05	Capt., D. of Wellington's, W. Riding Regt. Major, Tank Corps, Engineering Branch, 1919. *Wounded* (2). *Despatches.* M.C. D.S.O.
GERARD, W. G. G.	... I 12–16	R.N., Midshipman. H.M.S. *New Zealand.*
GEORGE, F. W. B. ... Major	... D 87–89	(Farming in Canada.) Major, 46th S. Saskatchewan Bn., Canadian Force.
GERY, H. T. WADE Major	COLL. 00–07	Capt., Oxf. and Bucks L.I. Temp. Major, Lancashire Fusiliers, 19th Bn. M.C.
GIBBES, F. D. ... Lieut.-Col.	... G 86–90	(B.N.C., Oxford. Lincolnshire Regt., 1894. S. African War. Retired as Major, 1912. Lieut.-Col., Lincolnshire Yeomanry, Reserve of Officers.

✠ GIBBS, D. A. ... ... G 12–16
2nd Lieut.   2nd Lieut., R.B., 2nd Bn., Scout Officer.
                              Killed, March 24th, 1918, *Pargny, near Chaulnes.*

GIBBS, L. C. M. ... I 10–15
Lieut.   Lieut., Hertfordshire Yeomanry.
                              A.D.C.
                              Coldstream Guards, 1918.

GIBSON, A. K. ... ... B 96–99   (Land Agent.)
Capt.   Capt., Oxf. and Bucks L.I., 1916.
                              Staff Capt., 1918–1919.
                              Despatches (3).
                              M.C.   Croix de Guerre.   O.B.E.

GIBSON, A. L. ... ... B 90–96   (Tea Planter, Ceylon.)
2nd Lieut.   2nd Lieut., R.B., 11th Bn., 1917.
GIBSON, G. H. ... ... B 89–94   (Tea Planter, Ceylon.)
Lieut.   Lieut., K.R.R.C., 1915.
                              Wounded.
                              Staff Lieut., 1919.

✠ GIBSON, H. O. S.   COLL. 97–04   (New Coll., Oxford.   Master at Lancing Coll.)
Lieut.   Lieut., London Regt., 11th Bn.
                              Gallipoli, 1915, Palestine, 1917.
                              Killed, April 19th, 1917, *Wadi Gazi.* 2nd
                                Battle of Gaza.

✠ GIBSON, R. B. ...   COLL. 08–13
Capt.   Capt., S. Staffordshire Regt., att. Bedfordshire
                                Regt.
                              Despatches.
                              Killed, July 11th, 1916, *Maricourt.*

GIDLEY, J.   ... ... C 80–85   (St. John's Coll., Oxford.   Solicitor.)
Capt.   Capt., Oxford and Bucks L.I., 1st Garrison Bn.,
                                1914.

GIFFARD, W. C.,   ... G 74–76   (Welsh Regt., 1880.   Capt., 1886.   Bt. Lieut.-
D.S.O.   Col., 1899.   Soudan, W. Africa, S. African
Lieut.-Col.   War.)

                              Lieut.-Col., Comm. W. Yorkshire Regt., 5th Bn.
GILBERT, J. C. W.   ... F 92–96   (Ch. Ch., Oxford.   Solicitor.)
Lieut.   2nd Lieut., R. Defence Corps.
                              Lieut., 1918.

✠ GILBERT, K. N. W.   ... F 02–07   (Lieut., Acting Capt., R.H.A.)
Lieut.   *Wounded.*
                              M.C.
                              Died in England, pneumonia, Oct. 15th, 1918.

✠ GILLESPIE, A. D.   COLL. 03–08   (New Coll., Oxford.)
     2nd Lieut.   2nd Lieut., Arg. and Suth. Highlanders.
                                           Killed, Sept. 25th, 1915, *Battle of Loos.*

✠ GILLESPIE, T. C.   ... K 05–11   (New Coll., Oxford.)
     Lieut.   Lieut., K.O.S.B.
                                           Killed Oct. 18th, 1914, *near La Bassée.*

GILLETT, H. V.   COLL. 92–97   (Exeter Coll., Oxford. Solicitor.)
     Capt.   2nd Lieut., Grenadier Guards, 1918.
                                           Temp. Capt., Education Officer, 1919.

GILLOTT, B. H.   ... G 93–96
     Capt.   Capt., R.A. Ordnance Corps, 1918.

GILLUM, W. W. ...   ... B 98–01   (R.F.A., 1903.)
     Major   Capt., R.F.A., 1914.
                                           Major, 1916.
                                           Officer of Coy. of G.C.'s, R.M. Academy, 1918.
                                           Wounded (2).   *Despatches* (2).
                                           D.S.O.

✠ GILROY, G. B.   ... H 02–08   (Magd. Coll., Oxford.)
     Capt.   Capt., Black Watch (Royal Highlanders), 8th Bn.
                                           M.C.
                                           Died July 15th, 1916, *of wounds received* July
                                                 14th, *at Longueval.*

GILROY, J. D. ...   ... H 12–15
     2nd Lieut.   2nd Lieut., 9th Lancers.

✠ GILROY, K. R.   ... H 05–10
     Lieut.   Lieut., Black Watch (Royal Highlanders),
                                           2nd Bn.
                                           Killed March 12th, 1915, *Neuve Chapelle.*

GISBORNE, W. G.   ... G 08–12
                                           9th Lancers, 1914.
                                           Lieut., 1915.
                                           War Office, 1918.
                                           Wounded.
                                           M.C.

GLOSSOP, G. C. ...   COLL. 10–15
     Lieut.   Lieut., R.F.A. Adjt.
                                           Acting Capt.
                                           Wounded.
                                           M.C.

GLOSSOP, W. G. C.   ... D 12–17   (King's Medal, Pollock Medal, Tombs Memorial,
     2nd Lieut.   R.M.A., 1918).
                                           2nd Lieut., R.F.A.

83

GODDARD, F. W. ... F 13–18
                                Cadet, R.A.F.

GODFREY, E. A. ... C 04–08 (Royal Scots, 1912.)
   Capt.   Capt., Royal Scots, 1915.
                                Adjt. to Tank Corps, 1917.
                                Wounded.

GODMAN, E. G. ... I 90–94 (Dorset Regt., 1896. Capt., 1902. S. African
   Lieut.-Col.   War. Retired, 1913.)
                                Temp. Major. Staff Capt.
                                A.P.M., Southern Command.
                                Temp. Lieut.-Col. Dep. P.M.
                                O.B.E.

GODSAL, H. ... ... H 81–86 (Trin. Coll., Camb. Barrister.)
   Capt.   Lieut., R.F.A.
                                Comm. London M.G. School.
                                Capt., 1918.
                                Wounded.   *Despatches.*

GODSON, C. L. ... COLL. 05–11
   Lieut.   Lieut., Worcestershire Regt., Gas Officer.
                                  Temp. Lieut., R.E., 1917.
                                Wounded.

GODSON, E. A. ... ... A 02–07
   Capt.   Acting Capt., R. Irish Fusiliers, 3rd Bn.
                                G.S.O.$_2$. Capt., 1918.
                                Wounded.
                                M.C. and Bar. Croix de Guerre.

GODSON, F. P. ... ... A 01–06 (Pemb. Coll., Camb.)
   Capt.   Acting Capt., E. Yorkshire Regt.
                                R.E. Tunnelling Coy.
                                M.C.

GODWIN, C. C. ... ... E 96–99 (Yorkshire Regt., 1903. W.A.F.F., 1907–09.
   Capt.   Capt., Yorkshire Regt., 1911. Egyptian
                              Army, 1913.)
                                Capt., Yorkshire Regt.
                                G.S.O.$_3$.
                                D.A.A.G., 1914–16.

GOFF, A. H. S. ... E 77–80 (R.F.A., 1883. Capt., 1892. Major, 1900.
   Lieut.-Col.   S. African War).
                                Lieut.-Col., R.F.A., 1915.
                                Despatches.
                                C.M.G.

GOLDBERGER. See GOULD.

GOMPERTZ, H. C. T.   COLL. 11–16
   2nd Lieut.   2nd Lieut., R.F.A.
                                       R.A.F. O.
                                       Reported Missing Nov. 10th, 1918. Returned
                                            Nov. 19th.

✠ GOOCH, E. S.   ...   ...   G 92–97   (7th Hussars, 1899. S. African War. Capt.
   Major   Berks Yeomanry, 1904.)
                                       Major, Berks Yeomanry.
                                       Despatches.
                                       Died of Wounds Sept. 21st, 1915, *Suvla Bay.*

GOODDY, R. W.   ...   A 01–05
   Lieut.   Lieut., R.A.S.C.
                                       M.C.

GOODE, C. B. C.   ...   A 08–09
   Capt.   Capt., R.A.S.C., 1915.

GOODENOUGH, Rev.   ...   C 79–84   (New Coll., Oxford).
   L. W. V.   C.F., att. Warwickshire Yeomanry.
   Lieut.   Demobilized, ill-health, 1916.
                                       Lieut., General List, 1917.
                                       Intelligence Officer, British Military Mission,
                                         Italian E.F.

GOODFELLOW, A. G. S.   F 13–18
   2nd Lieut.   2nd Lieut., Coldstream Guards, 1919.

GOODHART, J. H.   ...   I 08–12   (20th Hussars, 1913.)
                                       Lieut. and Adjt., 20th Hussars, 1915.
                                       Wounded.   *Despatches.*
                                       M.C.

GOODSON, D. F. J.   ...   I 12–16
                                       2nd Lieut., 8th Hussars, 1916.
                                       Lieut., 1918.
                                       M.G.C., 1918.

GOOLDEN, W. H. L.   COLL. 89–94   (Electrical Engineer.)
   Capt.   Capt., Asst. Proof and Experimental Officer.
                                         Despatches.
                                       O.B.E.

GORDON, Sir A. ...   ...   E 72–77   (R.A., 1880. Capt., 1888. Lieut.-Col., 1905.
   HAMILTON, C.B.   Afghan War. S. African War. G.S.O.$_1$,
   Lieut.-Gen.   H.Q., 1908. Director Military Operations,
                                         India, 1910.)
                                       Lieut.-General, G.O.C.-in-Chief, Aldershot, 1914
                                         –16. Comm. IXth Army Corps, 1917.
                                       Despatches (4).
                                       K.C.B. Commandeur Légion d'Honneur. Order
                                       La Couronne. Croix de Guerre.

GORDON, A. H. HAMILTON   D 11–16
  Lieut.
      R.H.A., 1917.
      Lieut., R.F.A., 1919.

✠ GORDON, C.   ...   ...   H 07–11
  Capt.
      Capt., London Regt., 2nd Bn.
      Wounded.   *Despatches.*
      Killed, August 16th, 1917, *Glencorse Wood,*
         near Ypres.

GORDON, J. H. ...   COLL. 99–05
  2nd Lieut.
      2nd Lieut., R. 1st Devon Yeomanry.
      Resigned Commission, ill-health.

GORE, St. J. C., C.B. ...   H 73–76
  Col.
      (5th D.G., 1879. Soudan. Lieut.-Col., 1899.
         S. African War. Retired, 1906.)
      Col. Assistant Military Secretary, Aldershot.
      Despatches.
      C.B.E.

✠ GORELL, Lord   ...   ...   E 95–00
  Major
      (Trin. Coll., Oxford. Harvard University.
         Barrister.)
      Major, R.F.A., 7th London Brigade.
      Despatches.
      D.S.O.
      Killed, Jan. 16th, 1917, *near Ypres.*

GORELL, Lord   ...   ...   E 97–97
  Col.
      (Ball. Coll., Oxford.)
      Capt. and Adjt., R.B.
      G.S.O.$_3$, G.S.O.$_2$.
      Col. Dep. Director, Dept. of Staff Duties
         (Education), 1918.
      Wounded.
      M.C. O.B.E.

GOSTLING, B. W. W. ...   H 04–06
  Capt.
      (R. Fusiliers, 1911.)
      Capt., R. Fusiliers, 1915.
      Staff Capt., 1916.
      Brigade-Major, 1918.
      Wounded (2).   *Despatches.*
      M.C.

✠ GOUGH, J. B. T.   ...   G 94–97
  Major
      (Solicitor.)
      Capt., Hertfordshire Regt. (att. E. Surrey Regt.
         O.C. Bn).
      Major, 1918.
      Killed, March 22nd, 1918, *Ste Emilie, near*
         Peronne.

GOULD, C. ... ... I 00–04   (Nat. Bank of Egypt.)
(formerly Goldberger)   Trooper, Canadian Contingent.
   2nd Lieut., R.F.A.
   Wounded.
   Resigned Commission, ill-health.
   Returned to Canada.

GOULD, E. ... ... B 92–97   (Yorkshire Regt. Lovat Scouts. 12th Lancers.)
   Capt., Intelligence Dept.

✠ GOULD, H. C. H. ... D 10–15
   2nd Lieut.   2nd Lieut., R.F.A.
   Died, April 15th, 1917, *from effects of gas shells,*
       Aubigny, near Arras.

GOULD, Rev. K. L. ... B 91–95   (Pemb. Coll., Camb.)
   Sergeant, R.A.S.C.

✠ GOULD, P. W. ... ... E 02–06
   2nd Lieut.   2nd Lieut., K.R.R.C.
   Killed, Aug. 25th, 1916, *Delville Wood.*

GOWER, C. E. G., ... H 91–95   (Lieut., Somerset L.I., 1900. S. African War.)
   LEVESON-   Capt., R.T. Asst. Military Landing Officer.
   Capt.

GOWER, C. O. G., ... H 88–91   (Cirencester Agricultural Coll.)
   LEVESON-   Capt., R.A.S.C., 1916.
   Capt.   *Despatches* (2).

GOWER, Rev. F. A. G., H 85–90   (Magd. Coll., Oxford. Rector, Singleton,
   LEVESON-   Sussex.)
   Chaplain to Forces.

GOWER, H. D. G., ... H 87–92   (Magd. Coll., Oxford. Stock Exchange.)
   LEVESON-   Lieut.-Col., R.A.S.C.
   Lieut.-Col.   *Despatches.*

GRÆME, E. H. HAMOND   H 91–94   (Trin. Coll., Camb. Hants Yeomanry, 1903.)
   Major   Major, Hampshire Carabiniers, 1916.
   Remount Officer, 1919.

GRÆME, P. LLOYD ... F 97–02   (K.R.R.C. Yorkshire Regt.)
   Major ...   Major, Gen. List, 1916.
   Empl. Ministry Nat. Service.
   M.C.

GRAHAM, A. ... ... B 05–08
   Capt.   Lieut., Highland L.I.
   Capt., 1917.
   G.S.O.$_3$.

GRAHAM, C. R. ...   ... G 03–07
    Capt.   Capt., 1916.   Intelligence Dept.
                                   G.S.O.₃.   Inspector of General Communications.
                                   Despatches.

GRAHAM, H. F.   ... G 03–09
    Lieut.
                                   2nd Lieut., R.F.A.
                                   Lieut., 1918, Act. Capt.
                                   Wounded.

GRAHAM, J. F. C.   ... B 13–18
                                   Gentleman Cadet, R.M. Coll.

GRAHAM, P. L. ...   ... C 11–15
    Lieut.
                                   2nd Lieut., R.F.A., 1916.
                                   Lieut., R.H.A., 1917.
                                   M.C.

GRAHAM, R. F. ...   ... E 90–94   (Trin. Coll., Camb.   Architect.)
    Lieut.   2nd Lieut., Arg. and Suth. Highlanders.
                                   Lieut., 1917.   Spec. Appt.

GRANET, G. E. A.   COLL. 01–04   (R.F.A., 1907.)
    Major   Major, R.F.A., 1917.
                                   Acting Lieut.-Col., 1918.   Brigade-Major.
                                   Despatches (3).
                                   M.C.   D.S.O.

GRANT, J. P.   ...   ... A 99–04   (Magd. Coll., Oxford.)
    Major   Lovat Scouts.
                                   Major, Cameron Highlanders, 10th.   Lovat
                                       Scouts Bn., 1916.
                                   Despatches.
                                   M.C.   T.D.

GRANT, P. C. H.   ... F 14–18
                                   Gentleman Cadet, R.M. Coll.

GRANT, R. C.   ...   ... F 08–12
    Capt.   Capt., Cameronians (Scottish Rifles).
                                   R.A.F.   A.
                                   Wounded
                                   Missing Sept 16th, 1918.

GRANTHAM, W. A. C.   H 13–17
    2nd Lieut.
                                   2nd Lieut., R.F.A., 1918.
                                   Wounded.

Correction: G.S.O.$_3$.

GRAY, D. F. B.   ... c 07–09
   Major
                            Major. Pr. Pat. Canadian L.I.
                            E. Ontario Regt.
                            G.S.O.$_2$.
                            Wounded.   *Despatches* (2).
                            D.S.O.

✠ GRAY, E. J.   ... ... A 11–16
   2nd Lieut.
                            2nd Lieut., R.B.
                            Killed March 31st, 1918, *near Arras.*

✠ GRAY, M.   ... ... B 03–08
   Capt.
                            Lieut., 2nd Dragoon Guards.
                            Capt., M.G.C., Cavalry.
                            Killed Aug. 9th, 1918, *Beaucourt en Santerre.*

GRAYSON, H. M., M.P.   F 79–82
   Hon. Lieut.-Col.
                            (Director Shipbuilding Co., Birkenhead.)
                            Hon. Lieut.-Col., R. Marines, unattached List.

✠ GREENFIELD, R. M.   ... H 70–73
   Brig.-Gen.
                            (Inniskilling Fusiliers, Capt., 1881. Lieut.-Col.,
                                1893. Col. 1899. Burmese Exped., Tirah
                                Exped.
                            Brigadier-General. Irish Command.
                            Died in England April 25th, 1916.

GREENSHIELDS, J. D.   ... B 93–98
   Capt.
                            (Oriel Coll., Oxford. Berks Regt., 1900–01.
                                Ship owner, Liverpool.
                            Major, The King's Liverpool Regt.
                            Resigned Commission 1917.
                            Despatches.

GREENSHIELDS, R. L.   ... I 06–10
   Lieut.
                            (1st D.G., 1915.)
                          Lieut., 1st Dragoon Guards, 1917.

GREENWELL, G. H.   ... c 09–14
   Lieut.
                            Lieut., Oxford and Bucks L.I., 4th Bn.
                          Acting Capt., 1917—1919.
                          Wounded.
                          M.C.

GREENWOOD, L. W.   COLL. 11–17
   2nd Lieut.
                          2nd Lieut., R.A.F., A. and S.

GREGSON, D. N. K.   ... I 09–14
   Capt.
                            Capt., London R.F.A.
                          Retired, ill health, Hon. Capt., 1917.

GREIG, D. G.   ... ... G 10–15
   Lieut.
                            Lieut., 16th Lancers, 1917.

GRESSON, F. H.   ... c 81–86
   Lieut.
                            (Schoolmaster.)
                          Lieut., Sussex Vol. Regt.

GREY, G. E. A.   COLL. 08–14
    Capt.

1917, Lieut., R.F.A. T.M.B.
Acting Capt., 1918.
Despatches.
M.C.

GREY, J.   ...   ... B 12–17
    2nd Lieut.   ...

2nd Lieut., R.B.

GREY, N. F. E.   ... G 04–09
    Lieut.

Lieut., R.F.A. A.D.C.
Staff Lieut., 1918.

GREY, W. A. S.   ... A 96–01
    Capt.

(B.N.C. Oxford. R. Fusiliers, 1904 I.A., 1906.
    Capt. 1913.)
Capt., I.A.

GRIFFITH, H. C.   ... E 08–11
    Lieut.

Lieut., S.W. Borderers, 1915.
Att. Gloucester Regt., 2/6th Bn.

✠ GRIFFITH, W. S. C.   ... H 96–00
    2nd Lieut.

(Solicitor.)
2nd Lieut., Leinster Regt.
Killed Aug. 9th, 1915, *Gallipoli, above Suvla Bay.*

✠ GRIFFITHS, A. R.   ... I 05–09
    2nd Lieut.

2nd Lieut., R.F.A.
Killed Aug. 9th, 1915, *near Ypres.*

GRIFFITHS, N. M.   ... E 90–94

(Local Govt. Board.)
Capt., R.A.S.C., 1915.
Q.M.G.'s Dept.
Staff Capt., 1918.
O.B.E.

GRIGG, E. W. M.   COLL. 93–98
    Temp. Lieut.-Col.

(New Coll., Oxford. "*Times*" Staff.)
Capt., Grenadier Guards.
G.S.O.$_3$. Brigade-Major.
Temp. Major, 1918. Temp. Lieut.-Col. G.S.O.$_1$.
Despatches (2).
M.C. D.S.O. C.M.G.

GROGAN, Sir E. I. B. ... B 86–90
    Bart.
      Col.

(R.B., 1893. Capt., 1900. S. African War.)
Lieut.-Col., R.B., 1915.
G.S.O.$_3$, 1915. G.S.O.$_2$, 1916. G.S.O.$_1$, 1918.
Brevet Col. Col., 1919.
Despatches (3).
D.S.O.
Greek Order of "Redeemer."

GROGAN, E. S. ... ... D 88–92   (Jesus Coll., Camb. S. Africa.)
Major   Major, Liaison Staff Officer, Belgian Congo.
  Despatches.
  D.S.O.. Order of Léopold.

GROVER, J. M. L. ... A 10–14
Capt.   Shropshire L.I., 1914.
  Lieut., 1916. Acting Capt., 1918.
  Officer Cadet Bn.
  Wounded (2).

GUEST, Hon. F. E. ... F 88–91   (1st Life Guards, 1897. Nile Exped. and
Capt.   S. African War.
  Capt., 1st Life Guards.
  Retired, 1917.
  Despatches (2).
  D.S.O. Chevalier Légion d'Honneur.

GUINNESS, A. R. ... B 08–14
Capt.   Capt. and Adjt., Manchester Regt.
  A.D.C.
  Wounded.

GUINNESS, H. E. ... B 11–15
Lieut.   Lieut., R.F.A., 1918.
  Wounded.

GUISBOROUGH, Lord ... F 71–72   (As R. G. W. Long: 6th D.G. Afghan War.
Major   3rd Hussars. Imp. Yeomanry. S. African
      War. As R. G. W. Chaloner: M.P., Wilts.)
  Major, 4th Reserve Regt. Cavalry.
  Relinquished Commission, 1917.

GUISE, V. R. ... ... I 98–01   (R.G.A., 1904.)
Capt.   Lieut., R.G.A.
  Capt., 1914.
  Prisoner of War, Kut.
  Repatriated, 1918.

GUNSTON, C. A.   COLL. 13–17
2nd Lieut.   2nd Lieut., K.R.R.C., 6th Bn., 1918.

GURNEY, H. L. G.   COLL. 12–16
Lieut.   2nd Lieut., K.R.R.C., 6th, att. 1st, Bn.
  Lieut., 1918.
  Wounded.

GUY, B. G. ... ... G 06–10
Lieut.   Lieut., R.F.A., 1917.
  M.C.

GUY, Rev. C. A. ... E 99–03 (Oriel Coll., Oxford.)
Chaplain, R.N.

✠ GWYER, C. ... ... I 00–02 (Ch. Ch., Oxford.)
2nd Lieut. 2nd Lieut., D. of Lancaster's Yeomanry.
Grenadier Guards, 1917.
Killed, Aug. 27th, 1918, *near St. Léger.*

✠ GWYER, C. P. ... ... I 96–00 ·(Welsh Regt., Lieut., 1903.)
Capt. Capt., Welsh Regt.
Killed, Aug. 8th, 1915, *Gallipoli.*

GWYN, H. G. MOORE- G 99–05 (R.B., 1906. Lieut., 1910.)
Capt. Capt., R.B., 1914.
Brigade-Major, 1917.
Despatches (3).
M.C. Croix de Guerre. D.S.O.

GWYN, J. G. MOORE- G 93–96 (Capt., Glamorgan Yeomanry, 1903.)
Major Major, Glamorgan Yeomanry.
Posted to Welsh Regt.
Resigned Comm., 1919, ill-health from Active
Service.

✠ HABERSHON, K. R. ... F 03–08
Capt. Capt., R.B.
Killed, Feb. 12th, 1916, *near Ypres.*

✠ HABERSHON, L. O. ... F 07–12
Capt. Capt., E. Yorkshire Regt.
Killed, Nov. 13th, 1916, *between Serre and*
Hebuterne.

✠ HABERSHON, P. H. ... A 07–11
2nd Lieut. 2nd Lieut., K.R.R.C.
Killed, Sept. 15th, 1915, *Hooge.*

✠ HABERSHON, S. H. ... A 03–08 (2nd Lieut., O.T.C., Eastbourne College.)
2nd Lieut. 2nd Lieut., Suffolk Regt., 1917.
Wounded.

Killed, April 10th, 1918, *Estaire, near Fleurbaix.*

✠ HADDEN, N. C. ... K 06–10
Capt. Capt., R.F.A.
Killed, April 9th, 1916, *San-i-yat.*

✠ HADEN, F. H. ... ... K 11–12
2nd Lieut. 2nd Lieut., R.B., att. T.M.B.
Killed, Nov. 4th, 1917, *Monchy-le-Preux.*

HADLEY, P. A. S. ... G 12–17
2nd Lieut. 2nd Lieut., R.F.A., 1918.
Wounded.

HAGEMEYER, A. G. COLL. 12–17

Cadet, R.F.A.

HAIG, A. B. ... ... D 99–03 (2nd Lieut., I.A., 1905.)
Capt.   Capt. and Adjt., I.A., 24th Punjabis, 1914.
                           Prisoner of War, Kut.
                           Escaped from Turkey, Aug.–Sept., 1918.
                           Wounded.   *Despatches* (2).

HAIG, A. E. ... ... B8 0–84 (Trin. Coll., Oxford. R.M. Coll. K.O.S.B.,
Lieut.-Col.   1887. Soudan, Tirah, Nile, S. African
                               War. Staff Capt., 1903. G.S.O.$_2$, 1905.
                               Major, 1905.)
                           Lieut.-Col., K.O.S.B., 1914.
                           Prisoner of War. Interned Holland.
                           Repatriated, 1918.
                           Wounded.   *Despatches.*

HAIG, A. G. ... ... B 80–84 (R.G.A., 1896. Capt., 1901. S. African War.)
Lieut.-Col.   Major, R.G.A., 1914.
                           Bt. Lieut.-Col., 1917.
                           Despatches (7).
                           D.S.O. Order of St. Anne. C.M.G.

HAIG, C. H. ... ... B8 7–89 (Leicester Regt., 1894. Capt., 1902. Major,
Lieut.-Col.   1914. S. African War.)
                           Lieut.-Col., Leicestershire Regt., 1915.
                           A.A.G., Irish Command, 1917.
                           Wounded.   *Despatches* (3).
                           D.S.O.

HAIG, H. G. ... ... D 93–00 (New Coll., Oxford. I.C.S.)
Capt.   Capt., 31st Lancers, I.A.

HAIG, R. C. ... ... B 86–89 (7th Dragoons. Capt., 1900. S. African War.)
Brig.-Gen.   Retired, 1903.
                           Bt. Lieut.-Col. R.B., att. Berkshire Regt.
                           Brigadier-General, 1917.
                           Wounded.   *Despatches* (4).
                           D.S.O. and 2 Bars.

HAIGH, A. D. ... ... I 07–10
Lieut.   Lieut., R. Sussex Regt.
                           Acting Capt., 1916.
                           Wounded.
                           M.C.

✠ HAIGH, C. R. ... ... I 02–07
Capt.   Capt. and Adjt., R.W. Surrey Regt.
                           Killed, Nov. 7th, 1914, *Klein Zillebeke, near
                               Ypres.*

93

✠ HAIN, E. ... ... A 01–06
    Capt.
                           Capt., R. 1st Devon Yeomanry.
                           Killed, Nov. 11th, 1915, *Gallipoli.*

HALE, T. W. ... ... I 77–80
    Col.
                           (Lieut., Wiltshire Regt., 1885. Major, 1903.)
                           Col., Army Ordnance Dept.
                           Director Ordnance Services, 1917.
                           Despatches.
                           C.M.G. C.B.

HALES, E. B. ... ... A 81–84
    Lieut.-Col.
                           (D.L.I., 1889. Capt., 1898. S. African War.
                              Retired, 1911.)
                           Major, Durham Light Infantry.
                           Temp. Lieut.-Col., Comm. Depot.

✠ HALES, G. O., BRUNWIN- A 03–07
    Capt.
                           Capt., Essex Regt.
                           R.A.F.
                         Killed, March 24th, 1917, *by Anti-Aircraft, near*
                                  Vimy Ridge.

✠ HALES, H. T., BRUNWIN A 06–10
    2nd Lieut.
                           2nd Lieut., Lincolnshire Regt.
                         Killed, Oct. 13th, 1915, *Hohenzollern Redoubt.*

HALES, Rev. J. P. ... A 84–87
    C.F.
                           (Jesus Coll., Camb.)
                         Chaplain to Forces, att. Sherwood Foresters.
                         D.A. Chaplain-General, IVth Corps.
                         D.S.O.

HALL, C. D. ... COLL. 11–14
    2nd Lieut.
                           2nd Lieut., R.F.A.
                         Wounded.
                         Retired owing to wounds, Nov., 1917.

HALL, F. G. ... ... C 96–98
    Capt.
                           Lieut., Dorset Regt.
                         Capt., Assistant Base Commandant.

HALL, F. H. H. COLL. 90–94
    Major
                           (R.M.L.I., 1895. Capt., 1901.)
                         Major, R.M.L.I., 1914.
                         H.Q., Chatham.

✠ HALL, G. E. ... ... I 94–99
    2nd Lieut.
                           (New Coll., Oxford. Stock Exchange.)
                         2nd Lieut., Norfolk Regt.
                         Wounded. Despatches.
                         Killed April 26th, 1917, *near Grenay.*

HALL, G. H. ... ... H 05–08
    Capt.
                           Lieut., Welsh Horse.
                         R.A.F. Capt. A.

HALL, H. E. ... ... I 03–08
    Lieut.   Lieut., Norfolk Regt.
                                Killed Nov. 23th, 1915, *Ctesiphon.*

HALL, P. M. ... COLL. 07–13
    Capt.   Lieut., R.F.A., Wessex Brigade.
                                Capt., G.S.O.$_3$, Staff Capt., 1918.
                                Despatches.
                                M.C.

HALL, R. E. ... ... I 96–02
                                (New Coll., Oxford.)
                                Gold Coast Volunteers.

Sen. Crown Commissioner, Gold Coast.

HALLIDAY, W. R. COLL. 99–05
(formerly Hoffmeister)   (New Coll., Oxford.)
    Lieut.   Lieut., R.N.V.R. H.M.S. *Theseus.*

HALLOWES, T. R. F. B. C 67–69
    Major   (Lieut., 6th D.G., 1876. Afghan War. Major,
                                    1891. Retired, 1893.)
                                Major, Shropshire Yeomanry, T.F.R.

HALLWARD, B. M. ... D 96–01
                                (Ball. Coll., Oxford.)
                                Lieut., R.B.
                                War Office.
                                Despatches.
                                D.S.O.

HAMES, G. C. HAYTER- B 12–16
    Lieut.   2nd Lieut., 1st Life Guards.
                                Lieut., Guards M.G. Regt.

✠ HAMILTON, A. B. BAILLIE B 90–94
    Capt.   (Seaforth Highlanders, 1901. S. African War).
                                  Capt., Seaforth Highlanders, 1st Bn.
                                Despatches.
                                Killed May 9th, 1915, *Festubert.*

HAMILTON, A. R. ... F 82–88
    Capt.   (New Coll., Oxford. Jamaica.)
                                  Capt., R.A.S.C.

HAMILTON, C. K. ... B 14–18
                                  Cadet, R.A.F.

HAMILTON, G. D. BAILLIE I 89–92
    Major   (R. Fusiliers, 1897. Malay State Guides.
                                      A. and S. Highlanders. S. African War.
                                      Capt., R. Scots, 1905.)
                                Major, Royal Scots, 1915.
                                Staff Capt., R.T. Dept., 1917.
                                Wounded.

✠ HAMILTON, G. E. A.   H 12–15
   FITZ GEORGE
    2nd Lieut.   2nd Lieut., Grenadier Guards.
                        Killed May 18th, 1918, *by aeroplane bomb,*
                           Warlencourt.

✠ HAMILTON, H. A.   I 93–97
    Major   (R.A., 1899. S. African War.)
                        Major, R.F.A., Inspection Staff.
                        Despatches (2).
                        Killed Jan. 25th, 1916, *Poperinghe.*

HAMILTON, J. M.   G 00–05
   Brevet Major   Capt., Brevet Major, Gordon Highlanders, 1915.
                        Staff Capt. Brigade-Major. G.S.O.$_2$.
                        Despatches (4).
                        D.S.O.

✠ HAMILTON, M. J.   G 93–97
    Capt.   (Lancs. Fus., 1899. Capt., 1903. Egyptian
                          Army. S. African War.)
                        Capt., Gordon Highlanders.
                        A.P.M.
                        Killed Nov. 28th, 1914, *Poperinghe.*

HAMILTON, R. N.   F 09–13
    Lieut.   H.A.C., 1914.
                        Lieut., R. Bucks Hussars, 1916.
                        Hon. Lieut., R.A.F., A. and S.

✠ HAMMOND, G. P.   H 05–08
    2nd Lieut.   2nd Lieut., K.O.S.B.
                        Killed, Sept. 26th, 1914, *Le Cateau.*

HANBURY, Rev. G. S.   H 00–06
    C.F.   Chaplain to Forces, 79th Brig., R.G.A.
                        O.B.E.

HANHAM, Sir J. L.   F 11–16
   Bart.
    Lieut.   2nd Lieut., Grenadier Guards.
                        Lieut., 1918.
                        Wounded.

✠ HANKINSON, R. P.   COLL. 04–09
    2nd Lieut.   2nd Lieut., Corps of Guides.
                        Att. 56th Rifles, I.A.F.F.
                        Died Feb. 23rd, 1917, *of wounds received near*
                           Kut.

HANSARD, A. C.   A?69–73
    Col.   (R.A., 1874. Capt., 1883. Lieut.-Col., 1900·
                          Col., 1904.)
                        Col., R.A.
                        Despatches.
                        C.M.G.

HANSON, C. O. ... ... H 85–88

Assist. Surveyor, Forest of Dean.
M.B.E.

✠ HARBORD, S. G. ... F 03–07
Capt.

Lieut., Acting Capt., R.F.A.
Staff Capt.
Despatches.
M.C.
Killed, Aug. 14th, 1917, *near Ypres.*

✠ HARDCASTLE, J. B. ... H 06–10
Capt.

Capt., Oxford and Bucks L.I.
Killed July 30th, 1916, *near Guillemont.*

✠ HARDINGE, Hon. H. R. G 09–13
2nd Lieut.

2nd Lieut., R.B.
Despatches.
Killed May 9th, 1915, *Fromelles.*

HARDY, E. G. ... ... H 80–83
Col.

(1st R. Dragoons, 1887. Capt., 1894. S. African
War.)
Temp. Col., Remount Service.
Deputy Director, 1917.
Despatches.
C.M.G.

HARDY, W. K. ... ... I 78–82
Brig.-Gen.

(Lieut., R.A., 1884. Major, 1903. Lieut.-
Col., 1913.)
Brigadier-General, R.G.A., 1917, Peshawur.

HARLAND, C. C. ... C 02–05
Capt.

Lieut., Hampshire Regt.
Capt., att. S. Staffordshire Regt., 1915.
Staff Capt., 1918.
Wounded (3).
Despatches.
M.C.

HARMAR, C. d'O ... I 91–95
Col.

(R.M.L.I., 1897. Capt., 1903.)
Temp. Col., R.M.L.I.
G.S.O.,1.
D.S.O. Chevalier Légion d'Honneur.

HARRIS, Rt. Hon. F. ... A 78–80
LEVERTON
Capt.

(M.P.)
Hon. Lieut., R.N.V.R., 1914.
Hon. Capt., 1915. Commander.
Parliamentary Under Sec. of Blockade, 1916.
Officier, Légion d'Honneur.

HARRIS, G. M. ... ... E 82–87
Lieut.   Lieut., R. Sussex Regt., Vol. Bn.
                                O.B.E.

HARRISON, A. C. GRAEME   F 02–06
Lieut.   Lieut., Intelligence Corps.
                                Att. 4th Dragoon Guards.
                                Invalided, 1916.
                                Despatches.

HARRISON, F. E. H. ... I 95–01   (Lieut., 1st Northern R.G.A., Vol., 1904.)
Major   Major, R.F.A.
                                Relinquished Comm., ill health, 1918.

HARRISON, H. E. HYDE   D 88–90   (Engineer.)
Major·   Capt., R.E., 112th Railway Coy.
                                Acting Major, 1918.

HARVEY, A. FOX.   ... I 88–93   (St. John's Coll., Oxford. Solicitor.)
                                2nd Lieut., R. Irish Rifles.
                                Wounded.

HARVEY, H. le F. F. ... H 04–08   (R.A., 1910.)
Capt.   Capt., R.F.A., 1916.
                                Acting Major, 1916-18.
                                Brigade-Major, 1919.
                                Wounded.   Despatches.
                                M.C.

HARVEY, R. K. ... ... H 79–82   (B.N.C., Oxford.)
Lieut.-Col.   Lieut.-Col., East Surrey Regt.
                                T.D.

✠ HARVIE, E. A. G.   ... F 01–05
Sub-Lieut.   Sub.-Lieut., R.N. Division, Public Schools' Coy.
                                Killed Nov. 13th, 1916, *near Beaumont Hamel.*

✠ HASLER, J.   ... ... B 82–85   (The Buffs, 1888. Capt., 1898. Bt. Lieut.-Col.
Brig.-Gen.   1906. S. African War.)
                                Brigadier-General, 11th Infantry Brigade.
                                Despatches (2).
                                Killed April 27th, 1915, *St. Jean, near Ypres.*

HAUGHTON, H. L.   ... F 97–01   (I.A., 1904. Capt., 1911.)
                                Major, 36th Sikhs I.A., 1917.

✠ HAWARDEN, VISCOUNT ... B 04–08
Lieut.   Lieut., Coldstream Guards.
                                Killed Aug. 25th, 1914, *Cambrai.*

98

✠ HAWKER, C. W. S.   ... E 01–05
     Lieut.
       Lieut., Hampshire Regt.
       Resigned Comm.
       Died in Switzerland, March, 1918.

HAWKER, H. G.   ... G 79–84
     Capt.
       (Univ. Coll., Oxford. Capt., S.W. Borderers,
         1891.)
       Capt., Devonshire Regt., 11th Bn. and Depot.

HAWKER, H. L. L.   ... A 09–14
       Sergeant Instructor, Cambridge O.T.C.
       Att. R.E. Signal Service.

HAWKER, M. L.   ... A 03–08
     Lieut.
       Lieut., A.P.D.

✠ HAWKER, R. S.   ... E 03–06
     Capt.
       Capt., R. 1st Devon Yeomanry.
       M.G.C., Infantry.
       Killed Nov. 9th, 1917, *Kantara, Palestine.*

HAWKINS, C. F.   ... F 93–00
     Major
       (2nd Lieut., Hants Regt., 1900. In Canada.)
       Canadian Contingent.
       Temp. Major, M.G.C., Tank Corps.
       Acting Lieut.-Col., 1918-1919.
       Relinquished Comm., 1919.
       Wounded.   *Despatches.*
       M.C.   D.S.O.

HAWKINS, E. B. B.   ... H 04–08
     Acting Lieut.-Col.
     Brevet Major
       (West Yorkshire Regt., 1909   K.A.R., 1912.)
       Capt., West Yorkshire Regt., 1914.
       Major, K.A.R., 4th Uganda Bn.
       D.A.A.G., Staff Officer, 1916.
       Acting Lieut.-Col., 1919.
       Despatches (2).
       D.S.O.

HAWKINS, E. J. E.   ... F 95–00
     Major
       (R. Sussex Regt., 1904, to I.A. Retired.
         Canada.)
       R.A.F., Major, Balloons.
       Relinquished Comm., 1918.

HAWKINS, G. E....   ... H 07–10
     Capt.
       2nd Lieut., Welsh Regt., 1914.
       Lieut., R. Berkshire Regt., 1916.
       K.A.R., 4th Bn.
       Acting Capt., 1916-17.
       Wounded.
       M.C.

HAWKINS, H. V. ... F 93–97 (Engineer)
Capt. Temp. Capt., R.E., 1915.
Resigned Comm.

✠ HAWKINS, L. H. ... I 00–03
Lieut. Lieut., 1st Dragoon Guards.
Killed Oct. 31st, 1915, *near Messines.*

HAWKSLEY, E. B. ... B 89–94 (Univ. Coll., Oxford. Solicitor.)
2nd Lieut. 2nd Lieut., Welsh Guards, 1918.

✠ HAWORTH, P. T. ... G 10–15
Capt. Capt., R.F.A.
Died May 3rd, 1917, *at Etaples of wounds
received* April 28th *at Gavrelles.*

HAY, I. A. G. ... ... B 77–81 (Coldstream Guards, 1884. Lieut.-Col, 1900.
RICHARDSON DRUMMOND- S. African War. Brevet Col. Retired,
Lieut.-Col. 1911.)
Lieut.-Col. Comm., Coldstream Guards, 1914
Despatches.
Retired.

✠ HAYCOCK R. H. HINE ... F 05–09
Capt., Yorkshire L.I.
Wounded.
Killed May 3rd, 1917, *Henin sur Cojeul.*

HAYDEN, F. A. COLL. 73–79 (Duke of Wellington's, 1881. Major, 1898.
D.S.O. S. African War. Lieut.-Col., 1908.
Lieut.-Col. Retired, 1912.)
Lieut.-Col., Duke of Wellington's, W. Riding
Regt., 1914.
Comm. Training Reserve, 8th Bn., 1916-1919.
C.B.E.
Despatches.

HAYDON, A. D. ... ... B 03–07
Lieut. Lieut., R.A.M.C., till 1917.

HAYES, W. E. ... ... E 07–11
2nd Lieut. 2nd Lieut., R.E.
Relinquished Comm., 1918.

HAYTER, W. G. ... COLL. 82–88
Counsel to Sultan of Egypt.
C.B.E.

✠ HAYWARD, E. R. ... K 11–15
2nd Lieut. 2nd Lieut., R.F.A.
Killed Dec. 17th, 1917, *near Salonica.*

HEARN, G. R. ... Lieut.-Col.	COLL. 84–88	(R.E., 1890. Capt., 1901. Major, 1910.) Brevet Lieut.-Col., R.E., 1918. Lieut.-Col., 1919. *Despatches* (3). D.S.O.
HEARN, H. S. ... Major	COLL. 89–92	(R.G.A., 1895. Capt., 1901.) Major, R.G.A., 1914. With Egyptian Army, 1907-1917. D.A.A.G., 1917, War Office. *Wounded. Despatches.* Order of " The Nile."
HEATH, R. ... Capt.	COLL. 02–08	Capt., R.E., 1917.
HEATHCOTE, R. ST. A. Capt.	COLL. 02–07	Late Capt., R.A.M.C.
✠ HEDLEY, W. A. C. Capt.	... H 08–10	Lieut., Acting Capt., E. Kent Regt. *Despatches.* *Killed* July 19th, 1918, *between Dickebusch and* *Mt. Kemmel.*
HELLYER, F. E. Major	... E 02–05	Capt., Hampshire Regt. Temp. Major, R.A.F., 1918. S.O. *Wounded* (2). *Despatches.* O.B.E.
✠ HELLYER, G. E. Capt.	... K 06–09	Capt., Hampshire Regt. *Died of wounds* Aug. 22nd, 1915, *Dardanelles.*
HELLYER, T. E. 2nd Lieut.	... K 12–17	2nd Lieut., R.F.A., 1918.
HELME, E. Major	... I 86–91	(Ch. Ch., Oxford. Glamorganshire Yeomanry, 1904.) Major, Glamorganshire Yeomanry, 1914. Staff Capt. G.S.O.$_3$. Comm. Welsh Regt., 15th Bn. Temp. Lieut.-Col. till 1919. *Wounded* (2). *Despatches.* D.S.O. and Bar.
HELME, Sir G. C. K.C.B., C.M.G. Col.	COMM. 56–60	(Lincolnshire Regt., 1862. Major, 1881. Lieut.-Col., Middlesex Regt. S. African War. Retired, 1889.) Hon. Col., West Yorkshire Regt.

101

✠ HENDERSON, A. W. ... I 08–13
    Capt.

Capt., R.B.
Killed July 1st, 1916, *Serre, 1st Battle of the Somme.*

✠ HENDERSON, G. B. ... A 97–02
    Lieut.

Lieut., London Regt., 2nd Bn.
Killed June 16th, 1917.

✠ HENDERSON, T. H. ... I 09–14
    Capt.

Capt. and Adjt., R.B.
Wounded. Despatches.
M.C. and Bar.
Killed Nov. 30th, 1917, *La Vacquerie, near Cambrai.*

HENDERSON, W. E. B. A 94–99
    2nd Lieut.

(Trin. Coll., Oxford. Barrister.)
2nd Lieut., R.G.A., 1917.

HENDRIKS, C. L. ... B 80–82
    Lieut.-Col.

(Munster Fusiliers, 1888. S. African War. Major, 1906. Retired, 1913.)
Lieut.-Col., Munster Fusiliers.
Wounded.
Reserve of Officers.

HERBERT, A. P. ... C 04–09
    Lieut.

Lieut., R.N. Division, Hawke Bn.
Wounded. Despatches.

✠ HERBERT, O. W. E. ... C 06–11
    Lieut.

Lieut., R.F.A.
Killed Oct. 26th, 1914, *near Neuve Chapelle.*

✠ HERMAN, G. A. COLL. 04–11
    Lieut.

Lieut., Cambridgeshire Regt.
Killed July 20th, 1916, *Givenchy.*

HERRINGHAM, ... COLL. 67–73
  Sir W. P., M.D.
    Major-General

(Keble Coll., Oxford. Physician.)
Surgeon-General. Lieut.-Col., R.A.M.C.
H.Q. Staff. Temp-Major-General.
Consulting Physician to E.F.
Despatches (4).
C.B. K.C.M.G.

HERRON, R. L. ... ... K 11–16
    2nd Lieut.

2nd Lieut., R.G.A., 1918.

✠ HESS, A. G. ... ... H 05–10
    Lieut.

Lieut., R.H.A.
Killed Feb. 25th, 1915, *near Ypres.*

HEWETT, H. M. P. ... c 04–09 (1st Dragoons, 1911.)
Capt.   Capt., 1st Royal Dragoons, 1916.
                                Att., R.A.F.
                                Wounded.   Despatches.

✠ HEWITT, D. G. W. ... G 11–15
2nd Lieut.   2nd Lieut., Hampshire Regt.
                                𝔙.ℭ.
                                Killed July 31st, 1917, *St. Julien, 3rd Battle
                                    of Ypres.*

HEWITT, A. W. W. ... G 14–18
                                Gentleman Cadet, R.M. College.

HEWSON, A. G. ... I 05–09   (R.A., 1911.)
Capt.   Capt., R.F.A., 1916.
                                Acting Major, 1918.
                                Wounded.   Despatches (2).
                                M.C.

HEYLAND, Rev. A. K. A 94–99   (Trin. Coll., Oxford.)
C.F.   Chaplain to Forces.

✠ HEYWOOD, B. C. P. ... c 78–81 (Trin. Coll., Camb. S. African War.)
Col.   Hon. Col., Manchester Regt.
                                Comm. 19th Bn.
                                Died in England, 1914.

HEYWOOD, G. G. P. ... c 80–84 (Trin. Coll. Camb. S. African War.)
Lieut.-Col.   Lieut.-Col., T.F.R. Served in Egypt, 1914–15.
                                Temp. Capt., 1st Vol. Bn. K. Shropshire L.I.
                                T.D.

✠ HICHENS, J. B. ... E 86–91   (Magd. Coll., Oxford. Stock Exchange.)
Lieut.   Lieut., K.R.R.C.
                                Wounded.
                                Killed July 16th, 1916, *Bois de Fourrousse.*

✠ HICKLEY, R. T. N. ... F 11–15
Lieut.   Lieut., Hertfordshire Regt.
                                Wounded (2).
                                Killed Mar. 24th, 1918, *near Maricourt sur
                                    Somme.*

✠ HICKS, F. A. ... ... K 10–14
Lieut.   Lieut., Royal Fusiliers.
                                Wounded.   Despatches.
                                M.C.
                                Killed Aug. 21st, 1918, *Courcelles.*

HICKS, K. B. ... ... K 14–18
                                Gentleman Cadet, R.M. College.

103

HICKS, P. H. W. ... r 09–13
Capt.
                     2nd Lieut., Warwickshire Regt., 1916.
                     Lieut., 1917.
                     Acting Capt., 1918.
                     Despatches (2).
                     M.C.

HILL, E. T. ... ... H 83–88 (19th Lancers, 1889. Capt., 1896. S. African
Major   War.)
                     Major, Gloucestershire Yeomanry, 1904.
                     Remount Service.
                     In France with Y.M.C.A., 1918.

✠ HILL, G. GRAY ... ... A 02–07
                     Singapore Vol. Rifles.
                     Died of pneumonia, July 16th, 1915, *after Singapore Mutiny.*

HILL, H. BURROW ... H 05–09 (Exeter Coll., Oxford.)
Capt.   Capt., Dorset Regt.
                     Staff Capt.
                     Despatches.
                     M.C.

✠ HILL, H. B. ... ... A 05–10
                     R.A.F.
                     Killed by accident, flying.

HILL, H. B. ... COLL. 83–86 (R.F.A., 1888. Capt., 1889. Major, 1904.
BERKELEY   Retired, 1909.)
Major   Major, R.A.
                     Staff Capt., Brigade-Major, S. Midland Div.

HILL, J. C. H. ... COLL. 05–11 (Magd. Coll., Oxford.)
Lieut.   Lieut., Worcestershire Regt.
                     Despatches.
                     D.S.O. Italian Medal for Valour.

HILL, J. S. B. ... ... D 99–04 (Magd. Coll., Oxford.)
Capt.   Capt., Oxford and Bucks L.I., 1916.
                     Staff Capt.
                     Despatches (3).
                     M.C. Croix de Guerre.

HILL, M. V. B. ... H 00–06 (New Coll., Oxford.)
Lieut.-Col.   2nd Lieut., R. Fusiliers, 1914.
                     Capt., 1915.
                     Temp. Lieut.-Col. Commanding Sussex Regt., 9th Bn.
                     Wounded.   *Despatches* (4).
                     M.C. D.S.O. and Bar.

✠ HILL, N. W. ... ... G 09–15
  Capt.
    2nd Lieut., Oxford and Bucks L.I.
    Capt., 1916.
    Wounded.
    M.C.
    Killed Jan. 16th, 1917, *near Courcelette.*

HILL, P. M. T. ... ... H 91–95
  Lieut.
    (Oriel Coll., Oxford.)
    Lieut., R.F.C., Equipment Officer, 2nd Class,
        1915.
    R.A.F., Lieut., T.

HILL, V. T. ... ... H 84–89
  Capt.
    (Oriel Coll., Oxford. Barrister.)
    Capt., K.R.R.C.
    Disciplinary Officer, Convalescent Camp, Bath,
        1918.

✠ HILL, W. E. ... ... C 06–09
  Lieut.
    Lieut., N. Staffordshire Regt.
    Killed Sept. 5th, 1914, *Battle of the Aisne.*

HILLS, A. C. ... ... I 82–84
  2nd Lieut.
    (Planter, etc., India.)
    2nd Lieut., 6th (K.E. Own) Cavalry I.A.

HILLS, E. H., C.M.G. ... C 77–80
  Major
    (Lieut., R.E. Major, 1901. Retired, 1905.)
    Major, R.E.
    Staff Officer to Chief Engineer, Midland Div.
    Despatches.
    O.B.E.

HIND, N. G. ... ... F 05–09
  Capt.
    (I.A., 1912.)
    Capt., 2nd Gurkha Rifles, 1915.

✠ HINDSON, L. R. P. ... B 08–13
  Lieut.
    Lieut., R.F.A.
    Killed June 10th, 1917, *Messines.*

HINDSON, R. E. ... B 06–08
  Capt.
    (R. Welsh Fusiliers, 1911.)
    Capt., R. Welsh Fusiliers, 1915.
    Wounded.
    Prisoner of War, interned Holland, Feb., 1918.
    Repatriated, Nov., 1918.

HITCHINS, L. R. S. ... B 13–18
    Gentleman Cadet. R.M. College.

✠ HOARE, G. C. ... ... I 12–17
  2nd Lieut.
    2nd Lieut., R.B., 6th Bn.
    Died July 31st, 1918, *of wounds received March,*
        1918.

105

HOARE, M. W. ... I 13–18

Cadet, R.F.A.

HOBBS, C. P. ... ... A 12–15
2nd Lieut.

2nd Lieut., R.F.A., 1918.

HOBHOUSE, E. W. N. B 01–07
Capt.

Capt., R.A.M.C.

✠ HODGE, G. G. HERMON ... H 97–01
Capt.

(R.F.A., 1903.)
Capt., R.H.A.
Died July 7th, 1916, *at Doullens of wounds received Battle of the Somme*, June 28th.

HODGE, Hon. H. B. COLL. 99–03
HERMON
Lieut.

(Magd. Coll., Oxford.)
Lieut., Nigeria F.F.

HODGE, Hon. R. E. U. H 96–00
HERMON
Major

(Oxford L.I. S. African War.)
Capt., Oxfordshire Hussars.
Major, 1918.
Wounded. *Despatches* (2).
D.S.O.

HODGE, HON. R. H. ... H 93–96
HERMON, M.V.O.
Brevet Lieut.-Col.

(Gren. Guards, 1899. Lieut., 1905. S. African War.)
Major, Grenadier Guards.
Brigade-Major. D.A.Q.M.G.
D.A.A.G., 1917.
Despatches (2).
D.S.O.

HODGKINSON, H. S. B.... A 67–70
Col.

(N. Lancs Regt., 1873. Capt., 1881. Major, N. Staffs Regt., 1890. S. African War. Lieut.-Col., 1901. Brevet Col., 1904. Ret. 1905.)
Col., T.F., Record Office, Preston.

HOERNLE, E. S. COLL. 00–05
Lieut.

Lieut., Temp. Capt., I.A.R.O.

HOG, R. D. ... ... F 11–15
Lieut.

2nd Lieut., Royal Highlanders.
R.M. Coll., 1916.
I.A. unattached list, 1917.
2nd Lieut. Lieut., 1918.

HOG, R. T. A. COLL. 06–11
Capt.

(R.A., 1912.)
Capt., R.F.A., 1916.
Acting Major, 1917.
Wounded (2). *Despatches.*

HOGARTH, D. G. ... G 76–81 (Magd. Coll., Oxford.)
    Commander   Lieut.-Commander, R.N.V.R.
                                       Commander, 1918.
                                       C.M.G. Order of " Nile."

HOGG, R. J. J. ... E 07–10
    Lieut.   2nd Lieut., E. Surrey Regt., 1917.
                                       Lieut., 1918.

HOLE, W. G. ... ... A 94–98 (Merton Coll., Oxford.)
    Major   Major, R. 1st Devon Yeomanry.
                                       Comm. 2nd Cyclist Division, Signal Squadron,
                                            R.E.

✠ HOLLINS, W. H.... ... I 09–14
    2nd Lieut.   2nd Lieut., Notts and Derby Regt., 1914.
                                       Killed June 15th, 1915, *Flanders.*

✠ HOLLIST, A. M. C. ... G 86–90 (Trin. Coll., Camb. W.I. Regt., 1900. S.
    Capt.   African War.)
                                       Capt., E. Kent Regt.
                                       Wounded.
                                       Killed Sept., 1915, *Loos.*

✠ HOLT, H. W. ... ... B 02–07
    2nd Lieut.   2nd Lieut., R.E.
                                       Wounded and prisoner Aug., 1915.
                                       Died of Wounds.

HOLTBY, E. ... ... I 03–07 (E. Yorkshire Regt., 1912. Lieut., 1913.)
    Major   Capt. and Adjt., E. Yorkshire Regt., 1915.
                                         Major, 1917. Brigáde-Major, 1918.
                                       Despatches.
                                     M.C.

HOME, J. M. ... ... H 79–83 (R.A., 1886. Capt., 2nd Gurkhas, 1897. Major,
    Brevet Col.   1904. Lieut.-Col., 1912.)
                                       Lieut.-Col., 1st Gurkha Rifles.
                                         G.S.O.$_1$, 1915. A.A.Q.M.G., 1916.
                                       Brevet Col., 1917.
                                       R.A.F., S.O.$_1$, 1918.
                                       Despatches.
                                       C.B.E. Order " St. Anne."

HONE, T. N. ... ... F 08–12
    Capt.   2nd Lieut., K.R.R.C., 1914.
                                         A.D.C.
                                       Capt., 1917. G.S.O.$_3$.
                                       Liaison Officer, American G.H.Q.
                                       Wounded (2).   *Despatches.*
                                       American D.S.M.

HOOD, R. JACOMB ... I 12–15
2nd Lieut.   2nd Lieut., K.R.R.C., 5th Bn., 1918.

✠ HOOPER, S. H. ...   ... C 81–85   (2nd Lieut., R.A., 1887. Capt., 1898. R.O.)
Lieut.-Col.   Lieut.-Col., R.F.A., 1914.
                                     D.A.A.G.
                                     Died on active Service May 31st, 1915.

HOPE, H. L.   ...   ... G 10–15
Lieut.   2nd Lieut., R.F.A., 1915.
                                     Lieut., 1917.
                                     Wounded (2).
                                     M.C.

HOPE, H. O.   ...   ... I 94–99
Lieut.   Lieut., K.R.R.C.
                                     R.A.F., Lieut., K.B.
                                     Croix de Guerre.

HOPE, J. F. R.   ... A 96–00   (K.R.R.C., 1902. Capt., 1914.)
Brig.-Gen.   Temp. Lieut.-Col., K.R.R.C., 1917.
                                     Comm. M.G.C. Bn., 1918.
                                     Temp. Brigadier-General.
                                     Wounded (3).   *Despatches* (4).
                                     D.S.O.

HOPE, W. G. I.   ... C 92–97   (Ch. Ch., Oxford.)
Capt.   Capt., Gen. List.
                                     Staff Lieut., 1918.
                                     Wounded.

HOPKINSON, H. C. B. ... H 81–85   (Seaforth Highlanders, 1891. Capt., 1899. Nile
Col.   Exp., Khartoum.)
                                     Col., Comm. Police, Egypt.
                                     Director-General of Municipality, Alexandria.
                                     Despatches (4).

HOPKINSON, H. S. P.   ... B 13–18
                                     Gentleman Cadet. R.M. Coll.

HOPWOOD, H. R.   ... C 85–89   (R.M.L.I., 1891. 33rd Cavalry I.A., 1899.
C.S.I.   Capt., 1901.)
Col.   G.S.O.$_2$., 1914. Temp. Brig.-General, 1916.
                                     G.S.O.$_1$, 1918.
                                     Temp. Major-General, 1917.

✠ HORN, R.   ...   ... C 95–98   (Seaforth Highlanders, 1900. Lieut., 1901.)
Lieut.-Col.   Lieut.-Col., Seaforth Highlanders.
                                     Wounded.   *Despatches* (3).
                                     M.C. D.S.O. and Bar.
                                     Killed April 18th, 1918, *Scherpenberg, Flanders.*

108

HORNBY, A. H. ...   ... I 07–12
    Capt.   Capt., R.H.A.
                                    Acting Major, 1918.
                                    Wounded.   Despatches.
                                    M.C.

HORNBY, H. S. ...   ... I 03–06
    Capt.   2nd Lieut., R.E.
                                    Temp. Lieut.
                                    1918, Temp. Capt., Base Commandant.
                                    Despatches (2).
                                    M.C.   Order of " Nile."

HORNBY, M. C. ST. J.   ... F 12–17
    2nd Lieut.   2nd Lieut., Grenadier Guards, 1918.
                                    Reserve of Officers, 1919.

HORNDON, D.   ...   ... E 77–81   (Exeter Coll., Oxford.)
    Lieut.   Lieut., Devon Vol. Regt.

HORNUNG, G.   ...   ... I 03–08
    Capt.   Lieut., R.F.A.
                                    Relinquished Comm., ill health, Hon. Capt.
                                        1918.

HOSKYNS, C. B. A.   ... A 09–12   (R.B., 1914.)
    Capt.   Lieut., R.B.
                                    Capt., 1917.
                                    M.G.C.
                                    Wounded.

HOTHAM, H. F.   ... B 13–17
    2nd Lieut.   2nd Lieut., Grenadier Guards, 1919.

HOUBLON, H. L. ARCHER   H 91–95   (Ch. Ch., Oxford. Berks Regt. E. Kent Regt.
    Capt.   Capt., 1904. S. African War.)
                                    Capt., Acting Major, E. Kent Regt.
                                    Army Ordnance Dept., 1918.
                                    Despatches.

HOUGH, G. de L.   ... K 07–13
    Capt.   Temp. Capt., R.W. Kent Regt.
                                    A.P.M., Cambridge, 1918.
                                    A.P.M., Bovington, 1919.
                                    Relinquished Comm., 1919.
                                    Wounded (2).   *Despatches.*

HOWARD, Hon. J. K. E.   B 00–02   (Canada.)
    Lieut.   Lieut., Hampshire Carabiniers, 1914.
                                    Reserve Regt., Household Cavalry.
                                    Guards M.G. Regt.
                                    Lieut., R. Horse Guards, 1919.

109

| HOWARD, T. F. K. | ... E 13–17 | |
| 2nd Lieut. | | 2nd Lieut., R.F.A., 1919. |

HOWE, J. C. ...   ... E 11–12
Lieut.
Lieut., R.G.A.
War Office.

HOWELL, A. A.   ... C 79–82 (Northumberland Fusiliers, 1885. Capt., I.A.,
Major   1896. Major, 1903. Lieut.-Col., 1911.
                             Retired, 1913.)
                         Major, Cambridgeshire Regt.
                         Relinquished Comm., 1918.

HUBAND, G. D.   ... E 11–16
Lieut.
2nd Lieut., R.G.A., 1917.
Lieut., R.A.F., 1918.
M.C.

HUDLESTON, W. H.   ... D 85–90 (Trin. Coll., Camb. Schoolmaster, Sedbergh.)
Capt.   Capt., D. of Wellington's, W. Riding Regt.
                               T.F.R.

HUGHES, F. ST. J.   ... F 80–83 (S.W. Borderers. Lieut., 1886. Capt., 1892.
Brevet Major   S. African War.)
                            Brevet Major, S. Wales Borderers.
                            Camp Commandant, No. 1 Base, 1915.
                            Despatches (2).
                            M.V.O.

✠ HULBERT, G. D....   ... D 12–18
2nd Lieut.
2nd Lieut., 18th Hussars.
Killed Aug. 9th, 1918, *De Luce, Battle of Amiens.*

HUME, B. M. ...   ... H 02–04

Trooper, Heidelberg Commando N. Forces,
   S. Africa.
Served with General Botha, German S.W.
Africa.

✠ HUME, E. A. ...   ... H 92–98 (Trin. Coll., Oxford. Barrister.)
Lieut.   Lieut., S. Staffordshire Regt., 1914.
                           Died at sea, Aug. 27th, 1915, *of wounds received*
                               Aug. 25th, *Gallipoli.*

HUMPHERY, H. C.   ... A 69–73

Inspector, City of London Special Police.

HUMPHERY, Sir J.   ... A 86–89
Lieut.-Col.
Lieut.-Col., Surrey Yeomanry, T.F.R.
Despatches.

110

HUMPHRY, J. M. ... B 10–15
    Lieut.

2nd Lieut., Arg. and Suth. Highlanders.
98th T.M. Battery.
Lieut., 1918.
Wounded (2).
M.C. Croix de Guerre.

HUNT, C. B. ... ... D 94–99
    Lieut.

(Ball. Coll., Oxford. High School, Leeds, 1905.)
Lieut., Oxf. and Bucks L.I.
Prisoner of War, 1918.
Wounded.
Repatriated, 1918.

✠ HUNT, J. H. S. C. ..., E 88–93
    2nd Lieut.

(Somerset House.)
2nd Lieut., London Regt., 23rd Bn.
Killed, Sept. 16th, 1916.

HUNTER, A. R. ... ... F 96–01
    Capt.

(New Coll., Oxford.)
Lieut., R.A.S.C.
Capt., 1917.

✠ HUNTER, H. M. ... C 05–10
    2nd Lieut.

2nd Lieut., Wiltshire Regt., 1914.
Despatches.
Died April 6th, 1915, *of wounds received at
    Neuve Chapelle.*

HUNTER, K. O. ... ... C 94–00
    2nd Lieut. ...

2nd Lieut., Coldstream Guards, 1918.

✠ HUNTER, L. W. ... COLL. 98–05
    Lieut.

(New Coll., Oxford.)
Lieut., Oxf. and Bucks L.I.
Killed Aug. 14th, 1916, *Pozières.*

HUNTER, R. C. ... ... C 92–97
    Lieut.

(Univ. Coll., Oxford. Solicitor. S. African
    War.)
Lieut., R. 1st Devon Yeomanry, 1910.
T.F.R.

✠ HUNTER, R. J. ... ... C 99–05
    Capt.

(B.N.C., Oxford.)
Capt., London R.B.
Killed Aug. 25th, 1918.

HUNTINGFORD, W. L. ... H 95–99
    Lieut.-Col.

(2nd Lieut., R.M. Artillery, 1899.)
Brevet Major, R.M.A.
On Staff of French C.O., Flagship *Courbet.*
Temp. Lieut.-Col., 1917.
Chevalier Légion d'Honneur. Order of " The
    Redeemer."

111

HUSON, A. C. ... COLL. 03–09
Capt. 2nd Lieut., R.G.A.
Lieut., 1918.
Acting Capt. and Adjt., 1918.

✠ HUTCHISON, R. H. COLL. 03–09 (B.N.C., Oxford.)
2nd Lieut. 2nd Lieut., Black Watch (Royal Highlanders).
Killed Oct. 13th, 1915, *Hohenzollern Redoubt.*

HUTTON, R. C. ... ... E 10–16
2nd Lieut. 2nd Lieut., Gloucestershire Yeomanry.

HYDE, J. G. ... ... I 77–81
Private, R. Fusiliers, 23rd Bn.

INCHBALD, G. H. E. ... F 09–15
Lieut. Lieut., Berkshire Yeomanry, 1917.
Imperial Camel Corps, 1916-18.
Wounded.

✠ INCHBALD, J. C. E. COLL. 07–13
Capt. Capt., Devonshire Regt.
Despatches.
Killed April 2nd, 1917, *Ecoust, near Bapaume.*

INGLIS, J. ... ... I 96–00 (Highland L.I., 1901. S. African War. Capt.,
Major 1912.)
Major, Highland L.I.
Officer Cadet Coy., R.M. College, 1916-17.
Acting Lieut.-Col, 1917-18.
Wounded.
D.S.O.

✠ INGLIS, J. N. ... ... I 01–03 (Arg. and Suth. Highlanders, 1906.)
Capt. Capt., Black Watch (Royal Highlanders).
Despatches.
M.C.

Killed April 22nd, 1916, *Sanna-i-yat.*

INGRAM, B. S. ... ... E 91–95 (Trin. Coll., Oxford. E. Kent Yeomanry.
Capt. *Illustrated London News.*)
Lieut., R.G.A.
Temp. Capt. Staff Capt., 1916.
Despatches (2).
M.C.

INGRAM, C. W. ... ... E 93–97
Capt. Lieut, St. John's School, Letherhead, O.T.C.
Capt., R.E.

INGRAM, F. M. COLL. 78–83 (Magd. Coll., Oxford.)
Major Major, Shrewsbury School O.T.C.
Despatches.

✠ INGRAM, G. S. ... ... E 04–07
2nd Lieut. 2nd Lieut., R.W. Surrey Regt.
Killed, October 21st, 1914, *Zonnebeke.*

INNES, J. A., D.S.O. ... G 89–94 (R.B., 1896. Capt., 1901. S. African War.)
Lieut.-Col. Lieut.-Col. Training Reserve.

✠ INNES, J. A. ... ... D 94–98 (Ship-broker.)
Motor Ambulance Driver, B.E.F.
Section Leader Red Cross, att. French Army.
Despatches.
Croix de Guerre.
Killed Sept. 9th, 1918, *Epernay.*

IONIDES, S. A. ... ... A 93–98
Central Ontario Regt.
Imperial Munitions Board, Ottawa.
British Acetones, Toronto.

IONIDES, T. H. ... ... I 79–83 (University Coll., London.)
Major Major, R.A.M.C.

IRVINE, A. F. ... ... G 96–00 (New Coll., Oxford.)
Lieut. Lieut., Grenadier Guards.
Wounded.
Retired, 1917.

IRVINE, A. L. ... COLL. 94–00 (Ch. Ch., Oxford. Asst. Master, Charterhouse.)
Lieut. Lieut., O.T.C., Charterhouse.

✠ IRVINE, G. B. C. ... I 94–96 (Leinster Regt., 1901. S. African War.)
Major Major I.A., 9th Bhopal Infantry.
Killed May 15th, 1917, *Amara, Mesopotamia.*

IRVINE, M. L. C. ... D 00–03 (Indian Med. Service, 1910.)
Capt. Capt., Indian Medical Service.
E. African Expeditionary Force.

IRWIN, Rev. R. J. B. D 93–97 (Keble Coll., Oxford. Government Chaplain,
C.F. Meerut.)
Chaplain to Forces.
D.A.C.G. 2nd Corps.
A.C.G. 4th Army.
Wounded (2). *Despatches* (2).
M.C. D.S.O. Croix de Guerre.
Relinquished Comm., 1919.

IRWIN, T. S.   ...   ... I 94–99   (1st Dragoons, 1901. S. African War. Capt.,
    Major   1910.)
                                       Major, 1st Royal Dragoons, 1916.
                                       Adjt., Westmorland Yeomanry.

JACKSON, B. H.   ... F 00–04
    Capt.   Lieut., R.H.A., West Riding.
                                       Capt., Acting Major, 1918.
                                       Despatches.
                                       M.C.

JACKSON, H. A.   ... C 98–03   (Trin. Coll., Camb. Asst. Master Win. Coll.)
    Lieut.   Lieut., K.R.R.C., 6th Bn.
                                       Acting Capt. and Adjt., 8th Bn., 1917.
                                       Wounded (2).
                                       Prisoner of War March, 1918.
                                       Repatriated Dec., 1918.

JACKSON, H. N.   ... F 94–98   (R.G.A., 1902. I.A.)
                                       Capt., R.F.A.

JACKSON, J. H. EVANS... I 02–05
    Lieut.   Lieut., R.N.V.R.

JACKSON, L. J. ...   ... B 13–17   2nd Lieut., R.F.A., 1918.

JACOB, E. F.   ...   ... D 07–13
    Capt.   Hampshire Regt., 1915.
                                       Lieut., 1917.
                                       Temp. Capt., O.C. Bn.
                                       Wounded (2).

JAMES, F.   ...   ... I 99–02   (2nd Lieut., I.A., 1904. Capt., 1913.)
    Capt.   Capt., 28th Light Cavalry, I.A.

JAMES, F. W. T.   ... D 12–16
                                       R.M. Academy, 1916. Invalided.

JAMIESON, A. G. A.   ... H 96–03   (New Coll., Oxford.)
    Lieut.   Lieut., Royal Scots and M.G.C.
                                       Adjt., M.G.C. School.
                                       Wounded.   *Despatches.*
                                       M.C.

JAMIESON, J. H. A.   ... D 92–97
    Lieut.   Lieut., Royal Scots and M.G.C.

114

JEFFREYS, F. V. ... F 73–76 (Lieut., R.E., 1879. Capt., 1889. Lieut.-Col.,
Brevet Col.   1905. Brevet Col., 1908. Retired, 1908.)
                              Brevet Col., R.E.

✠ JENKINS, G. P. ... ... D 11–15
2nd Lieut.   2nd Lieut., R.F.A.
                              Killed Sept. 7th, 1917, *Elverdinghe, near Ypres.*

JENKINS, S. S. ... ... E 95–01 (Ball. Coll., Oxford.)
Capt.   Capt., R.B., 1914.
                              Acting Major.
                              Acting Lieut.-Col., Comm. Bn. N. Stafford-
                                 shire Regt.
                              Wounded.
                              M.C.

JENNER, A. V., D.S.O. ... C 76–78 (Lieut., R.B., 1882. Capt., 1891. Major, 1897.
Lieut.-Col.   S. African War. Brevet Lieut.-Col., 1902.
                                Retired, 1904.)
                              Lieut.-Col. G.S.O.$_2$. Imperial General Staff.
                              Despatches.
                              C.M.G.

JERVOISE, F. H. T. ... E 87–92 (Ch. Ch., Oxford.)
Capt.   Capt., Hampshire Carabiniers.
                              Labour Corps, Acting Major, 1918.
                              Restored to Establishment, 1919.

JOHNSON, E. ... ... E 83–88 (B.N.C., Oxford.)
Major   Major, D. of Lancaster's Yeomanry, 1905.
                              T.D.

JOHNSON, E. S. T. ... A 11–15
Lieut.   2nd Lieut., 16th Lancers.
                              Lieut., 1918.
                              Wounded.   *Despatches.*
                              M.C.

JOHNSON, F. M. LUTTMAN C 06–10
Lieut.   Lieut., 19th Hussars.
                              M.G.C. Cavalry.
                              A.D.C. H.Q., 2nd Cavalry Division.
                              Capt., G.S.O.$_3$, 1919.

JOHNSON, R. A. ... COLL. 87–93 (New Coll., Oxford. Served with Imperial
Lieut.-Col.   Yeomanry, S. African War. Scotch Educa-
                                tion Dept.)
                              Lieut.-Col., Hampshire Regt., Cyclist Bn.

✠ JOHNSON, R. H. J. ... B 07–12
2nd Lieut.   2nd Lieut., Essex Regt.
                              Killed March 3rd, 1915, *Armentières.*

115

JOHNSTON, A. C. ... G 98–02 (Worcestershire Regt., 1903.)
    Lieut.-Col.   Capt., Worcestershire Regt., 1914.
                              G.S.O.$_3$. Brigade-Major, 1916. Brevet Major.
                              Lieut.-Col., Comm. Bn. Cheshire Regt., 1916–17.
                              Temp. Brig.-Gen., 1917.
                              G.S.O.$_1$. War Office. Lieut.-Col.
                              Wounded (3).   *Despatches* (5).
                              M.C. D.S.O. and Bar. Croix de Guerre.

JOHNSTON, G. S. ... A 13–18
                              Cadet, O.T.B., Oxford.

JOHNSTON, J. S.... ... A 11–16
    Lieut.   Lieut. and Adjt., R.F.A.
                              Acting Capt., att. H.Q., 74th Brigade.
                              Despatches.
                              M.C.

✠ JOHNSTON, R. GRAHAM COLL. 06–12
    Capt.   Capt., Seaforth Highlanders.
                              M.C.
                              Killed July 18th, 1916, *Delville Wood.*

JOHNSTONE, R. ... ... F 87–88 (K.R.R.C., 1895. Capt., 1901. Chitral Ex-
                                  pedition. S. African War. Retired, 1910.)
                              Major, K.R.R.C., 1915.

JONES, A. D. DERVICHE COLL. 85–91 (Solicitor.)
    Lieut.-Col.   ...   1914, enlisted Liverpool Scottish.
                              Lieut., Liverpool Regt., 3rd Bn.
                              1915, Capt.
                              1916, Capt., K.O.R. Lancs. Regt.
                              Brigade-Major, 142nd Infantry Brigade.
                              1917, Acting Major, Essex Regt., 13th Bn.
                              Temp. Lieut.-Col., London Regt., 8th Bn.
                              Wounded (3).   *Despatches* (3).
                              M.C. D.S.O. and Bar.

JONES, E. W. ... ... A 83–86 (S. Wales Borderers, 1889. Capt., 1897. S.
    Lieut.-Col.   African War.)
                              Major, S. Wales Borderers.
                              Lieut.-Col., 1917.

✠ JONES, L. O. W. ... A 90–95 (Essex Regt., 1897. Capt., 1900. S. African
    Col.   War. W. African F.F., 1904–1908.)
                              Temp. Brig.-General, 13th Brigade, 1915.
                              Brevet Lieut.-Col., Brevet Col.
                              Wounded.   *Despatches* (5).
                              D.S.O. Chevalier Légion d'Honneur. Officier
                                  SS. Maurizio e Lazzaro.
                              Died on Active Service, Bagneux, Sept. 14th, 1918.

JONES, O. CAMPBELL ... K 07–12
Lieut.   Private, H.A.C., 1914.
                                Lieut., R.F.A., 1918.

JONES, O. K. ... ... C 00–03   (Hertford Coll., Oxford.)
Lieut.   Lieut., R.F.A., 1917.

JONES, R. L. ... ... C 92–96   (King's Coll., Camb. Barrister.)
Lieut.   R.N.V.R. Anti-Aircraft Corps.
                                Lieut., R.G.A.

JOSEPH, H. W. B.   COLL. 80–86 (New Coll., Oxford. Bursar and Tutor.)
2nd Lieut.   2nd Lieut., Oxfordshire Vol. Regt.

JOWERS, R. F.   ... H 75–79
Lieut.-Col.   Lieut.-Col., R.A.M.C., 2nd Eastern.

JOY, F. D. H. ...   COLL. 93–99 (New Coll., Oxford.)
Capt.   Capt., K.O.S.B.
                                Intelligence Officer, Calais.
                                G.S.O.$_3$.
                                Despatches.

JOY, R. C. G. ...   ... K 12–16
Lieut.   2nd Lieut., 1st Royal Dragoons.
                                Lieut., 1918.

JOY, N. H.   ... E 02–06
Capt.   Capt., E. Yorkshire Regt.
                                Att. R.E., Special Brigade.
                                Comm. Corps, Gas School.
                                Wounded.

KATKOFF, N. ...   ... H 06–08
Sub-Lieut.   Sub-Lieut., Russian Navy.
                                Asst. to Naval Attaché, Russian Embassy,
                                    London.
                                D.S.M.

KAY, G.   ... B 00–03
Lieut.   Lce.-Cpl., 50th Gordon Highlanders, Canadian
                                    Contingent.
                                Lieut., Acting Capt., K.R.R.C., 1917.

KAYE, C.   ...   ... B 81–86 (Denbigh Regt., 1889. Capt., I.A., 1900.)
Lieut.-Col.   ...   Major, Gen. Staff, India.
                                Dep. Chief Censor.
                                Lieut.-Col., 1915. C.S.I. C.I.E.

KAYE, H. W., M.D. ... H 88–94 (Magd. Coll., Oxford.)
    Capt. Capt., R.A.M.C., 1915.
    . Ministry of National Service.

✠ KAYE, J. L. ... ... C 75–80 (R. Berks Regt., 1882. Central India Horse,
    Lieut.-Col.   Major, 1901.)
    Lieut.-Col., I.A.
    Retired, 1916.
    Died in England Nov. 17th, 1917.

KAYE, W. A. ... ... H 85–9) (Magd. Coll., Oxford. Solicitor.)
    R.N.V.R., Anti-Aircraft Corps. Retired, 1916.

✠ KEELING, F. H. ... B 99–04
    Sergt. Sergeant, D. of Cornwall's L.I.
    Killed 1916.

KEENE, H. L. RUCK- ... A 82–84 (2nd Lieut., Oxford L.I., 1889. Capt., 1898.
    D.S.O.   Major, Oxford and Bucks L.I., 1907.)
    Major Commandant Reinforcement Camp.
    Acting Lieut.-Col., Infantry Base Depot,
    1917–18.
    Despa'ches.
    O.B.E.

KELLY, A. L. ... COLL. 93–99 (Univ. Coll., Oxford. Barrister.)
    Capt. Lieut., K.R.R.C.
    Capt., Court-Martial Officer, 1917. Staff Capt.
    Despatches (2).
    O.B.E.

KELLY, M. H. ... ... G 04–10
    Capt. Lieut., R. West Surrey Regt.
    Capt., 1917.

KELLY, N. L. ... ... G 99–04 (Univ. Coll., Oxford.)
    2nd Lieut. ... Private, London Regt.
    2nd Lieut., Monmouthshire Regt., 1917.

KELWAY, K. S. ... E 07–12
    Lieut. Lieut., R.A.S.C., 1917.

KEMPTHORNE, G. A. ... F 89–94 (St. John's Coll., Camb. Lieut., R.A.M.C.,
    Major   1903. India.)
    Major, R.A.M.C., 1915.
    Temp. Lieut.-Col., 1916.
    Prisoner of War. Exchanged home.
    Wounded. *Despatches* (2).
    D.S.O.

KENAH, A. V. ... ... D 93–95 (Chartered Accountant.)
    . R.N.V.R., Canada.

KENDALL, E. A....   ... G 01–04
   Capt.   Capt., R. Lancaster Regt., 1915.
                                  Despatches.
                                  M.C.

KENNARD, C. G. H.   ... F 13–16
                                  Pte., Coldstream Guards, 1918.

KENNARD, C. H.   ... F 85–89   (B.N.C., Oxford.)
   Capt.   Capt., R.A.S.C.

KENNARD, E.   ...   ... D 85–89   (Trin. Coll., Camb.)
   Major   Major, R.A.S.C.
                                  Relinquished Comm., 1917.

✠ KENNEDY, H. T.   ... C 03–07
   Lieut.   Lieut., N. Staffs Regt.
                                  Att. R. Scots Fusiliers.
                                  Later att. R.E. Field Survey.
                                  Killed June 6th, 1917, *Nieppe.*

KENYON, E. A.   ... C 72–78   (Capt., Bombay V.R.C.)
   Major   Temp. Capt., T.F.R.   Record Office, Shrews-
                                       bury.
                                  Temp. Major, 1918.

KENYON, E. R. ...   ... C 67–71   (R.E., 1874. Major, 1894. Lieut.-Col., 1901.
   Major-Gen.   Col., 1906.)
                                  Chief Engineer, Gibraltar, 1911. Retired.
                                  Brigadier-General. Chief Engineer, H.Q.
                                  Hon. Major-General, R.E.
                                  Wounded.   *Despatches* (4).
                                  C.M.G.   C.B.   Order Corona d'Italia.

KENYON, Sir F. G.   COLL. 75–82
   K.C.B.   Major., O.T.C.
   Lieut.-Col.   Temp. Lieut.-Col.   G.S.O.$_3$.
                                  T.D.
                                  Despatches.

KENYON, H. E. ...   ... C 95–98   (R.G.A., 1901.)
                                  Major., R.G.A.   Brigade-Major.
                                  Despatches (4).
                                  D.S.O.   Croix de Guerre.

KENYON, L. R.   ... G 81–85   (R.A., 1887. Major, 1906.)
   Col.   Lieut.-Col., R.G.A., 1914. Brevet Col., 1915.
                                  Temp. Brigadier-General, 1918.
                                  Despatches.
                                  C.B.

KER, A. M. ... COLL. 05–11
Capt.
Lieut., N. Lancs. Regt. Capt., 1916.
Ministry of Munitions.
Asst. Superintendent, Ordnance Factory.
Wounded.

KIDD, F. S. ... ... I 91–96
Capt.
(Trin. Coll., Camb. London Hospital.)
Capt., R.A.M.C.

KIDD, H. L. ... ... I 92–97
2nd Lieut.
(Trin. Coll., Camb. Lloyd's.)
2nd Lieut., Egyptian Camel Transport Corps.

KILBURN, D. ... ... K 13–17
2nd Lieut.
2nd Lieut., Grenadier Guards, 1918.

✠ KILBY, A. F. G. ... F 98–02
Capt.
(S. Staffs Regt., 1905.)
Capt., S. Staffs. Regt.
Wounded. *Despatches.*
M.C. Ⅴ.Ⅽ.
Killed Sept. 25th, 1915, *Railway Triangle,
La Bassée.*

KINDERSLEY, N. H. ... E 14–18
Gentleman Cadet. R.M. Academy, 1918.

KING, A. H. ... ... B 02–08
Lieut.
2nd Lieut., E. Surrey Regt.
1915, Lieut. Employed Ministry of National
Service.
Wounded.

KING, C. F. E. ... ... H 10–14
Civilian Prisoner in Germany, 1914–1918.

✠ KING, L. H. ST. A. ... A 08–12
2nd Lieut.
2nd Lieut., K.R.R.C.
Wounded.
Killed May 8th, 1915.

KING, W. H. ... ... D 84–88
Capt.
(Inniskilling Dragoons, 1902. S. African War.)
Capt., Connaught Rangers.
Asst. Director Remounts.

KINGDON, J. ... ... B 97–01
Capt.
(Ch. Ch., Oxford. Devonshire Regt., 1905.
I.A., 1907.)
Capt., 86th Carnatic Infantry, I.A., 1914.
Brigade-Major, Bareilly Brigade.
K.A.R., 1912–14
Somaliland Camel Corps, 1914–15

✠ KINGTON, W. M. ... D 89–90
D.S.O.
Capt.
(R. Welsh Fusiliers, 1896. S. African War.)
Capt., R. Welsh Fusiliers.
Killed Oct. 21st, 1914, *Zonnebeke.*

KITSON, Sir G. C. ... E 69–73 (60th Regt., 1876. Lieut.-Col., 1896. Col.,
  K.C.V.O., C.B.   1900. Comm. R.M. Coll., 1902.)
  Major-Gen.   Major-Gen., 1907.
                      Comm. 2nd Division, Rawal Pindi, 1912–16.

KNIPE, C. ... ... E 84–88 (Oriel Coll., Oxford.)
  Capt.   Capt., R. Inniskilling Fusiliers.
                      General List.

KYRLE, Rev. C. L. MONEY- E 82–86
  C.F.   Chaplain to Forces.
                      R.F.A., 1st Division.
                      Despatches.
                      M.C.

LAFFAN, Rev. R. S. du C., D 67–71
  C.F.   Chaplain to Forces, 1916.
                      Despatches.

LAIDLAW, W. ... ... I 02–07
  Capt.   Capt., Royal Scots.

LAIDLAY, N. ... ... K 05–10
  Lieut.   Lieut., R. Fusiliers, 24th Bn., 1917.
                      Ministry of Munitions.
                      Wounded.

LAILEY, G. P. B. ... F 01–06
  Capt.   Capt., D. of Cornwall's L.I.
                      Wounded.
                      Court-Martial Officer, Western Command.

LAKE, E. D. C. ... ... C 91–96 (New Coll., Oxford.)
  Lieut.   Lieut., Charterhouse O.T.C.

LAMB, S. E. ... ... C 77–79 (Trin. Hall, Camb. Barrister.)
                      Major, Dorset Regt., Reserve of Officers.

LAMBERT, J. E. H. ... G 04–09
  Capt.   Lieut., K.A.R., 4th Uganda Bn.
                      Capt. and Adjt.
                      M.C.

LAMBERT, R. S. ... I 08–12 (Grenadier Guards, 1913.)
  Capt.   Capt. and Adjt., Grenadier Guards, 1916.
                      Staff Capt., 1918. Brigade-Major
                      Wounded. *Despatches.*
                      M.C.

121

LAMBERT, R. U....   COLL. 10–15
   Lieut.   2nd Lieut., R.F.A.
                      Lieut., 1918. Employed at War Office.

LAMBERT, W. R.   ... B 08–12   (I.A., 1914.)
   Capt.   Lieut., 97th Deccan Infantry.
                      Acting Capt., 1917.
                      Capt. and Adjt., Delhi Regt.
                      Wounded.

LAMOTTE, F. G. L.   ... C 78–80   (Lieut., Oxford L.I., 1883. Major, 1900. S.
   Brig.-Gen.   African War. Col., 1911. Retired, 1913.)
                      Hon. Brig.-Gen., Reserve of Officers.
                      Despatches (2).
                      C.M.G.

LANCASTER, H. M.   ... I 89
   Lieut.   2nd Lieut., R.A.S.C., Motor Transport.
                      Labour Corps.
                      Lieut., 1918. Food Production Dept.

LANE, E. F. C.   ... C 96–00   (Transvaal.)
   Capt.   Capt., R.G.A. S. African Defence Force.
                      G.S.O.$_3$. Staff Capt., 1917.

LANE, R. C.   ...   ... H 85–91   (New Coll., Oxford. Barrister. S. Africa.)
   Major   Lieut., Middlesex Regt., 11th Bn.
                      Capt. and Adjt., R.A.F. Park Commander.
                      Major, T.

LANE, W. ARBUTHNOT ... K 11–14
   Lieut.   2nd Lieut., R.A.F.
                      Lieut., Airships.

LANE, W. A. P.   ... H 92–96   (Solicitor.)
   Capt.   Lieut.-Commander, R.N.V.R.
                      R.N. Division.

                      Capt., 1st Cadet Bn., London Regt.
                      Wounded.

LANG, W. H.   ...   ... E 98–01   (I.A., 1904. Capt., 1913.)
   Major   Major, 16th Cavalry, I.A., 1917.
                      G.S.O.$_3$, 1916–18.
                      Despatches (2).
                      O.B.E.

LANGHORNE, C. C.   ... C 04–07   (I.A., 1911.)
   Capt.   Capt., 24th Punjabis, I.A., 1915.
                      Wounded.

122

LARKEN, E. ... ... D 91–94 (Solicitor.)
    Lieut.-Col.   Major, Lincolnshire Yeomanry.
    Temp. Lieut.-Col., Inspector, Q.M.G.'s Services,
        1917.
    Despatches
    O.B.E.

LASCELLES, F. W. ... A 03–08
    Capt.   Capt., Sussex Yeomanry.
    Posted to R. Sussex Regt., 16th Bn., till 1918.
    Wounded.
    M.C.

✠ LASCELLES, J. F. ... A 09–14
    Lieut.   Lieut., R.B.
    Att. R.A.F.
    Despatches.
    M.C.
    Killed July 31st, 1915, *France.*

LATHAM, F. H. ... G 91–96
    Sergt.-Major   Private, N.Z. Contingent.
    Sergt.-Major, Education Department.

LATHAM, G. C. ... D 00–05 (Magd. Coll., Oxford.)
    Lieut.   Lieut., N. Rhodesia Police.
    E. Africa Campaign.
    Capt., 1917.
    Despatches.
    Croix de Guerre.

✠ LAURENCE, D. S. ... A 11–15
    2nd Lieut.   2nd Lieut., R.B.
    Killed Nov., 1916.

LAW, C. A. ... COLL. 84–90 (Oriel Coll., Oxford. Wiltshire Regt., 1895.
    Major   Capt., 1902. A.S.C., 1902–06.)
    Major, Wiltshire Regt., 1914.
    Prisoner of War.
    Interned in Holland.
    Wounded.

LAW, G. E. ... COLL. 05–11
    Private, 1st Rhodesian Regt.
    Wounded.

✠ LAWFORD, H. M. B. ... F 01–03 (Oriel Coll., Oxford.)
    Capt.   Capt., R. Fusiliers, 9th Bn.
    Wounded.
    Killed Oct. 7th, 1916, *Gueudecourt on R. Somme.*

LAWRENCE, H. R. ... D 92–97 (Pemb. Coll., Camb. R.A., 1900. Lieut., I.A.,.
    Major   1901.)
                                 Major 58th Vaughan's Rifles, I.A.

✠ LAWRENCE, G. F. COLL. 05–12
    Lieut.   Lieut., S. Staffordshire Regt.
                                 Capt., A.D.C.
                                 Lieut., Grenadier Guards, 1917.
                                 Despatches.
                                 Killed Aug. 27th, 1918, *near Arras.*

LAWRENCE, P. ... ... I 03–08
                                 Cadet Household Brigade, O.C., Bn., 1918.

✠ LAWSON, A. B. ... ... E 96–00 (11th Hussars, 1901. Lieut., 1902.)
                                 Brevet Major, 11th Hussars.
                                 Brigade-Major. G.S.O.$_2$.
                                 Lieut.-Col., Comm. Bn. Worcestershire Regt.
                                 Comm. Bn. Gloucestershire Regt., 1918.
                                 Wounded.   *Despatches* (3).
                                 D.S.O. and Bar. Order S. Stanislas.
                                 Killed June 24th, 1918, *between Calonne-s.-Lys*
                                      and Roebecq.

LAWSON, Sir DIGBY, ... E 95–97 (Trin. Hall., Camb.)
    Bart.   Capt., Yorkshire Hussars.
    Major   Acting Major, 19th Hussars, H.Q. of Regt.
                                   Despatches.

✠ LEACH, G. P. ... COLL. 99–03 (R.F.A., 1905.)
    Capt.   Capt., R.H.A.
                                   Killed Aug. 20th, 1915, *Dardanelles.*

LEACH, G. S. ... COLL. 98–04 (New Coll., Oxford.)
    Capt.   Capt., K.O. Yorkshire L.I.
                                 M.C.

LEAN, A. I. ... ... G 86–89 (R. Fusiliers, 1892. S. African War. Capt.,.
    Lieut.-Col.   A.P.D., 1903. Major, 1907. Lieut.-Col..
                                 A.P. Dept., 1912.)
                                 Despatches.
                                 D.S.O.

LEAN, J. V. ... ... I 98–01 (Lieut. Suffolk Yeomanry, 1904.)
    Lieut.   Lieut., 6th Reserve Regt., Cavalry, 1914.
                                   Employed Artillery Horse Lines.
                                 Att. Suffolk Regt.

LEATHER, J. H. ... D 08–13 (R.A., 1915. Lieut., 1917.)
    Capt.   Acting Capt., and Adjt. R.F.A., 1917.

LEATHER, P. C. du S.   A 80–86 (New Coll., Oxford. Durham L.I., 1900. S.
   Capt.   African War. Major, 1903.)
                                   Capt., Yorkshire Regt.
Wounded.
Employed Musketry Duties.
Relinquished Comm., ill health.

LECONFIELD, Lord ... I 86–89 (Life Guards, 1892. Lieut., 1894. Retired,
   Major   1899. S. African War.)
Major, Sussex Yeomanry.
Temp. Lieut.-Col., Sussex Vol. Regt.

LEDGARD, R. S.   ... G 97–01 (Yorkshire Regt., 1903. Capt., 1911.)
   Capt.   Capt., Yorkshire Regt.
Prisoner of War. Exchanged home, 1918.
Wounded.   *Despatches.*

LEE, A. C. ... ... C 81–84 (Nat. Provincial Bank.)
   Capt.   Capt., R.B.
Att. R. Fusiliers, 35th Bn.
104th Labour Coy.
Record Office, R.E., Chatham.

LEE, E. C. ... ... E 90–96 (Univ. Coll., Oxford.)
   Lieut.   Lieut., R.G.A.

LEE, G. M. ... ... C 92–95 (R. Fusiliers, 1898. Capt., 1903.)
   Major   Capt., R. Fusiliers. Major, 1915.
Brigade-Major.
Wounded.   *Despatches* (2).
M.C. D.S.O.

LEE, P. W. ... ... K 12–15
   Lieut.   2nd Lieut., Cameron Highlanders, 1917.
Lieut., 1918.
Wounded.

LEE, A. C. L. D. ... D 00–05 (Shropshire L.I., 1909.)
   Capt.   Capt., Shropshire L.I., 1915.
Served with W.A.F.F., 1913–16.
Acting Major, 1917.
War Office.
Despatches.

LEES, G. W. M. ... F 05–09
   Lieut.   Lieut., 17th Lancers, 1916.

LEES, L. M. ... ... B 12–17
   2nd Lieut.   2nd Lieut., Labour Corps.

LEESE, N. ... ... I 85–89   (Mining, N. Zealand and Mexico. S. African
    Lieut.-Col.   War.)
                                 Major, R.A.S.C.
                                 Acting Lieut.-Col., 1918.
                                 Despatches (3).
                                 D.S.O. O.B.E.

LEESE, V. F. ... ... I 83–88
                                 Dep. Surveyor of New Forest
                                 O.B.E.

LEESON, N. A. ... ... K 06–08   (E. Lancs. Regt., 1912.)
    Major   Capt., E. Lancashire Regt.
                                   Major, 1917.
                                 Wounded (2).

LEESON, S. S. G. COLL. 05–11   (New Coll., Oxford.)
    Lieut.   2nd Lieut., Middlesex Regt.
                                   Sec. for Service at Admiralty.
                                 Lieut., R.N.V.R., app. to *President*.

LEGARD, D'A. ... ... c 86–89   (New Coll., Oxford. 17th Lancers, 1895. S.
    Col.   African War. Major, 1905. G.S.O.$_3$., 1907.
                                 Brig.-Major, 1907–11. G.S.O.$_1$, 1914.)
                                 Lieut.-Col. Comm. 17th Lancers, 1915.
                                 Brigade Commander, 1916.
                                 Col., 1919.
                                 Despatches (2).
                                   D.S.O. C.M.G.

LEGG, L. G. WICKHAM c 90–96   (New Coll., Oxford.)
    Lieut.   Lieut., R.N.V.R.
                                   Admiralty, Intelligence Dept.

LEGGATT, W. M. ... c 14–18
                                   Gentleman Cadet, R.M. Academy.

✠ LEITCH, V. B. ... ... F 06–11
    2nd Lieut.   2nd Lieut., Liverpool Regt.
                                   Killed April 17th, 1915, *Hill* 60, *Ypres*.

LE MESURIER, A. G. ... I 89–93   (Business in Genoa.)
    Major   Temp. Major.
                                   Dep. Assistant Director Railway Transport,
                                 Rome.

LENANTON, G. F. ... K 10–15
    Capt.   R.A., 1915.
                                   Lieut., Acting Capt., R.H.A., 1917.
                                   Relinquished Comm., 1919.
                                 Wounded (2).

LENNARD, S. A. H. F. ... c 13–17
    2nd Lieut.   2nd Lieut., Scots Guards, 1919.

LESLIE, A. J. R. M.   ... e 04–08   (R.A., 1910.)
    Capt.   Capt., R.G.A., 1916.
                               Acting Major, 1917.
                               Instructor Gunnery, School of Instruction, Anti-
                                   Aircraft.

LESLIE, J.   ...   ... g 02–07
    Capt.   2nd Lieut., 12th Lancers, 1914.
                               Lieut., att. 16th Lancers.
                               Capt. and Adjt., Tank Corps., 1918.
                               Relinquished Comm., 1919.
                               Despatches (3).
                               M.C. D.S.O.

LEVESON, L. I. G.   coll. 98–03
    Lieut.   Lieut., R.N.R. H.M.S. *Emperor of India.*
                               Resigned Comm.

LEWIN, E. O.   ...   ... e 92–97   (King's Coll., Camb. R.F.A., 1900. Lieut.,
    Lieut.-Col.   1902. Capt., 1911.)
                               Major, R.H.A. Brigade-Major, 1915.
                               G.S.O.$_2$, 1916. G.S.O.$_1$, 1917.
                               Brevet Lieut.-Col., 1917.
                               Despatches (4).
                               D.S.O. C.M.G. Croix de Guerre.

LEWIS, G. D.   ...   coll. 93–98   (New Coll., Oxford. Business in Liverpool.)
    Lieut.   Private K. Shropshire L.I.
                               Att. Army Pay Corps, 1916.
                               Lieut. Gen. List, War Office, 1916–1917.

✠ LEWIS, R. P.   ...   ... a 87–92   (Lieut., Devon Regt., 1903. S. African War.
    Lieut.-Col.   K.A.R., 1904.)
                               Capt., Devonshire Regt.
                               Intelligence Officer, Cairo.
                               Acting Lieut.-Col., Comm. Bn. Manchester Regt.
                               Wounded.
                               Killed Sept. 7th, 1917, Ypres.

LIBERTY, I. STEWART   ... g 00–05   (Ch. Ch., Oxford.)
    Capt.   Capt., Oxford and Bucks L.I.
                               Wounded.
                               M.C.

LIDDELL, Hon. G. W.   c 82–86
    Capt.   Capt., R. Defence Corps. T.F.R.

✠ LIDDELL, J. H. T.   ...   I 04–06
    Lieut.   Lieut., K.R.R.C.
                       Died Nov. 17th, 1916, *of Wounds received* Nov.
                       13th, *Beaumont Hamel.*

LIDDERDALE, A. W.   ...   E 99–04   (Ball. Coll., Oxford.)
                       Foreign Office. Contraband Dept.
                       O.B.E.

LIDDERDALE, W. D.   ...   E 90–92
    Lieut.   Troop Sergt., Natal Carabiniers.
                       Lieut., Dorset Yeomanry.
                       Despatches.
                       M.C.

✠ LILLIE, F. S.   ...   ...   A 85–91   (Emm. Coll., Camb. Irish Regt., 1893. Capt.,
    Major   1901.)
                       Major, R. Irish Regt.
                       Killed March 15th, 1915, *St. Eloi.*

LILLINGSTON, E. G. G.   K 06–11
    Lieut.   2nd Lieut., 4th Dragoon Guards, 1915.
                       Lieut., 1916.
                       Army Signal Service, 1915–18.
                       Despatches.

LINDLEY, Hon. F. O.   ...   G 88   (Diplomatic Service.)
                       British High Commissioner for Northern
                       Russia, 1918.
                       C.B.

LINDLEY, Hon. J. E.   ...   G 73–78   (Trin. Hall, Camb. 1st Dragoons, 1882. Major,
    Major-Gen.   1897. S. African War. Col., 1st Royal
                       Dragoons. Major-Gen., 1910.)
                       Retired, 1917.
                       Despatches.

LINDLEY, Hon. L. H.   ...   G 81–85   (Magd. Coll., Oxford. Physician.)
    Capt.   Capt., R.A.M.C., H.Q., Aldershot, 1915.

LINDSAY, Hon. W. P.   E 86–90   (Engineer.)
    Capt.   Capt., Middlesex Regt., 1914.
                       Att. 1st Garrison Bn., Notts and Derby Regt.
                       Wounded.

LING, J. R.   ...   ...   B 93–95   (Civil Engineer.)
    Lieut.   Lieut., R.E.
                       Acting Capt., 1917.

LING, W. N.   ...   ...   A 87–90   (Corn Merchant, Carlisle.)
                       Pte., Cumberland Vol. Regt.

✠ Linton, C. S. ... ... G 94–98 (Lieut., Worcestershire Regt., 1904. S. African
Lieut.-Col.   War.)
Lieut.-Col. Worcestershire Regt.
Despatches (4).
M.C. D.S.O.
Killed Nov. 20th, 1917, *Cambrai.*

Lister, A. R. ... ... C 08–10
Lieut.   Lieut., R.F.A.
Staff Lieut., 1917.
M.C.

Lister, J. C. ... ... C 14–18

Cadet, Household Brigade, O.C.B.

Lister, W. A. ... ... C 10–15
Lieut.   2nd Lieut., K.R.R.C., att. 8th Bn.
Lieut., 1918.
Wounded.

Little, C. W. ... COLL. 82–89 (New Coll., Oxford. Staff Win. Coll.)
Capt.   Capt., Winchester College O.T.C.

Littledale, H. A. P. ... E 96–97 (Yorkshire L.I., Lieut., 1901.)
Major   Major, K.O. Yorkshire L.I., 1915.
G.S.O.$_3$. Imperial Gen. Staff.
Retired, 1918.

Livingston, P. J. C. ... E 74–77 (Black Watch, 1879. Capt., 1887. S. African
Lieut.-Col.   War. Lieut.-Col., 1902.)
Lieut.-Col., Black Watch (Royal Highlanders).
Comm. Depot.
Retired, 1918.
Despatches.

Llewellyn, G. R. P. H 99–04 (New Coll., Oxford.)
Capt.   Capt., Glamorganshire Yeomanry.
A.D.C.
Intelligence Officer, 6th Mounted Brigade,
    E.E.F., 1918.
Despatches.

Llewellyn, J. B. ... H 04–08

Sergt., E. African Supply Corps.

Lloyd, J. C. ... ... B 11–15
Lieut.   Lieut., R.F.A., 1917.
M.C.

Lloyd, M. A. ... ... I 01–05
Lieut.   Lieut., R.N.V.R. H.M.S. ' *Valiant.*'

LOCH, Lord ... ... B 87–89 (Gren. Guards, 1893. Capt., 1899. Soudan.
D.S.O., M.V.O.   S. African War. Lieut.-Col.)
Major-Gen.   Lieut.-Col., Grenadier Guards.
                                 Brevet Col., 1916.
                                 Temp. Brigadier-Gen. Gen. Staff, 1915.
                                 Major-Gen., 1919.
                                 Despatches (5).
                                 C.M.G. C.B. Officier Légion d'Honneur.

✠ LOCKETT, G. B. ... ... I 11–15
Capt.   2nd Lieut., Cheshire Yeomanry.
                                 Posted to Cheshire Regt.
                                 Acting Capt., 1918.
                                 M.C., 1919.
                                 Died of wounds Nov. 4th, 1918.

LONG, A. DE L.   ... D 94–99 (New Coll., Oxford.)
Lieut.-Col.   Capt., Gordon Highlanders, 1915.
                                 Lieut.-Col., R. Welsh Fusiliers, 1916.
                                 Major, acting Lieut.-Col., Gordon Highlanders,
                                     T.F. Bn., 1917.
                                 Brevet Lieut.-Col.
                                 Wounded.   *Despatches.*
                                 D.S.O.

LONG, S. C.   ... ... H 83–87 (Magd. Coll., Oxford. K.R.R.C., Lieut., 1890.
Bt. Lieut.-Col.   R.B., 1893. S. African War. Bt. Major,
                                     1907. Retired, 1913.)
                                 Temp. Lieut.-Col., R.B., 1917. Bt. Lieut.-Col.
                                 Asst. Director Railways till Sept., 1918.
                                 Despatches (4).

LONG, W. J.   ... ... G 84–89 (K.R.R.C., Capt., 1899. Burmese Expedition
Bt. Lieut.-Col.   and S. African War.)
                                 Bt. Lieut.-Col., K.R.R.C., 4th Bn.
                                 Wounded (2).   *Despatches* (3).
                                 C.M.G.

LONGFIELD, L. ... ... F 88–93
Major   Temp. Major, R.A.S.C., 1916.
                                 Despatches.

LONGFIELD, R. W. ... F 87–92   (3rd Dragoons, Capt., 1900. Retired, 1902.)
Major   Major. Railhead Commandant.
                                 Assistant Embarkation Officer.
                                 Retired, 1917.

130

✠ LONGFORD, EARL OF ... G 78–82   (Ch. Ch., Oxford. Life Guards, Capt., 1895.
    K.P., K.C.V.O.   S. African War, Lieut.-Col., 1901.)
      Brig.-Gen.   Lieut.-Col., Irish Horse.
Brigadier-Gen., 2nd Midland Mounted Brigade.
Despatches (2).
Chevalier Légion d'Honneur.
Killed, Aug. 21st, 1915, *above Suvla Bay.*

LONGSTAFF, R. ... D 92–97   (New Coll., Oxford. R.F.A., Lieut., 1901.)
    Lieut.-Col.   Major, R.F.A., 1914.
Acting Lieut.-Col., 1918, T.F.
Wounded.   *Despatches* (3).
D.S.O.   Chevalier Légion d'Honneur.

LOVERIDGE, S. G. ... E 01–05
    Capt.   Capt., Staffordshire Yeomanry, 1916.

Low, J. M. B. ... A 96–97
    Capt.   2nd Lieut., Northamptonshire Regt.
Capt., 1917.   A.D.C.

Low S. ... ... G 01–07
    Major   Major, R.G.A., London Brigade.
Retired, 1919.
Wounded.   *Despatches* (2).
D.S.O.

Low, S. P. ... ... G 97–02   (Magd. Coll., Oxford. Barrister.)
    Major   Major, Hampshire Regt.
Wounded.

✠ LOWE, R. C. ... COLL. 08–13
    Lieut.   Lieut., Warwickshire Regt.
Wounded.   *Despatches.*
M.C.
Killed, Aug. 18th, 1916, *between Thiepval and
     Ovilliers, Somme.*

LOWNDES, D. G. ... G 13–17
                     Indian Cadet, Quetta.

LOWNDES, M. ... ... B 82–87   (R. Dublin Fusiliers, 1889. Capt., 1898. S.
    Bt. Major   African War. Bt. Major, 1902. Retired,
     1909.)
Bt. Major, R. Dublin Fusiliers, Reserve of
     Officers.

✠ LOWNDES, R. F. ... G 11–15
     2nd Lieut.   2nd Lieut., K.R.R.C.
Killed, Nov. 14th, 1916, *near Beaumont Hamel.*

✠ Lowson, C. P. F. ... B 10–15
    Lieut.
                   Lieut., R.B.
                   R.A.F., O.
                   Killed in Accident, Nov. 3rd, 1917.

Lowther, Sir C. B.,   C 94–96
    Bart.
    Bt. Lieut.-Col.
                   (8th Hussars. Lieut., 1900. Capt., 1905.)
                   Major, acting Lieut.-Col., Northants Yeomanry.
                   Bt. Lieut.-Col.
                   Despatches (2).
                   D.S.O. Croix de Guerre.

Lowther, J. G. ... C 99–01
    Capt.
                   (11th Hussars, 1905.)
                   Capt., 11th Hussars, 1914.
                   D.A.Q.M.G., 1915.
                   Adjt., Northants Yeomanry.
                   Wounded.   *Despatches.*
                   M.C., D.S.O.

Luard, F. B. ... ... H 75–78
    Major
                   (W.I. Regt., 1880. Capt., 1894. Retired, 1902.)
                   Major, E. Surrey Regt., Depot.

Luard, W. Du C. ... H 76–79
    Major
                   (Lieut., R.E., 1882. Soudan. Major, 1899.
                        Retired, 1903.)
                   Major, R.E.

✠ Lucas, H. C. M. ... G 99–05
    Lieut.
                   Lieut., 2nd Gurkha Rifles.
                   Killed, Nov. 2nd, 1914, *Neuve Chapelle.*

Lumley, F. D., C.B. ... A 72–73
    Brig.-Gen.
                   (77th Regt., 1875. Capt., Middlesex Regt.,
                        1884. S. African War. Lieut.-Col., 1901.
                        Col., 1907. Retired, 1911.)
                   Hon. Brigadier-General, Chatham.
                   Despatches.

Lund, O. M. ... I 05–09
    Capt. (Bt. Major)
                   Capt., R.F.A.
                   Acting Major, 1916.
                   Despatches (2).
                   D.S.O.

Luxmoore, A. A. ... D 94–99
    (formerly Wilson)
    Capt.
                   (Trin. Coll., Oxford.)
                    Capt., W. Yorkshire Regt.
                    R. Defence Corps.

Lyall, G. H. H. ... G 85–90
    (formerly Pile)
    Capt.
                   (New Coll., Oxford. Solicitor.)
                   Staff Capt., R.A.F.

Lyon, F. H. ... coll. 99–04 (Magd. Coll., Oxford.)
Capt.   Lieut., Intelligence Corps.
                          Staff Capt.
                          Capt., 1919. Retired, 1919.
                          Despatches (2).

Lyon, W. R. ... ... d 69–70 (Insurance Broker. Lieut., 3rd W. Surrey
                              Regt.)
                          Pte., City of London National Guard, Scottish
                              Coy.

✠ Lysons, N. L. S. ... i 89–93 (Lancaster Regt., 1897. Capt., 1901. S.
Major   African War.)
                          Major, K.O. Lancaster Regt.
                          Killed, Oct. 21st, 1915, *Armentières*.

Maberly, C. J. A. ... i 94–98 (S. African War. Lieut., 17th Lancers, 1904.
Lieut.   20th Hussars. 5th Lancers.)
                          Temp. Capt., 6th Reserve Regt. Cavalry.
                          Acting Capt. and Adjt., E. Riding Yeomanry,
                              1917.

✠ McAndrew, C. A. W. ... e 11–16
2nd Lieut.
                          2nd Lieut., R.F.A.
                          Killed, April 26th, 1917, *Vermelles, near Bethune.*

McAndrew, G. A. ... e 07–13
Lieut.
                          Lieut., Hampshire Regt.
                          Acting Capt., 1918.

✠ Macandrew, I. M. ... i 05–10 (New Coll., Oxford.)
Lieut.   Lieut., Seaforth Highlanders.
                          Wounded.   Despatches.
                          Killed, Dec. 23rd, 1914, *Festubert.*

McAndrew, R. L. ... e 14–18
                          Cadet, R.F.A.

✠ McArthur, H. D. ... i 02–07
2nd Lieut.
                          2nd Lieut., Gloucester Regt., 3rd Bn.
                          Killed, 1914.

McArthur, V. G. ... i 97–01 (Indian Army, 1903.)
Major   Capt., Berkshire Regt.
                          Major, 6th Bn.
                          Retired, 1919.
                          Wounded.
                          M.C.

MACARTNEY, C. A.   COLL. 08–14
   Lieut.   Lieut., R.F.A.
                                    Wounded.

McCALMONT, B. C., C.B.   G 75–76   (11th Regt., 1881.   Capt., 1888.   Lieut.-Col.
   Lieut.-Col.   1899. S. African War. Retired, 1900.)
                                      Lieut.-Col. Warwickshire Regt.
                                      Despatches.

McCAUSLAND, C. E.   ... B 12–16
   2nd Lieut.   2nd Lieut., Irish Guards, 1918.

McCLINTOCK, H. F.   ... E 85–89   (New Coll., Oxford. G.P.O. S. African War.)
   Major   Major, London Regt., P.O. Rifles.
                                      Director Army Postal Service.

McCONNEL, D. F.   ... I 06–11   (R.A., 1912.)
   Capt.   Capt., R.F.A., 1916.
                                      Acting Major, 1916–19.
                                      Wounded.   *Despatches* (3).
                                      D.S.O.

McCONNEL, J. K.   ... B 05–10   (20th Hussars, 1912.)
   Major   Capt., 20th Hussars, 1915.
                                        Instructor, M.G.C., Training Centre, 1916–17.
                                      Acting Major, 1917. G.S.O.$_3$, 1917.
                                      Brigade-Major, 1918. G.S.O.$_1$.
                                      Brevet Major, 1919.
                                      Wounded (2).   *Despatches* (2).
                                      M.C. and Bar. D.S.O.

✠ McCONNEL, M. H.   ... F 98–02   (R.F.A., 1904.)
   Major   Major, R.F.A.
                                        Despatches (2).
                                      Killed, Sept. 14th, 1917, *near Poperinghe.*

MACDONALD, A. J.   COLL. 13–18
                                      Gentleman Cadet, R.M. Academy.

✠ MACDONALD, R. M.   ... G 04–09
   Lieut.   Lieut., Cameron Highlanders.
                                      Killed, Nov. 2nd, 1914, *Veldhoek.*

MACDONALD, S. H.   ... G 06–10
   Capt.   Acting Capt., Cameron Highlanders, 1918.
                                      Wounded.

MACDONELL, A. G.   COLL. 09–14
   Lieut.   Lieut., R.F.A., 1st Highland Brigade.
                                      Wounded.

MACDONELL, J. F.　　... I 04–09
　　Capt.
　　　　　　　　　　　　　　　Capt., R.F.A., 1st Highland Brigade.
　　　　　　　　　　　　　　　Acting Major, 1918.
　　　　　　　　　　　　　　　Despatches.
　　　　　　　　　　　　　　　M.C.

✠ McDONNEL, J. ...　　... F 92–97
　　Lieut.-Col.
　　　　　　　　　　　　　　　(King's Coll., Camb.　Leinster Regt.　Ca t.,
　　　　　　　　　　　　　　　　　　1908.)
　　　　　　　　　　　　　　　Lieut.-Col., Leinster Regt.
　　　　　　　　　　　　　　　Killed, Sept. 29th, 1918, *near Ypres.*

✠ MACDUFF, A.　...　　... D 97–03
　　Capt.
　　　　　　　　　　　　　　　(New Coll., Oxford.)
　　　　　　　　　　　　　　　Capt., Cameron Highlanders, 2nd Bn.
　　　　　　　　　　　　　　　Killed, April 23rd, 1915, *Ypres.*

MACFARLANE, R. C.　　... F 06–11
　　Major
　　　　　　　　　　　　　　　Capt., Arg. and Suth. Highlanders.
　　　　　　　　　　　　　　　Major, 1918.
　　　　　　　　　　　　　　　Wounded.
　　　　　　　　　　　　　　　M.C.

MACGEORGE, J. B.　　... G 10–15
　　Lieut.
　　　　　　　　　　　　　　　2nd Lieut., R.B., 1st Bn., 1916.
　　　　　　　　　　　　　　　Lieut., 1st Bn., 1917.
　　　　　　　　　　　　　　　Wounded.
　　　　　　　　　　　　　　　G.H.Q., Gt. Britain.

MACGEORGE, R. A.　　... G 13–17
　　2nd Lieut.
　　　　　　　　　　　　　　　2nd Lieut., R.B., 2nd Bn., 1918.
　　　　　　　　　　　　　　　A.D.C., 1919.

✠ McGUSTY, G. R.　　... K 07–11
　　2nd Lieut.
　　　　　　　　　　　　　　　2nd Lieut., R. Irish Rifles.
　　　　　　　　　　　　　　　Died of Wounds, June 14th, 1916, *Battle of the
　　　　　　　　　　　　　　　　　Somme.*

MACINTYRE, D. H.　　... B 12–15
　　Lieut.
　　　　　　　　　　　　　　　2nd Lieut., Arg. and Suth. Highlanders, 1916.
　　　　　　　　　　　　　　　R.A.F., Lieut., A, 1916.
　　　　　　　　　　　　　　　Prisoner of War.　Interned in Holland, 1918.
　　　　　　　　　　　　　　　Repatriated, 1919.

McINTYRE, J. G.　　... F 10–14
　　Capt.
　　　　　　　　　　　　　　　Lieut., Ayrshire Yeomanry.
　　　　　　　　　　　　　　　Posted to R. Scots Fusiliers, 12th Bn.
　　　　　　　　　　　　　　　Capt., 1918.
　　　　　　　　　　　　　　　Wounded (2).
　　　　　　　　　　　　　　　M.C. and Bar.

MacIVOR, R. S. P.　　... E 05–08
　　Capt.
　　　　　　　　　　　　　　　(I.A., 1914.)
　　　　　　　　　　　　　　　Lieut., 129th Baluchis, I.A.
　　　　　　　　　　　　　　　Capt., 1917.

MACKARNESS, A. J. C. ...   H 78–83   (Trin. Coll., Oxford. Solicitor.)
    Capt.   Capt., Hampshire Vol. Regt.
    Relinquished Comm., 1917.

McKECHNIE, H.   ...   C 12–17   Cadet, Cambridge Garrison Infantry.

✠ McKENNA, J. M.   ...   B 09–13
    Lieut.   Lieut., K.R.R.C.
    Att. R.A.F.
    Killed, Oct. 2nd, 1917, *Wasnes-au-Bac, near Cambrai*.

McKENNA, T. M.   ...   I 07–12   (Univ. Coll., Oxford.)
    Capt.   Lieut., 8th Hussars.
    R.A.F. Capt. Staff Capt. G.S.O.₃.
    Relinquished Commission, ill-health, 1917.

✠ MACKENZIE, C. R.   ...   I 05–10   (Trin. Coll., Camb. St. Thomas Hospital.)
    Commander   1914, Vol. Medical Probationer, H.M.S. *Spitfire*.
    1915, R.N.A.S.
    1916, Flight-Commander.
    Despatches.
    D.S.O. Croix de Guerre.
    Killed, Jan. 24th, 1917, *Bihucourt, near Bapaume*.

MACKENZIE, H. D.   ...   K 06–10
    Capt.   Lieut. and Adjt., Lovat Scouts, 1916.
    A.D.C., Staff of Vth Army.
    Capt., 1919.
    Despatches.
    M.C.

MACKENZIE, H. G. G. ...   G 83–88   (Magd. Coll., Oxford. Ordained, 1894. Curate,
    M.D.   St. John's, Kennington. Capt., R.A.M.C.,
    Lieut.-Col.   1913.)
    Lieut.-Col., R.A.M.C., 1915.
    Despatches (3).
    D.S.O.

✠ MACKENZIE, M. K.   ...   H 01–07   (Magd. Coll., Oxford.)
    Lieut.   Lieut., K.R.R.C.
    Killed, Sept. 25th, 1914, *Soupir, near Soissons*.

✠ MACKENZIE, R. I.   ...   K 09–11
    2nd Lieut.   2nd Lieut., Black Watch (Royal Highlanders).
    Killed, April 11th, 1915, *near Bethune*.

MACKENZIE, W. N. ... E 07–12
    Lieut.
                         Lieut., R.F.A., 1916.
                         Acting Major, 1918.
                         M.C.

MACKEY, H. J. A., ... F 9C–93
    M.V.O.
    Brig.-Gen.
                         (R.F.A., 1896. Capt., 1902. Major, 1912.)
                         Lieut.-Col., R.F.A., 1917.
                         Temp. Brigadier-General, 1918.
                         Despatches (4).
                         D.S.O. C.M.G. Order S. Stanislas.

✠ MACKINTOSH, A. H. ... A 93–98
    Capt.
                         (Cameron Highlanders, Lieut., 1901. S. African
                               War.)
                         Capt., Cameron Highlanders.
                         Killed, Sept. 14th, 1914, *Battle of the Aisne.*

MACKWORTH, J. D. ... E 00–05
    Lieut.-Col.
                         (Ch. Ch., Oxford. W. Sussex Regt., 1909.)
                         Capt., R. West Surrey Regt., 1915.
                         R.A.F.
                         Lieut.-Col., acting Col., Dep. Director Kite
                               Balloons, 1918
                         O.B.E. Officier Légion d'Honneur.

MACLAREN, T. G. ... B 75–
    Lieut.-Col.
                         (Trin. Coll., Camb. K.O.S.B., Major, 1904.
                               Tirah Exp. S. African War. Lieut.-Col.,
                               Seaforth Highlanders. Retired, 1908.)
                         Lieut.-Col., Depot, K.O.S.B.

MACLEOD, G. F. ... D 09–13
    Capt.
                         Lieut., Arg. and Suth. Highlanders.
                         Capt. and Adjt., 1917.
                         M.C. Croix de Guerre.

MACLEOD, J. M. N. ... D 05–09
    Lieut.
                         Lieut., R.N.V.R., Motor Launch.

MACLEOD, M. C. ... G 07–12
    Lieut.
                         Lieut., Seaforth Highlanders.
                         A.D.C.
                         Wounded.
                         Relinquished Commission, 1918.

MACMILLAN, J. E. ... I 08–12
    Capt.
                         Capt., Arg. and Suth. Highlanders, 1915.
                         Wounded.
                         M.C.

McNab, A. J. ... ... E 78–81   (King's Coll., London. Major, I.M.S., 1902.
    Bt. Col.   Lieut.-Col., 1910.)
                                        Bt. Col., Indian Medical Service.
                                        G.H.Q.
                                        Asst. Director Medical Service, 1915–1918.
                                        Despatches (3).
                                        C.B. C.M.G.

✠ Macnamara, C. C. ... c 89–93   (R. Irish Rifles, 1896. Capt., 1902.)
    Lieut.-Col.   Lieut.-Col., R. Irish Rifles.
                                          Despatches.
                                        Killed, July, 1916, *Battle of the Somme.*

McNeill, N. A.   B 91–97   (Scots Guards. S. African War. Capt., 1904.)
    Capt.   Capt., Scots Guards, Reserve of Officers.

Maconchy, G. A.   ... G 10–14
    Lieut.   Lieut., 5th Gurkha Rifles, I.A., 1915.
                                          Acting Capt., 1916–17.
                                        Despatches.

Maconochie, R. H.   ... H 97–02   (Univ. Coll., Oxford.)
    Lieut.   Lieut., Gen. List. Recruiting Duties.
                                          Ministry of National Service.
                                          Relinquished Commission, 1919.
                                        O.B.E.

Macpherson, A. D.   ... F 01–06   (R.A., 1908).
    Major   Capt., R.F.A., 1914.
                                          D.A.A.G., 1917.
                                        Major, 1918.
                                        Despatches.
                                        M.C. D.S.O.

✠ Macpherson, G.   ... I 09–15
    Lieut.   2nd Lieut., E. Kent Regt.
                                          Lieut., 1916.
                                          Tank Corps.
                                        Killed, Sept. 15th, 1916, *near Albert, first advance of Tanks.*

✠ Macpherson, G. D. ... F 75–79   (Munster Fusiliers, 1882. S. African War.
    Major   Major, 1904.)
                                          Major, Munster Fusiliers.
                                      Killed, Sept. 26th, 1915, *Hill* 70, *near Loos.*

MACPHERSON, R. C. ... G 11–14
Lieut. 2nd Lieut., **Black Watch** (Royal Highlanders),
1915.
Lieut., 1917.
R.A.F.
Prisoner of War. Interned in Holland, 1918.

✠ MACPHERSON, R. C. ... H 10–12
Capt. Lieut., R.H.A., 2nd Highland Brigade.
Capt.
Despatches.
Died of Wounds, April 18th, 1918, *Ham en
Artois.*

MAGRATH, C. J. K. ... E 96–00 (Oriel Coll., Oxford.)
Y.M.C.A., 1914, Ypres.
O.B.E.

MAITLAND, F. J. ... E 88–89 (Capt., Sussex Artillery, 1896.)
Major Hon. Major, R.G.A., Reserve of Officers.

MAITLAND, R. C. F. ... G 96–99 (R.F.A., 1901. Lieut., 1902.)
Major Capt., R.F.A., 1914. A.D.C.
Major, R.H.A., 1915.
Wounded. Despatches.
D.S.O.

MAJENDIE, B. J. ... I 89–92 (K.R.R.C., 1890. Capt., 1902. S. African War.,
Brig.-Gen. Bt. Lieut.-Col., K.R.R.C.
Comm., Hampshire Regt., 12th Bn., 1915.
Comm., K.R.R.C. Bn., 1916.
Temp. Brigadier-General, 1918.
Comm., 67th Infantry Brigade.
Despatches (3).
D.S.O. C.M.G. Officier Légion d'Honneur.

MAJENDIE, J. H. A. ... C 84–87 (Lieut., Royal Scots, 1880.)
Col. Brigadier-Gen., on Staff of French Army, 1915.

MAJENDIE, V. B. H. ... C 99–03 (Somerset L.I., 1905. Served with W.A.F.F.,
Lieut.-Col. 1908–1913.)
Acting Lieut.-Col., Somerset L.I., 1916–18.
Bt. Major.
Lieut.-Col., 1919.
Despatches (4).
D.S.O.

139

MAKINS, E., D.S.O.   ...   D 83–87   (Ch. Ch., Oxford. 1st Royal Dragoons, 1892.
     Brig.-Gen.   S. African War. Major, 1902. Col., 1913.)
                                     Brigadier-General, 1st Cavalry Brigade, 1914–
                                     1918.
                                     Despatches.
                                     C.B. Order SS. Maurizio e Lazzaro.

✠ MAKINS, G., M.V.O.   ...   D 92–93   (K.R.R.C. S. African War. Capt., 1904.)
     Capt.   Capt., K.R.R.C., 3rd Bn.
                                     Died of Wounds, Aug. 23rd, 1915.

MALAN, A. G. ...   ...   A 90–95   (New Coll., Oxford.)
     2nd Lieut.   Pte., Devonshire Regt.
                                     2nd Lieut., Labour Corps, 1917.

MALCOLM, J. W. K.   ...   F 13–17
                                     Pte., London Scottish, London Regt., 14th Bn..

MALET, C. H. W.   ...   H 90–93
     Capt.   Lieut. and Adjt., R. 1st Devon Yeomanry.
                                     Posted to Devonshire Regt., 16th Bn.
                                     Temp. Capt., 1917.
                                     Staff Capt., L.O.C., Jerusalem, 1917.
                                     Despatches.

MALLET, V. A. L.   ...   F 06–11
     Capt.   Capt., Cambridgeshire Regt.
                                     A.D.C.
                                     Staff Capt., 1918–1919.

✠ MALLOCK, C. H.   ...   C 91–95   (R.F.A., 1897. Capt., 1905.)
     Major   Major, R.F.A.
                                     D.S.O.
                                     Died, Nov. 5th, 1917, *from effects of gas, near*
                                         St. Julien, Nov. 2nd.

MALLORY, G. H. L.   COLL. 00–05
     2nd Lieut.   2nd Lieut., R.G.A.

MANGLES, C. G.   ...   G 99–04   (20th Hussars, 1906. Capt., 1912.)
     Major   Capt., 20th Hussars.
                                     Motor M.G.C.
                                     Acting Lieut.-Col., T.F., 1918.
                                     Major, 1918.
                                     Wounded (2).   *Despatches.*
                                     M.C. Italian and Egyptian Medals.

MANN, J. G.   ...   ...   E 11–16
     Lieut.   2nd Lieut., R.F.A.
                                     Lieut., 1918.

MANSFIELD, R. S. ... c 05–09
   Capt.

Capt., R.E. Motor Cyclist.
Staff Capt., Signal Service Training Centre,.1918.
O.B.E.

MANUEL, A. ... ... A 92–
   Capt.

(Physician.)
Capt., R.A.M.C.
Relinquished Commission, ill-health, 1919.

MAPLES, F. C. ... ... G 90–95
   Lieut.

(Solicitor.)
2nd Lieut., R.F.A., 1916.
Lieut., 1918.

✠ MAPLES, K. J. ... ... G 91–96
   Capt.

(S. Staffs. Regt. S. African War.)
Capt., S. Staffs Regt., 2nd Bn.
Killed, May 16th, 1915, *Festubert*.

✠ MAPLES, W. E. ... ... G 93–97
   Major

(D. of Wellington's Regt., 1899. S. African
   War. Capt., 1904.)
Major, D. of Wellington's, West Riding Regt.
Killed, Dec. 14th, 1916, *Mesopotamia*.

MARCHANT, J. ... ... A 83–86
   Major

(R.M.L.I., 1887. Capt., 1896. Major, 1910.)
Major, A.P.D., 1916.
Retired, 1916.

MARDEN, B. J. N. ... F 06–10
   (late Deakin)
   Capt.

(9th Lancers, 1912.)
Capt., 9th Lancers, 1915.
G.S.O.$_3$, 1919.
Wounded (2).

MARLBOROUGH, DUKE OF H 84–89
   K.G.

Lieut.-Col. G.S.O.$_2$. Retired.

✠ MARSH, D. C. E. ... A 11–16
   2nd Lieut.

2nd Lieut., 6th Dragoon Guards.
Died, April 8th, 1918, *at Rouen, of wounds
   received* April 1st.

MARSHALL, REV. C. B. c 82–87
   Chaplain.

Chaplain, R.N., H.M.S. *Endymion*.

MARSHALL, E. A. ... A 07–11
   Capt.

Capt., Royal Marines.

MARSHALL, E. T. ... I 79–82
   Major

(B.N.C., Oxford. E. Yorkshire Regt., 1889.
   Capt., 1897. S. African War.)
Major, Warwickshire Regt. Comm. Depot.

MARSHALL, G. ... COLL. 95–01
   Capt.

(New Coll., Oxford.)
Capt. and Adjt., Hampshire Regt., 1916.

MARTIN, A. C.	F 89–94	(Architect.)
Capt.		2nd Lieut., R. Fusiliers, Public School Bn.
		Capt., Coy. of Cadets, R.M. College.
MARTIN, C. C. WYKEHAM-	B 06–11	
Capt.		2nd Lieut., Oxford and Bucks L.I., 1914.
		Lieut., 1916.
		Temp. Capt., 1918.
		Despatches.
MARTIN, E. S. D. ...	K 07–11	(5th Dragoon Guards, 1913.)
Capt. .		Capt., 5th Dragoon Guards, 1916.
		M.G.C. Cavalry, 1916.
		Wounded. *Despatches.*
		M.C. D.S.O.
MARTIN, R.	D 84–86	(Highland L.I., 1891. I.A., 1900. R. Irish,
Lieut.-Col.		1903. Capt.)
		Major, R. Irish Regt., 1915.
		Temp. Lieut.-Col., E. Lancs. Regt., 1916.
		D.A.A.G., H.Q., India.
		Wounded.
MARTINDALE, M. H. ...	B 06–10	
Lieut.		2nd Lieut., R.A.S.C., M.T., 1915.
		Lieut., 1917.
✠ MARTINDALE, W. F. ...	B 07–12	
2nd Lieut.		2nd Lieut., Scots Guards.
		Killed, Sept. 15th, 1916, *Guinchy.*
MASON, E.	A 93–97	(Stock Exchange.)
Capt.		Capt., R.A.S.C.
		D.A.Q.M.G., 1918.
		Despatches.
MASON, H. C.	A 89–93	
Capt.		Capt., R.A.S.C., 1915.
		Despatches (2).
MASON, H. S.	A 95–99	
Lieut.		Lieut., R.N.V.R.
MASON, J. R.	A 87–93	(Solicitor.)
Lieut.		Sub-Lieut., R.N.V.R.
		Lieut., 1918.
MASSAREENE & FERRARD,	C 87–91	(17th Lancers, 1895. S. African War. Bt.
Visct., D.S.O.		Major, 1902. Major, 1904. Ret., 1907.)
Lieut.-Col.		Major.
		Lieut.-Col., N. Irish Horse to 1919.
		A.Q.M.G.
		Despatches (2).

MATHESON, I. M.A.   ... A 09–14
    Capt.   Lieut., Lothian and Border Horse.
                                       Seaforth Highlanders.
                                       R.A.F., Capt. A. A.D.C. to G.O.C. Salonica.
                                       Despatches.
                                       O.B.E.   Order Serbian White Eagle.

MATTHEWS, A. S.   ... C 97–00
                                       Pte., Devonshire Regt.

MATTHEWS, B. H.   ... I 88–93   (Bristol Univ. Coll.)
    Major   Major, N. Somerset Yeomanry.
                                       Employed War Office.
                                       Wounded.   *Despatches.*

MATTHEWS, E. C.   ... D 07–08
    Lieut.   Lieut., Middlesex Regt.

MATTHEWS, REV. H. J.   D 03–08
    C.F.   Chaplain, R.N., H.M.S. *Malaya.*

MATTHEWS, J. C. G.   ... A 89–93
    Capt.   Capt., Suffolk Regt.
                                       Wounded (2).
                                       M.C.

MATTHEWS, T. F. V.   ... F 09–14
    Capt.   Capt., Worcestershire Regt.
                                       Prisoner of War, 1918.
                                       Wounded.
                                       M.C.

MAUDE, A.   ...   COLL. 72–78
    Capt.   Capt., R.A.M.C. 1st Home Counties Field
                                           Ambulance.

MAULE, W. H. F.   ... D 03–08
    Capt.   Capt., N. Lancashire Regt., 1916.
                                       Wounded (2).
                                       D.S.O.

MAUNSELL, C. R. W.   ... B 12–15
    Capt.   2nd Lieut., Warwickshire Regt.
                                       Lieut., 1916.
                                       Acting Capt., 1917.
                                       M.C.

MAURICE, T. J. BONNOR-   G 01–06
    Capt.   Capt., Montgomeryshire Yeomanry.
                                       Posted to R. Welsh Fusiliers, 25th Bn.

MAXWELL, G. A. ... E 95–00
    Capt.

Capt., Yorkshire Regt.
Prisoner of War, 1918.
Wounded.   *Despatches* (3).

✠ MAXWELL, W. G. ... E 02–07
    Bt. Major

Capt., Gordon Highlanders, 8th Bn.
Brigade-Major, 1916.
G.S.O.$_2$, Bt. Major, 1917.
M.C.
Wounded (2).   *Despatches* (3).
Died on active service, Dec. 11th, 1918, *Le Tréport.*

MAY, C. H. ... ... A 00–05
    Capt.

Lieut., Sussex Regt.
Capt., Tank Corps, 1917.
M.C.

✠ MAY, H. C. ... ... H 12–17
    2nd Lieut.

2nd Lieut., K.R.R.C., 6th Bn., 1918.
Killed, Sept. 29th, 1918, *Villers Farm, near Ypres.*

MAY, R. L. G. ... ... K 10–14
    Capt.

2nd Lieut., R. Fusiliers, 1915.
Lieut., 1916.
R.A.F., Capt., Administrative Branch.
Wounded.

✠ MAY, R. T. ... ... A 03–09
    Capt.

Lieut., Sussex Regt., 7th Bn.
Capt., 1916.
Despatches.
Killed, July 7th, 1916, *Ovillers, Battle of the Somme.*

MAYHEW, C. L. ... COLL. 88–94
    Lieut.-Col.

(R.M.L.I., 1895. Capt., 1901.)
Major, R.M.L.I., 1913, H.M.S. *Swiftsure.*
Lieut.-Col., G.S.O.$_1$, at Hong Kong, 1918.

MAYNE, C. E. M. ... F 93–97
    Major

(Lieut., I.A., 1901.)
Major, Indian Army, 1915.
Superintendent Remount Dept.

✠ MEAD, J. F. ... ... G 05–10
    Lieut.

Lieut., Royal Fusiliers.
Killed, Aug. 23rd, 1914, *Mons.*

✠ MEAD, R. J. ... ... G 09–14
    2nd Lieut.

2nd Lieut., Royal Fusiliers.
Killed, Aug. 2nd, 1915, *Armentières.*

✠ MEDLEY, B. A. ...   COLL. 08–14
    Lieut.   Lieut., Highland L.I., att. 2nd Bn.
                                    Wounded.   Despatches.
                                    Killed, Sept. 25th, 1915, *Givenchy.*

MEDLEY, J. D. G.   COLL. 04–10
    Major   Capt., Welsh Regt.
                                    A.D.C.   Staff Lieut.
                                    Temp. Major.   R.T. Officer, 1918.
                                    With British Mission at French G.H.Q.

MEDLICOTT, W. B.   ... F 86–91   (Architect.)
    Lieut.   2nd Lieut., R. Fusiliers.
                                    M.G.C.
                                    Tank Corps.   Acting Capt.   Assistant In-
                                        structor, 1918.
                                    Wounded.

MEDLICOTT, REV. R. S.   F 83–88   (Magd. Coll., Oxford.)
    C.F.   Chaplain to Forces, att. Hampshire Regt.

MELLOR, G. E. ...   ... I 10–14
    Capt.   Lieut., Welsh Horse.
                                    Att. Denbighshire Yeomanry.
                                    Posted R. Welsh Fusiliers, 25th Bn.
                                    Capt., 1918.

MELVILL, J. C. D.   ... F 91–94
    Lieut.   Hon. Lieut. and Quartermaster, R.M.

MELVILL, M. G. D.   ... F 93–98 (New Coll., Oxford.)
    Major   Capt., Manchester Regt., 6th Bn., 1916.
                                    Acting Lieut.-Col., 1917.
                                    Temp. Major.
                                    M.C.

MERCER, N. B. ...   ... D 00–02
    Capt.   Lieut., West Surrey Regt.
                                    Capt., 1917.   Staff Lieut.

✠ MEREWETHER, C. K.   ... H 04–09 (Oriel Coll., Oxford.)
    Capt.   Capt., Wiltshire Regt.
                                    A.D.C.
                                    Wounded.
                                    Died, Dec. 19th, 1917, *at Port Said, of wounds
                                        received at Mesmyeh.*

MERRIMAN, C. A.   H 01–03   (R.N.)
    Lieut.-Commander   Lieut.-Commander, R.N.
                                    Despatches.
                                    Chevalier, Star of Roumania.

145   L

MERRIMAN, E. C. B.   ... E 98–01   (6th Dragoons.)
    Lieut.   2nd Lieut., Coldstream Guards.
                                     Lieut., 1918.
                                     Wounded.
                                     Retired, ill-health from wounds, 1919.

MERRIMAN, F. B.   ... H 93–98   (Barrister.)
    Major, K.C.   Major, Manchester Regt.
                                     D.A.A.G.
                                     Retired, 1919.
                                     Despatches (3).
                                     O.B.E.

✠ MERRIMAN, G. H.   ... H 98–02   (R.F.A., 1904.)
    Lieut.   Lieut., R.H.A.
                                     Killed, May 12th, 1915, *Ypres*.

✠ MERRIMAN, W. R. H. COLL. 94–01   (New Coll., Oxford. Home Civil Service.)
    2nd Lieut.   Enlisted H.A.C., 1914.
                                     2nd Lieut., R.B.
                                     Despatches.
                                     Killed, Aug. 15th, 1916, *Longueval*.

MEYNELL, G.   ...   ... C 84–87   (Shropshire L.I. Capt., 1899. I.A.)
    Brig.-Gen.   G.S.O.₂. Brigade-Major. A.A. and Q.M.G.,
                                     1915.
                                     Lieut.-Col., Comm. K. Shropshire L.I., 1st Bn.,
                                     1918.
                                     Brigadier-Gen., 171st Infantry Brigade.
                                     Wounded.   *Despatches* (4).
                                     C.M.G.

MICKLEM, H. A., D.S.O. B 85–88   (R.E., 1891. Capt., 1902. Egyptian Army.
    Lieut.-Col.   S. African War. Retired, 1909.)
                                     Lieut.-Col., R.E., Dep. Director Railways.
                                     Despatches.
                                     C.M.G. O.B.E.

MICKLEM, J.   ...   ... G 02–07   (R.B., 1910. Capt., 1912.)
    Brig.-Gen.   Capt. and Bt. Major, R.B.
                                     Acting Lieut.-Col., Gloucestershire Regt.
                                     Dep. Assistant Director S. and T.
                                     Lieut.-Col., Tank Corps, 1917.
                                     Temp. Brigadier-General, 1918.
                                     Wounded (2).   *Despatches* (4).
                                     M.C. D.S.O.

MICKLEM, L. O.   ... G 87–92   (Queensland Mounted Infantry.   S. African
    Capt.   War.)
                                     Capt., Northamptonshire Regt. Retired.
                                     Capt., Northamptonshire Vol. Regt.

MIDDLEDITCH, R. H. ... I 08–12
Lieut.   2nd Lieut., Yorkshire Regt., 1914.
                          Lieut., 1915.
                          Prisoner of War. Interned Switzerland.
                          Repatriated, 1918.
                          Wounded.

MIDDLETON, A. D. ... D 06–10 (Northants Regt., 1911.)
Capt.   Capt., Northamptonshire Regt., 1915.
                          Wounded.

MIDDLETON, J. A. ... D 08–14
Capt.   2nd Lieut., R.F.A., 1st W. Riding Brigade.
                          R.A.F., acting Capt., S.O.
                          Wounded.

MIDDLETON, R. C. ... F 05–08
Major   2nd Lieut., Liverpool Regt.
                          Major, Gen. List.

✠ MILDMAY, B. W. ST. J. ... C 12–17
2nd ·Lieut.   2nd Lieut., R.A.F.
                          Killed accidentally in flying, April 16th, 1918,
                              Doullens.

MILDMAY, G. ST. J. ... C 68–74 (C.C.C., Oxford. Barrister.)
Major   Capt., Somerset L.I., 1914.
                          Capt., R.B., 15th Rès. Bn.
                          Staff Capt., H.Q., Southern Command, 1915–16.
                          Major, Labour Corps, Plymouth Garrison, 1917.
                          Retired, 1918.

MILES, W. H. ... · ... C 01–04 (Dorset Regt., 1909.)
Capt.   Capt., Dorset Regt., 1915.
                          Adjt., T.F., 1917.
                          Wounded.

MILFORD, R. S. COLL. 78–84
Capt.   Capt., Cheshire Vol. Regt.

MILLER, A. B. ... ... F 92–96 (New Coll., Oxford. Barrister.)
Capt.   Capt., R.F.A.
                          War Office, G.S.O.$_3$, 1918.

MILLER, A. G. ... ... H 95–00 (Magd. Coll., Oxford.)
Lieut.   Lieut., Sussex Yeomanry.
                          Posted to 16th R. Sussex Regt.
                          Acting Capt. and Adjt., 1917–19.

147

MILLER, C. H. ... ... B 08–12
    Capt.

                            2nd Lieut., 18th Hussars, 1914.
                            Lieut., 1915.
                            Temp. Capt.
                            Capt., M.G.C. Cavalry, 1917.
                            Wounded (2).

MILLER, C. T. G. R. ... H 13–13
    2nd Lieut.

                            2nd Lieut., R.A.F., A. and S.

MILLER, D. M. ... I 78–92
    Capt.

                            (14th Hussars, 1887. Capt., 1893. S. African
                                War. Retired, 1902.)
                            Capt., 13th Reserve Regt. Cavalry. Retired.

MILLER, J. A. T. ... F 01–06
    Capt.

                            Capt. and Adjt., 14th Hussars, 1916.

MILLS, J. P. ... ... I 03–08

                            Trooper, Assam Valley Light Horse.

MILLS, R. B. Y. ... G 13–18

                            Gentleman Cadet, R.M. Coll.

✠ MILLS, W. R. G. COLL. 11–15
    2nd Lieut.

                            2nd Lieut., R.F.A.
                            Killed, Feb. 16th, 1917, *Ypres*.

✠ MILNE, A. R. ... ... A 09–14
    Capt.

                            Capt., Hertfordshire Regt.
                            Killed, July 31st, 1917, *St. Julien*.

MILSTED, G. H. ... ... B 89–94
    Lieut.

                            (Trin. Coll., Oxford. Publisher.)
                          2nd Lieut., R.G.A.
                          Lieut., 1918.
                          Retired.

MITCHELL, D. J. ... ... H 03–08
    Capt.

                            (K.R.R.C., 1911.)
                          Capt., K.R.R.C., 1916.
                          A.D.C.
                          G.S.O.$_3$, 1915.
                          M.C. Croix de Guerre. Orders: Serbian, White
                                Eagle; Greek, Redeemer.

MITCHELL, F. A. ... H 02–07
    Major

                          (Ch. Ch., Oxford.)
                          Capt., Gloucestershire Yeomanry.
                          Major, 1918.
                          Despatches.
                          M.C.

MOBERLY, A. H. ... G 99–03
    Capt.

                          (King's Coll., Camb.)
                          Capt., 1st Surrey Rifles, London Regt., 21st
                                Bn., 1916.
                          Comm. Coy. of Cadet Unit till 1919.
                          Wounded.

MOBERLY, B. R. ... c 90–93 (Lieut., I.A., 1899. Capt., 1906. G.S.O.$_3$, 1914.)
Brig.-Gen.   Lieut.-Col., I.A., 56th Punjabis.
                               G.S.O.$_2$, 1915. G.S.O.$_1$. D.A.A. and Q.M.G.
                               D.A.A.G., 1918.
                               Temp. Brigadier-General, Director of Military
                                    Operations, Gen. Staff, India.
                               Wounded.   *Despatches* (3).
                               D.S.O.

MOBERLY, G. H. ... c 05–10
Capt.   Lieut., Lancaster Regt.
                               M.G.C., 1916.
                               Acting Capt., 1918.
                               Despatches.
                               M.C.

MOBERLY, G. K. ... c 84–87 (Worcester Coll., Oxford.)
Lieut.-Col.   Lieut.-Col., R.A.M.C., S. Africa.
                               E. Africa Expedition.

MOBERLY, G. S. ... c 10–14
Lieut.   2nd Lieut., R.F.A.
                               Lieut., 1917.

MOBERLY, H. W. ... c 08–12
2nd Lieut.   2nd Lieut., Duke of Cornwall's L.I.
                               Wounded.
                               M.C.

MOBERLY, J. E. ... d 88–91 (University Coll., London. Civil Engineer.)
Lieut.   Lieut., R.A.S.C., 1915.
                               Ministry of Munitions.
                               Despatches.
                               M.B.E.

MOBERLY, REV. R. H. COLL. 96–03 (New Coll., Oxford.)
C.F.   Chaplain to Forces, 1917.
                               Wounded.

MOBERLY, W. H. ... g 95–00 (New Coll., Oxford.)
Capt.   Lieut., Oxford and Bucks L.I., 1917.
                               Acting Capt., 1917.
                               Wounded (3).   *Despatches* (2).
                               D.S.O.

✠ MOLINEUX, G. K. ... e 01–06
Capt.   Capt., Northumberland Fusiliers.
                               Killed, May 8th, 1915, *Ypres.*

149

MONCRIEFF, A. R.　　...　I 93–95　(Seaforth Highlanders, Lieut., 1900.　S. African
　　Major　　　　　　　　　　　　War.　2nd Dragoons.)
　　　　　　　　　　　　　　　　Capt., 6th Dragoons, att. 2nd Dragoon Guards.
　　　　　　　　　　　　　　　　G.S.O.₃, 1916.
　　　　　　　　　　　　　　　　Acting Major, 1918.
　　　　　　　　　　　　　　　　Wounded.
　　　　　　　　　　　　　　　　M.C.

MONCRIEFF, C. K.　　COLL. 03–98
　　SCOTT-　　　　　　　　　　Capt., K.O.S.B.
　　　　Capt.　　　　　　　　　Press Officer, G.H.Q., France, 1918.
　　　　　　　　　　　　　　　　Wounded.
　　　　　　　　　　　　　　　　M.C.

MONCRIEFF, M. M.　　...　E 89–91　(6th Dragoon Guards, Capt., 1900.　S. African
　　Capt.　　　　　　　　　　　　War.)
　　　　　　　　　　　　　　　　Capt., Gen. List.　Recruiting Duties.

✠ MONRO, K. E.　...　...　C 07–11
　　Lieut.　　　　　　　　　　Lieut., Northamptonshire Regt.
　　　　　　　　　　　　　　　　Died of Wounds, Boulogne, May 14th, 1915.

MONRO, N. H.　...　...　C 00–02
　　Lieut.　　　　　　　　　　Lieut., R.A.S.C.

MONSON, C. E. J.　...　D 92–95
　　Capt.　　　　　　　　　　Capt., Lincolnshire Regt., 1916.
　　　　　　　　　　　　　　　　Draft Conducting Officer.

MONTGOMERIE, H. S.　...　F 85–89　(Trin. Coll., Oxford.　Solicitor.)
　　Major　　　　　　　　　　Major, Middlesex Regt., 1912.

MONTGOMERY, G. W. C.　E 12–16
　　2nd Lieut.　　　　　　　2nd Lieut., R.F.A., 1917.

MONTGOMERY, H. E. L.　D 09–14
　　Lieut.　　　　　　　　　　2nd Lieut., N. Irish Horse.
　　　　　　　　　　　　　　　　Lieut., 1916, Army Cyclist Corps.
　　　　　　　　　　　　　　　　M.C.

MONTGOMERY, H. W.　...　D 89–93　(17th Lancers, Lieut., 1896.)
　　Major　　　　　　　　　　Capt., 17th Lancers, 1914.
　　　　　　　　　　　　　　　　Temp. Major.
　　　　　　　　　　　　　　　　A.P.M.

MOON, N. L.　...　...　F 02–05
　　Lieut.　　　　　　　　　　2nd Lieut., 13th Hussars.
　　　　　　　　　　　　　　　　Lieut., 1918.
　　　　　　　　　　　　　　　　R.A.F., Lieut., A, 1918.
　　　　　　　　　　　　　　　　Relinquished Commission, 1918, ill-health from
　　　　　　　　　　　　　　　　　　service.

MOON, R. O. ... ... E 78–84
    Major ...   Major, R.A.M.C.
                                  1st Serbian Hospital.
                                  49th General Hospital, Salonica.

MOREING, A. C. ... ... B 05–08
    Capt.   Capt., London Regt., 3rd Bn., 1916.

MOREING, A. H. ... B 04–06
    Capt.   Capt., R.F.A., T.F., 1916, 4th London Howitzer
                                      Brigade.
                                  Lieut., R.A. Motor Reserve.
                                  Despatches.

✠ MORGAN, A. C. O. ... F 99–03
    Lieut.   (Trin. Coll., Camb.)
                                  Lieut., R.F.A., N. Midland Brigade.
                                  Despatches.
                                  Killed, Oct. 13th, 1915, *Hohenzollern Redoubt.*

✠ MORGAN, G. W. S. ... H 08–13
    Capt.   (Ch. Ch., Oxford.)
                                  Capt., R. Welsh Fusiliers.
                                  Killed, Sept. 25th, 1915, *Loos.*

✠ MORGAN, R. C. ... ... F 97–02
    Capt.   (Land Agent.)
                                  Lieut., R. Welsh Fusiliers.
                                  Asst. Labour Commandant, 3rd Army H.Q.,
                                        Capt., 1918.
                                  Died of pneumonia, Feb. 18th, 1919.

MORISON, R. P. ... ... G 14–18
                                  Cadet, Household Brigade, O.C. Bn., 1918.

MORLEY, H. C. C. ... G 03–07
    Capt.   (E. Kent Regt., 1912.)
                                  Capt., E. Kent Regt., 1915.
                                  Att. R.A.F., 1916.
                                  Wounded (2).

✠ MORLEY, M. R. H. ... ,E 07–13
    Lieut.   Lieut., K.O.Y.L.I.
                                  Killed, July 1st, 1916, *near Thiepval, Battle oj*
                                      the Somme.

MORRAH, D. M. ... ... I 09–14
    Lieut.   Lieut., R.E., E. Lancashire Divisional Engineers
                                Army Signal Service.
                                  London Westminster Rifles, 1918.
                                  Wounded.

MORRES, E. R. ... ... B 87–92
    Lieut.   (Magd. Coll., Oxford.)
                                  Capt., R.A.S.C.
                                  Lieut., Guernsey Militia, 1916.

MORRES, H. F. M. ... B 89–93
2nd Lieut.
2nd Lieut., Eastbourne Coll. O.T.C.
Worcestershire Regt., 1st Garrison Bn.

✠ MORRIS, A. G. A. ... I 00–03
Lieut.
Lieut., R. Lancaster Regt.
Killed, Oct. 13th, 1914, *Meteren*.

MORRIS, C. A. ... ... G 12–15
Lieut.
2nd Lieut., 12th Lancers, 1916.
Lieut., 1918.

✠ MORSE, C. C. ... ... D 12–15
Lieut.
Lieut., R.A.F.
Killed accidentally, Nov. 14th, 1917, *Tantonville,
near Nancy*.

MORSE, F. J. ... COLL. 11–14
Capt.
2nd Lieut., K.R.R.C.
R.A.F., Capt., A, 1918.
Croix de Guerre.

MORSE, G. G. ... ... E 09–14
Capt.
Lieut., E. Surrey Regt.
Capt., 1917.
Wounded.
M.C.
Relinquished Commission, 1919, ill-health.

MORSHEAD, H. T. ... E 96–00
Lieut.-Col.
(R.E., 1901. Lieut., 1904. Capt., 1912.)
Major, R.E., 1916.
Acting Lieut.-Col., 1918.
Despatches.
D.S.O.

MORSHEAD, J. ... ... E 13–18
2nd Lieut.
2nd Lieut., 4th Res. Regt. Cavalry, 1919.

MORSHEAD, J. T. ... E 02–06
Pte., Princess Patricia's L.I., Canada.
Invalided.

MORSHEAD, J. V. COMM. 60–64
ANDERSON-
(Univ. Coll., Oxford. Barrister.)
Pte., 1st Vol. Bn. Devonshire Regt.

MORSHEAD, L. T. ... E 08–13
Capt.
2nd Lieut., R.E., 1914.
Capt., 1917.
Adjt., 1918. G.S.O.$_3$.
Wounded. (2)   *Despatches.*

MORSHEAD, P. E. ... A 96–00   (C.C.C., Oxford.)
  ANDERSON-   Lieut., R.F.A., 1915.
    Capt.   Acting Capt., Cadet Unit, 1917.
                               Wounded.

MORSHEAD, R. S. ... E 00–05
    Capt.   Capt., R.A.M.C.
                               M.C.

MORSHEAD, V. H. ... E 89–93   (Bank of England.)
    Lieut.   Lieut., R.F.A., 4th Wessex Brigade.
                               A.D.C., 1917.
                               Despatches.

MORT, M.   ...   ... G 88–94   (Magd. Coll., Oxford. Barrister.)
    Lieut.   Lieut., Northumberland Fusiliers.
                               Employed Ministry of National Service.

MOSELEY, G.   ...   ... F 96–01   (Ch. Ch., Oxford.)
    Capt.   Capt., Yorkshire Regt., 5th Bn., 1916.

MOSLEY, O. E. ...   ... H 09–12
    Lieut.   2nd Lieut., 16th Lancers, 1914.
                               Lieut., 1916.
                               R.A.F.
                               Ret., h.p., ill-health, 1917.
                               M.P. for Harrow, 1918.

MOTION, G. J. ...   ... B 01–04
    Lieut.   2nd Lieut., R.A.S.C.
                               Lieut., 1918.

MOULLIN, O. MANSELL ... D 99–04
    Lieut.   R.A.F., Lieut., A., 1918.
                               Interned in Holland till Nov., 1918.

MOXLY, S. H. S.   COLL. 99–00
    Commander   R.N., Commander.

MOXON, G. A. ...   ... C 12–14
    Lieut.   2nd Lieut., R.G.A., 1915.
                               Lieut., 1917. Staff Lieut.
                               Wounded.

MUGGERIDGE, C. E. ... G 90–94
    Major   Capt., R.A.S.C.
                               Temp. Major. G.S.O.$_2$. K.A.R.
                               M.C. O.B.E.

✠ MUNRO, H. C. S. ... G 08–13
    Major   Capt., Seaforth Highlanders. A.D.C.
                                   Temp. Major.
                                   M.C.
                                   Wounded.
                                   Killed, Oct. 23rd, 1918, *near Valenciennes.*

MUNTZ, F. A. I. ... D 12–17
    2nd Lieut.   2nd Lieut., R.E., 1918.

✠ MURE, G. A. S. ... ... D 94–99   (Univ. Coll., Oxford. K.R.R.C, 1901.
    Capt.   S. African War.)
                                   Capt., Arab Rifles.
                                   Killed, Jan. 3rd, 1916, *Kofi, E. Africa.*

MURE, J. G. D. ... B 97–98
                                   H.A.C.
                                   Private, Artists Rifles.

✠ MURRAY, A. J. G. ... H 08–12
    2nd Lieut.   2nd Lieut., Cameron Highlanders.
                                   Killed, Sept. 14th, 1914, *Battle of the Aisne.*

MURRAY, D. G. ... D 05–10
    Lieut.   R.A.F., Lieut., A. and S.
                                   Interned in Holland.
                                   Repatriated, 1918.

MURRAY, K. ... ... G 05–10
    Capt.   Capt., Cameron Highlanders, 10th Lovat Scouts
                                        Bn.
                                   Relinquished Comm., ill-health from wounds,
                                        1918.
                                   Wounded.

MUSGRAVE, A. G. ... F 01–06
    WYKEHAM-   Capt. and Adjt., Gloucestershire Yeomanry,
    Capt.   1916.
                                   Despatches.
                                   M.C.

MUSGRAVE, F. P. ... E 89–92
    Capt.   Lieut., Sussex Yeomanry.
                                   A.D.C. Staff Capt.
                                   Capt., 1919. Assistant Camp Commandant.
                                   M.B.E.

MYRES, J. L. ... COLL. 82–88   (New Coll. and Ch. Ch., Oxford.)
    Lieut.-Commander   Lieut.-Commander, R.N.V.R.
                                   Despatches.

154

NEAL, D. ... ... D 08–13
    Capt.   Capt., Warwickshire Regt.
                            Despatches.

NEEDHAM, E. J. ... A 02–02
    Capt.   Capt., Northamptonshire Regt.
                            A.D.C.
                            R.A.F., Capt., S.O.
                            Despatches.

✠ NEPEAN, E. C. ... F 07–11
    Lieut.   Pte., London Scottish.
                            2nd Lieut., R. Scots Fusiliers.
                            Lieut., att. R. Fusiliers.
                            Killed, Oct. 4th, 1918, *Le Catelet.*

NEVE, E. J. ... ... E 83–89
    Col.   (New Coll., Oxford. 2nd Lieut., Berkshire
                               Regt. Capt., A.P.D., 1898.)
                            Lieut.-Col., Staff Paymaster, A.P.D., 1910.
                            Col., Chief Paymaster, 1918.
                            Despatches.
                            O.B.E.

NEVILE, G. C. ... ... D 97–02
    Major   (Trin. Coll., Camb. Capt., R.A., 1912.)
                            Major, R.F.A., 1915.
                            Brigade-Major, 1916.
                            D.S.O.

✠ NEVILL, R. ... ... K 11–15
    Capt.   Capt., S. Lancashire Regt.
                              M.C. and Bar.
                            Wounded.
                            Killed, April 10th, 1918, *Pont d'Achelles, near
                              Nieppe.*

NEWBOLT, A. F. ... B 06–11
    Capt.   Capt. and Adjt., Oxford and Bucks L.I., 1915.

NEWTON, H. W. ... D 98–02
    GOODWIN   (King's Coll., Camb.)
    Lieut.   2nd Lieut., Somerset L.I.
                            Lieut., 1916.
                            Prisoner of War.
                            Wounded.

NICHOLAS, W. L. J. ... K 05–09
    Capt.   Capt., R.W. Surrey Regt.
                            Att. E. Kent Regt., 7th Bn.
                            R.A.F. Experimental Station, Orfordness.
                            Wounded (2).   *Despatches.*
                            M.C.

NICHOLS, P. B. B. ... c 09–13
    Capt.
                                Capt., Suffolk Regt.
                                Staff Capt.
                                Brigade Major, 1918.
                                Wounded (2).   *Despatches.*
                                M.C.

NICHOLS, R. M. B. ... c 07–09
    2nd Lieut.
                                  2nd Lieut., R.F.A.
                                  Relinquished Commission.

NICHOLSON, A. C. ... g 78–82
    Lieut.-Col.
                                  (Ch. Ch., Oxford. Hants Yeomanry, 1888.
                                        Major, 1901. S. African War.)
                                Lieut.-Col., Hampshire Carabiniers, T.F.R.

✠ NICHOLSON, A. S. ... p 02–06
    Lieut.
                                  Lieut., Cameron Highlanders.
                                  Killed, Sept. 14th, 1914, *Battle of the Aisne.*

NICHOLSON, C. J. H. ... g 07–12
    Lieut.
                                  Lieut., Suffolk Regt.
                                  A.D.C. to Governor Leeward Islands, 1918.
                                  Wounded.

NICHOLSON, C. ... ... g 12–16
    Lieut
                                  2nd Lieut., 16th Lancers, 1916.
                                  Lieut., 1918.

✠ NICHOLSON, E. H. ... d 93–98
    Lieut.-Col.
                                  (R. Fusiliers, 1900. Lieut., 1903. S. African
                                        War.)
                                  Lieut.-Col., Royal Fusiliers.
                                  Att. E. Surrey Regt.
                                  D.S.O. and Bar.
                                  Killed, Oct. 4th, 1918, *Le Catelet, attack on*
                                        Hindenburg Line.

NICHOLSON, R. ... h 81–87
    Major
                                  (Trin. Coll., Camb. With Mounted Infantry
                                        in S. African War.
                                  Capt., Sussex Regt., 1904.
                                  Major, Hampshire Carabiniers.

✠ NICOL, W. E. ... ... d 96–99
    Major
                                  (Gren. Guards, 1900. Lieut., 1904. S. African
                                        War.)
                                  Major, Grenadier Guards.
                                  Despatches.
                                  D.S.O.
                                  Died, Oct. 1st, 1915, *of wounds received at Loos,*
                                        Sept. 29th.

NICOLL, D. A. ... ... G 06–08   (R.A., 1913.)
    Capt.   Lieut., R.F.A.
                                     Capt., 1917.
                                     Wounded.

NICOLLS, A. E. J. ... G 01–06
    Capt.   Lieut., K.A.R.
                                     Capt. and Adjt., 4th Bn.

✠ NIELD, W. H. E. ... H 03–09
    Lieut.   Lieut., Royal Fusiliers.
                                     Wounded.
                                     Killed, July 1st, 1916, *near Carnoi.*

NIELSEN, E. E. M. ... E 06–11
    2nd Lieut.   2nd Lieut., Norfolk Regt.
                                   Wounded.
                                 Relinquished Commission.

NISBET, R. S. ... ... F 13–17
    2nd Lieut.   2nd Lieut., Cameron Highlanders, 1919.

✠ NISBET, F. S. ... ... A 92–94   (Manchester Regt., Capt., 1901. S. African
    Capt.   War.)
                                   Capt., Manchester Regt.
                                   Adjt., 2nd Bn.
                                   Killed, Aug. 26th, 1914, *Le Cateau.*

NORMAN, H. N. ST. V.   A 10–15
    Lieut.   2nd Lieut., R.G.A., 1915.
                                   Lieut., 1917, att. R.E. for Army Signal Service.

NORTHCOTE, D. S. ... D 05–08
    Lieut.   2nd Lieut., Oxf. and Bucks L.I.
                                   Lieut., 1918.
                                   Wounded.

NORRINGTON, A. L. P.   COLL. 13–18
    2nd Lieut.   2nd Lieut., R.F.A., 1919.

NORTHCROFT, A. G. C.   B 08–12
    Lieut.   2nd Lieut., R.G.A.
                                   Lieut., 1918.

NORTON, L. G. ... ... C 12–16
    Lieut.   2nd Lieut., R.A.F.
                                   Lieut., Tank Corps, 1918.
                                 Acting Capt.

NORTON, W. C. ... C 09–14
    Capt.   Capt., R. Sussex Regt.
                                   Staff Capt., Demobilization, E. Command.
                                 Despatches.
                                 M.C.

NOSWORTHY, R. S. ... D 13–18
2nd Lieut.   2nd Lieut., Coldstream Guards, 1919.

✠ NUGENT, A. ... ... K 12–17
2nd Lieut.   2nd Lieut., R.A.F.
Killed, June 1st, 1918, *Damery-sur-Marne.*

NUGENT, A. B. ... ... H 93–97
Lieut.   Lieut. Staff Lieut.$_2$.
Censor's Office, A.P.O., Calais.
Interpreter, Prisoners of War Camps.

NUGENT, F. H. ... ... H 93–98
BURNELL-
Bt. Lieut.-Col.   (R.B., 1899. S. African War, Capt., 1905.)
Lieut.-Col., R.B.
Temp. Brigadier-General, 167th Brigade, 1916.
Bt. Lieut.-Col., 1916.
Despatches (2).
D.S.O. C.B.E.

O'BRIEN, Hon. D. ... H 93–98
2nd Lieut.   (Ch. Ch., Oxford. Barrister.)
2nd Lieut., Irish Guards, 1914.
Relinquished commission, ill health, 1915.

✠ O'BRIEN, T. D. ... E 09–13
2nd Lieut.   2nd Lieut., 16th Lancers.
R.A.F.
Killed March 31st, 1916, *near Poperinghe.*

ODLING, C. J. ... ... A 09–13
Lieut.   2nd Lieut., R.F.A. 2nd Wessex Howitzer
Brigade.
Lieut., 1918.
Acting Captain and Adjutant, R.F.A.

OKEDEN, Rev. C. S. G.   C 01–06
PARRY-
C.F.   Chaplain to Forces.
M.C.

OKEDEN, H. D., PARRY-   D 71–75
Capt.   (Exeter Coll., Oxford)
Capt., R.A.S.C.

OLIVER, C. A. ... ... H 74–78
       Assistant Director, Navy Contracts.
Admiralty.
C.B.E.

✠ OLIVER, R. M. ...   ... A 95–01   (New Coll., Oxford. Solicitor.)
   Lieut.   Capt., E. Kent Regiment.
                                    Lieut., R. Horse Guards, Household Bn.
                                    Grenadier Guards.
                                    Killed Aug. 27th, 1918, *St. Léger, near Arras.*

OLIVER, W. J. ...   ... c 00–04   (Oriel Coll., Oxford.)
   Capt.   Capt., Durham L.I., 1917.
                                    M.C.

OLLIVANT, A. H.   ... E 84–87   (R.A., 1891. Capt., R.G.A., 1899. G.S.O.$_3$,
   Brig.-Gen.   1911. G.S.O.$_2$, 1913.)
                                    Lieut.-Col., R.A. G.S.O.$_1$, 1914.
                                    Brevet Col. Temp. Brig.-General, 1918.
                                    Despatches (4).
                                    C.M.G., C.B., Order St. Anne.

OLLIVER, C. O. ...   ... A 04–09   (R.A., 1911.)
   Capt.   Capt., R.G.A., 1916. G.S.O.$_3$.
                                    Acting Major, 1917.

ONSLOW, G. C. ...   ... F 97–00   (Engineer.)
   Lieut.   2nd Lieut., Gloucestershire Regiment.
                                    Lieut., R.E., 1918.

✠ ORFORD, W. K.   ... F 09–13
   2nd Lieut.   2nd Lieut., Manchester Regt.
                                    Killed July 1st, 1916, *near Albert.*

ORMOND, E. C.   ... H 10–15
   Lieut.   Lieut., R.F.A., 1917.
                                    Wounded.

✠ ORMSBY, V. A. ...   ... c 78–83   (E. Surrey Regt., 1885. Capt., I.A., 1891.
   Brig.-Gen.   3rd Gurkhas.)
                                    Brig.-General.
                                    Despatches (4).
                                    C.B.
                                    Killed May 2nd, 1917, *Villers Faucon.*

ORR, J. E. H. ...   ... F 69–73   (R.A., 75–82. Capt., C.I.V., S. African War.)
   Capt.   Capt., R.H.A.
                                    Adjutant, 10th Reserve Brigade, Woolwich.
                                    Retired.

OSBORNE, J. E. ...   ... H 99–02   (Lieut., Middlesex Regt., 1905. Oxford and
   Major   Bucks L.I.)
                                    Major, Oxford and Bucks L.I., 1915.

159

✠ OSLER, E. R.   ...   ...   c 10–12
    Lieut.

                         Lieut., Canadian A.M.C.
                         R.F.A.
                         Died Aug. 29th, 1917, *of wounds received in Flanders.*

OSMASTON, C. A. F.   ...   H 80–83
    Lieut.-Col.

                         (R.M. Artillery, 1884. Capt., 1895. Lieut.-Col., 1913.)
                         Lieut.-Col., R. Marine Artillery.
                         Ordnance Committee.
                         Ministry of Munitions, 1917.
                         C.B. C.B.E.

OSMASTON, D. F.   ...   K 06–11
    Capt.

                         Lieut., R.E.
                         Capt., 1918.
                         Despatches.

✠ OSMASTON, R. S.   ...   K 09–13
    2nd Lieut.

                         2nd Lieut., Sussex Regt.
                         R.A.F.
                         M.C.
                         Killed, Sept. 24th, 1916, *flying, near Arras.*

OSWALD, R. A. ...   ...   F 12–16
    2nd Lieut.

                         2nd Lieut., I.A., unattached, 1918.

OVERTON, A. E.   ...   F 06–11
    Lieut.

                         2nd Lieut., R.E.
                         Lieut., 1917.
                         M.C.

✠ OVERTON, T. D.   COLL. 08–13
    Lieut.

                         Lieut., Lincolnshire Regt.
                         Killed, July 30th, 1915, *Cape Helles, Gallipoli.*

OWEN, A. V.   ...   ...   H 13–17

                         Cadet, R.F.A.

OWEN, O. S.   ...   ...   K 13–18

                         Gentleman Cadet, R.M. College, 1918.

OXLEY, J. C. S.   ...   A 88–89
    Major

                         (St. Thomas Hospital. Indian Medical Service. Lieut., 1900.)
                         Major, I.M.S.

PAGE, R. ... COLL. 97–02   (New Coll., Oxford.)
    Capt.   Lieut., Hampshire Regt.
                         M.G.C. Infantry.
                         Acting Capt., 1918.

✠ PAGET, S. J. ... COLL. 08–14
    Capt.   Capt., Norfolk Regt.
                         G.S.O.$_3$. Brigade-Major, 1918.
                         Killed, March 26th, 1918, *Framerville sur Somme.*

PAIN, C. H. ... ... A 00–05   (Canada.)
                         Pte., 90th Winnipeg Rifles.
                         Prisoner of War, 1914.
                         Repatriated, 1918.
                         Wounded.

PAIN, N. S. ... ... A 05–10
    Capt.   Lieut., Cheshire Regt.
                         Acting Capt. and Adjt., 53rd Bn. Manchester
                              Regt.
                         Relinquished Commission, ill-health, 1919.

PAINE, K. H. ... ... B 12–17
    2nd Lieut.   2nd Lieut., R.A.F., A.

PAISH, F. W. ... ... H 11–16
                         2nd Lieut., R.F.A., 1916.
                         Woundèd.
                         M.C.

PAKENHAM, HON. E. M.   G 79–81   (Coldstream Guards, Capt., 1897. S. African
    Major   War. Retired 1905.)
                         Capt., Coldstream Guards.
                         Major.

PALMER, A. N. ... ... B 00–05   (Univ. Coll., Oxford. Journalist.)
    Capt.   Capt., Berkshire Regt., 1918.

PALMER, C. D. ... ... C 11–15
    Lieut.   2nd Lieut., Arg. and Suth. Highlanders, 1916.
                         Lieut., R.A.F., 1917.

✠ PALMER, D. W. O. ... A 08–10
    Lieut.   Lieut., Yorkshire Regt.
                         Killed, June 4th, 1916, *Bertrancourt.*

PALMER, H. G. ... ... I 02–07
    Lieut.   Lieut., R.E., 1916.
                         Employed under Admiralty.

✠ PALMER, HON. R. S. A.   C 02–07
                         Capt., Hampshire Regt.
                         Died of Wounds, Jan. 21st, 1916, *Mesopotamia.*

PALMER, HON. W. J. L.   B 08–11
    Lieut.   Lieut., Hampshire Regt., 1916.
                                    A.D.C. to Governor of Bengal.

PANCKRIDGE, H. R.   COLL. 00–04
    Capt.   Capt., S. and T. Corps.
                                    Brigade Supply Officer.
                                    Despatches.

PAPILLON, P. H.   ... G 86–90   (Tea Planter, Ceylon.)
    Capt.   Capt., S. Lancashire Regt.
                                    Relinquished Commission, 1917.

PAPILLON, P. R.   ... G 78–83   (Univ. Coll., Oxford. Barrister. Sussex
    Lieut.-Col.   Militia.)
                                    Lieut.-Col. Comm. Essex Regt., 13th Bn.
                                    Relinquished Commission, 1917.
                                    Despatches.
                                    D.S.O.

✠ PARKE, J. A. ... ... B 06–11
    Lieut.   Lieut., Durham L.I.
                                    Wounded.
                                    Killed, Sept. 25th, 1915, *Loos.*

PARKE, L.   ... ... H 74–77   (Durham L.I., 1881. Major, 1900. S. African
    Lieut.-Col.   War. Retired, 1901.)
                                    Lieut.-Col., Hampshire Regt., 7th Bn.

✠ PARKE, W. E. ... ... B 05–09
    Lieut.   Lieut., Durham L.I.
                                    Despatches.
                                    Killed, Oct. 13th, 1914, *near Hazebrouck.*

PARKER, E. C. L.   ... E 87–   (Solicitor.)
    Capt.   Capt., R.A.S.C.

PARKER, F. W. L.   COLL. 11–15
    Mc C.   2nd Lieut., R.E., 1916.
    Lieut.   Lieut., 1918.

PARKER, G. D. S.   ... E 08–13   (Trin. Coll., Cambridge.)
    Capt.   2nd Lieut., R.B., 1914.
                                    Capt., 1917.
                                    Wounded.

PARKER, R. M. B.   ... E 94–00   (Trin. Coll., Cambridge.)
    Lieut.   2nd Lieut., R.G.A., 1916.
                                    Lieut., 1918.

162

✠ PARKER, W. M.... ... E 00–05
    Capt.
                    Capt. and Adjt., R.B.
                    Killed, July 30th, 1915, *Hooge*.

PARKIN, G. R. ... ... K 09–12
    Lieut.
                    Lieut., Canadian Artillery.
                    Lieut., R.E., 1918.

✠ PARNELL, J. A. P. ... C 08–13
    Lieut.
                    Lieut., Gloucestershire Regt.
                    Killed, Sept. 8th, 1916, *High Wood*.

PARR, J. W. ... ... A 04–10
    Lieut.
                    (New Coll., Oxford.)
                    2nd Lieut., Highland L.I.
                    Lieut., 1917.
                    Wounded.
                    Prisoner of War, Oct.–Dec., 1918.

PARR, M. W. ... COLL. 05–11
    Capt.
                    Capt., Highland L.I.
                    Staff Capt.
                    Wounded.

✠ PARSONS, D. C. ... E 03–08
    Capt.
                    Capt., Irish Guards.
                    Wounded.
                    Killed, Sept. 15th, 1916, *Guinchy, Battle of the Somme.*

PATERSON, T. S. ... A 98–03
    Capt.
                    (I.A., 1905.)
                    Capt., 19th Lancers, I.A., 1914.
                    M.C.

✠ PATON, J. E. ... ... I 09–14
    2nd Lieut.
                    2nd Lieut., Monmouthshire Regt., 2nd Bn.
                    Despatches.
                    Killed, Dec. 31st, 1914, *near Le Bizet*.

PATON, R. R. D. ... I 12–17
    2nd Lieut.
                    2nd Lieut., Welsh Guards.
                    M.C.

✠ PATTEN, F. H. ... K 12–16
    Lieut.
                    Lieut., R.A.F.
                    Killed accidentally in England, Jan. 14th, 1918.

PATTEN, J. R. ... ... K 10–15
    Lieut.
                    2nd Lieut., R.F.A., 1916.
                    Lieut., 1917.
                    M.C.

PATTENSON, E. C. TYLDEN- Bt. Lieut.-Col.	... B 85–89	(R.E., Capt., 1903.) Bt. Lieut.-Col., R.E., Sappers and Miners, Retired. *Despatches* (2). D.S.O.
PATTENSON, W. B. TYLDEN- Major	... D 69–73	Major. Superintendent, Remount Squadron. Retired, 1919.
PATTON, B. M. ... Capt.	... I 89–93	(Engineer, G.W. Railway.) Capt., R.A.S.C.
PAWSON, A. C. ... Capt.	... B 95–00	(Ch. Ch., Oxford. Solicitor.) Capt., Sherwood Rangers. Yeomanry.
PAWSON, A. G. ... Capt.	... B 01–07	Lieut., W. Yorkshire Regt. Training Reserve, 88th Bn. Capt., 1918. R.T.O.
PAXTON, R. G. WAVELL Capt.	B 97–00	(Magd. Coll., Oxford.) Capt., Coldstream Guards. Prisoner of War. Interned in Holland, 1918. Repatriated, 1919. *Wounded.*
PAYNE, J B. ... Lieut.	COLL. 96–02	(Univ. Coll., Oxford.) 2nd Lieut., York and Lancaster Regt. Lieut., 1917, Officer Cadet Bn.
PEACOCK, F. L. ...	... E 13–17	Cadet, O.T.B.
✠ PEARCE, C. S. ... Capt.	... C 07–13	Capt., E. Surrey Regt. *Killed,* July 1st, 1916, *near Montauban.*
PEARCE, P. M. Capt.	COLL. 97–03	(R.G.A., 1905.) Capt., R.G.A., 1914. Acting Major, 1916.
✠ PEASE, J. F. B. Lieut.	... D 96–01	(K.R.R.C., 1904.) Lieut., K.R.R.C. *Killed,* April 29th, 1915, *Ypres.*
PEARSON, A. D. B. 2nd Lieut.	... D 13–18	2nd Lieut., Scots Guards, 1918.

PEARSON, G. C.   ... D 05–09
    Capt.
                                        2nd Lieut., R. Fusiliers, 1915.
                                        Lieut., 1916.
                                        Acting Capt., G.S.O.$_3$, 1917.
                                        M.C.

✠ PEASE, C. Y.   ...   ... c 99–04
    Capt.
                                          Lieut., Yorkshire Hussars.
                                        Capt., att. W. Yorkshire Regt., 9th Bn.
                                        Killed, May 9th, 1918, *Givenchy.*

PEASE, E.   ...   COLL. 94–99
    2nd Lieut.
                                          (Trin. Coll., Cambridge. Soudan Civil Service.)
                                        Trooper, King Edward's Horse.
                                        M.G.C.
                                        2nd Lieut., Special List.
                                        Wounded.
                                        Oriental Linguist Censor.

PEASE, T. O. C.   ... A 05–09
    Capt.
                                          Lieut., Middlesex Regt.
                                        R.A.F., Capt., T., 1918.

✠ PEEL, L.   ...   ... c 98–02
    Capt.
                                          (Lieut., Yorkshire Regt., 1905.)
                                        Capt., Yorkshire Regt.
                                        Despatches.
                                        Presumed killed, Oct. 23rd–24th, 1914.

✠ PEEL, REV. HON. M. B.   E 87–91
    C.F.
                                          (New Coll., Oxford. St. Paul's, Beckenham.)
                                        Chaplain to Forces.
                                        Wounded.   *Despatches* (2).
                                          M.C. and Bar.
                                        Killed, May 14th, 1917, *Bullecourt.*

PEEL, R.   ...   ... c 94–00
    Bt. Major
                                          (New Coll., Oxford. Barrister.)
                                        Capt., Q. Westminster Rifles.
                                        D.A.A.G.
                                        Despatches.

PEEL, W. C.   ...   ... E 84–87
    Major
                                          (3rd Dragoon Guards, Lieut., 1892.)
                                        Capt., Remount Service.
                                        Dep. Assistant Director, Southern Command,
                                              1915.
                                        Major, 1919.

PEEL, W. R.   ...   ... c 00–05
    Lieut.-Col.
                                          Capt., Yorkshire Regt.
                                        Major, 1916.
                                        Lieut.-Col., Manchester Regt., 10th Bn.
                                        Wounded.   *Despatches.*
                                        D.S.O. and Two Bars.

✠ PELL, A. J. ... COLL. 77–82 (Merton Coll., Oxford. Barrister.)
  Major Major, Suffolk Regt.
  G.S.O. Brigade-Major, T.F.R.
  Divisional Musketry Officer, Western Command,
  Died in England on Military Service, Aug. 18th,
  1916.

PENNYCUICK, J. COLL. 12–17
  2nd Lieut. 2nd Lieut., Coldstream Guards, 1919.

PENROSE, J. ... ... C 00–05 (Ch. Ch., Oxford. R.A., 1908.)
  Major Capt., R.F.A., 1914.
  Major, 1918.
  Assistant Superintendent, Ordnance Factory,
  1915–17.
  Wounded. Despatches (3).
  M.C.

✠ PEPPER, C. W. ... ... G 08–09
  2nd Lieut., Somerset L.I.
  Died in England, 1915.

PERRY, W. A. C. ... H 01–04
  Capt. Lieut., R.E.
  Staff Lieut.
  Temp. Capt., 1917.

PERSSE, D. S. ... ... K 08–10
  Lieut. Lieut., D. of Lancaster's Yeomanry.
  Att. Manchester Regt.
  R.A.F.
  Tank Corps, 1918–19.

PESKETT, A. H. ... C 07–11 (R.F.A., 1913.)
  Capt. Capt., R.F.A., 1917.
  Acting Major, 1918.
  Wounded (2).

✠ PETERKIN, C. G. GRANT I 92–97
  Capt. Lieut., Scottish Horse.
  Capt., att. Gordon Highlanders.
  Killed, Sept. 14th, 1917, *near Proven*.

PETERS, J. H. G. ... F 09–13
  Lieut. Lieut., E. Kent Regt.
  Lieut., 51st Sikhs, I.A.

PETERS, J. W. P. ... F 78–80 (7th Dragoon Guards, Major, 1897. Retired.
  Major S. African War.)
  Major; 7th Dragoon Guards. R.T.O.
  Despatches (3).
  D.S.O.

166

PETO, R. H. ... ... I 90–91 (Diplomatic Service.)
    Capt.   Capt., 10th Hussars.
                            R.A.F. S.O.₂.

PHILIPS, L. F. ... ... I 83–88 (K.R.R.C., 1890. S. African War. Major,
    Brig.-Gen.   1905.)
                            Lieut.-Col., K.R.R.C., 1915.
                            Brigadier-General, 1915.
                            Base Commandant, Rouen, 1917.
                            Wounded.   *Despatches* (4).
                            D.S.O. C.M.G. C.B.E.

✠ PHILIPPS, HON. R. E. ... F 03–07
    Capt.   Capt., Royal Fusiliers.
                            Wounded.
                            Killed, July 7th, 1916, *Battle of the Somme.*

PHILIPSON, J. T. ... E 07–10
    Capt.   2nd Lieut., R.F.A., 1914.
                            Capt., 1917, A.D.C.

PHILLIMORE, G. W. ... E 93–98 (Ch. Ch., Oxford.)
    Capt.   Capt., Oxford and Bucks L.I.
                            Att. Highland L.I.
                            Prisoner of War.
                            Wounded.
                            Repatriated, 1918.

PHILLIMORE, REV. ... E 95–00 (Ch. Ch., Oxford. Vicar of Seaforth, near
    HON. S. H.   Liverpool.)
    C.F.   Chaplain to Forces to Coldstream Guards, 4th
                                Bn., 1917.
                            Chaplain to Forces to Grenadier Guards, 3rd
                                Bn., 1917–19.
                            M.C. and Bar.

PHILLIPS, H. SEYS ... A 05–11
    Capt.   Capt., Bedfordshire Regt., 1916.

PHILLIPS, H. DE T. COLL. 75–79 (R.F.A., 1881. Major, 1899. S. African War.
    Brig.-Gen.   Col., 1913.)
                            Brigadier-General, R.F.A., 1916.
                            Despatches (3).
                            C.M.G. C.B.

PHILLIPS, J. C. ... ... G 95–96 (New Coll., Oxford. Barrister.)
    SPENCER   Major, R.A.S.C., 1st Mounted Division.
                            Despatches.
                            D.S.O.

167

✠ PHILLIPPS, C. ... ... B 79–83 (R.A., 1887. Capt., 1897. Canada, 1909–12.)
   Lieut.-Col. Lieut.-Col., R.G.A., 1914.
   Invalided, 1917.
   Died in Hospital, Jan. 10th, 1919.

PHILPOTTS, R. B. COLL. 85–90 (Ball. Coll., Oxford. Barrister.)
   Lieut. Lieut., R. 1st Devon Yeomanry.
   A.D.C. Staff Capt. T.F.R.

✠ PHIPPS, C. J. ... ... H 07–10 (Liverpool Regt., 1913.)
   Major Capt., Liverpool Regt., 1915.
   Comm. 2nd Signal Coy., 2nd Div., 1916–17.
   Major, 1917.
   Wounded (2).   *Despatches* (2).
   M.C. D.S.O.
   Died of Pneumonia at Duren, Feb. 19th, 1919.

✠ PHIPPS, C. P. ... · ... H 09–12
   Lieut. Lieut., Oxford and Bucks L.I.
   Killed, July 20th, 1916, *Laventie*.

PHIPPS, N. L. ... ... F 92–95
   Capt. Lieut., R.E., Cornwall, Army Troops Coy.
   No. 2 Army Workshop Coy.
   Capt., 1919.

PIDCOCK, R. G. ... COLL. 93–99 (New Coll., Oxford. Headmaster, Preparatory
   2nd Lieut.   School.)
   Pte., Inns of Court O.T.C.
   Cadet, 4th O.C.B., Oxford.
   2nd Lieut., K.R.R.C., 5th Bn.
   Wounded.

PIERREPONT, G. E. ... C 94–99 (Engineer, India.)
   Capt. Capt., Gen. List. Interpreter to Indian troops.
   Staff Capt.
   Despatches.
   M.C. Croix de Guerre. Order, La Couronne.

PIGOTT, V. R. ... ... D 80–84 (Cheshire Regt. Capt., Warwickshire Regt.
   Lieut.-Col.   S. African War. Major, 1905.)
   Lieut.-Col., Warwickshire Regt., 1914.
   Comm. 15th Bn. Training Reserve, 1916;
      267th Bn., 1917.
   Wounded.

PIGOTT, W. G. ... ... B 98–01
   Capt. R.N.A.S., Flight-Lieut.
   R.A.F., Acting Major, K.B., 1918.

PILDITCH, P. H.   ... E 04–09
    Lieut.   Lieut., R.F.A., 7th London Brigade, 1916.
                                   Acting Major, 1918.

PILE, G. H. H.   See LYALL.

PILKINGTON, D. F.   ... E 07–09
    Lieut.   Lieut., R.A.S.C., 1915.
                                   M.B.E.

PILKINGTON, E. F.   ... E 99–04   (Trin. Coll., Cambridge.)
    Major   Major, Manchester Regt., T.F.R.

✠ PILKINGTON, H. B.   ... E 00–03   (Trin. Coll., Cambridge.)
    Capt.   Capt., Manchester Regt.
                                   Despatches.
                                   Killed, June 4th, 1915, *Krithia Nullah, Gallipoli.*

PILKINGTON, L. G.   ... D 90–94   (Served as Sergt. S. African War.)
    Capt.   Capt., R. Warwickshire Regt., 1914.
                                   G.S.O.$_3$. Brigade-Major.
                                   Temp. Major, G.S.O.$_2$, 1918.
                                   Despatches.
                                   M.C. ˙Croce di Guerra.

PINNEY, SIR R. J.   ... B 77–81   (R. Fusiliers, 1884. Capt., 1891. Major, 1898.
    Major-Gen.   S. African War. Lieut.-Col., 1903.)
                                   Brigadier-General, 1914.
                                   Major-General, 1915.
                                   Despatches (6).
                                   C.B. Comm. Légion d'Honneur. K.C.B.

PINSENT, J. R. ...   ... E 02–07   (R.E., 1909.)
    Capt. (Bt. Major)   Capt., R.E., 1915.
                                   Acting Major, 1917.
                                   H.Q., Signalling Coy.
                                 Despatches (3).
                                 D.S.O. Officier Légion d'Honneur.

✠ PINSENT, L. A. ...   COLL. 08–13
    Lieut.   Lieut., N. Staffordshire Regt.
                                   Killed, Aug. 15th, 1915, *Gallipoli.*

✠ PINSENT, P. R.   ... E 11–15
    2nd Lieut.   2nd Lieut., R.A.F.
                                   Killed, Sept. 24th, 1916, *Allonville.*

PIPON, R. H. ... ... F 95–98 (R. Fusiliers, 1901. Capt., 1910. Served with
Lieut.-Col. K.A.R.)
Major, R. Fusiliers, 1916.
Lieut.-Col., 24th Bn.
Wounded. *Despatches.*
M.C. D.S.O. and Bar. Chevalier Légion
d'Honneur.

PIRIE, P. T. ... ... E 10–14
Capt. 2nd Lieut., Gordon Highlanders, 1915.
Lieut., 1917.
Acting Capt. and Adjt., 1918.

PLAISTER, A. J. ... C 10–14
Lieut. Lieut., R.F.A., 1917.

PLAYNE, W. H. ... ... I 84–88 (New Coll., Oxford. Major, Gloucestershire
Lieut.-Col., T.D. Yeomanry, 1902. S. African War.)
Lieut.-Col., Gloucestershire Yeomanry, T.F.R.
Wounded.

✠ PLEYDELL, J. M. MANSEL- E 97–03 (Trin. Coll., Cambridge. Canada.)
2nd Lieut. 2nd Lieut., R.F.A
A.D.C.
Died of Wounds, Sept. 22nd, 1916, *Amiens.*

POLLOCK, D. W. ... B 91–97 (New Coll., Oxford. Architect.)
Lieut. Lieut., R.E., 1916.

POOLEY, E. H. ... ... D 90–95 (Pemb. Coll., Cambridge. Barrister.)
Lieut. Lieut., R.N.V.R.
Lieut., R.G.A., 1918.

POPE, A. V. ... ... B 00–04 (14th Hussars, 1908.)
Capt. Capt., 14th Hussars, 1917.
Despatches (2).

POPE, C. J. ... ... I 00–01
Lieut.-Commander Lieut.-Commander, R.N.

Lent to Australian Government.

✠ POPE, C. M. ... COLL. 02–07
Lieut. Lieut., Worcestershire Regt.
Killed, October 24th, 1914, *Polygon Wood.*

✠ POPE, E. A. ... ... B 89–92 (Welsh Regt., Capt., 1899. S. African War.)
Lieut.-Col. Lieut.-Col., Welsh Regt., 3rd Bn.
Late Comm. S.W. Borderers, 12th Bn.
Despatches.
D.S.O.
Died, April 10th, 1919, *in Hospital, London.*

✠ POPE, H. E.   ...   ... I 95–00   (New Coll., Oxford.)
    Capt.   Capt., R.G.A., 1/2nd Lancashire Heavy Battery.
    M.C. and Bar.
    Killed, Aug. 24th, 1918, *Bayon-Villers, near
    Amiens.*

POPE, P. F.   ...   ... B 94–00   (Univ. Coll., Oxford. Lancs. Fusiliers, 1903.
    Major   I.A., 1905.)
    Capt. and Adjt., 1st Brahmans, I.A., 1912.
    Major, 1918.
    Wounded.

POPE, P. M.   ...   ... I 06–10
    Capt.   Capt. and Adjt., K.R.R.C., 1917.
    Prisoner of War, 1918.
    Wounded.
    Repatriated, Dec., 1918.

✠ POPE, P. P.   ...   ... B 96–01   (New Coll., Oxford. Barrister.)
    Lieut.   Lieut., Welsh Regt.
    Killed, Oct. 2nd, 1915, *Hohenzollern Redoubt.*

POPE, S. F.   ...   ... B 93–98   (Univ. Coll., Oxford. Solicitor.)
    Major   Capt., Devonshire Regt.
    D.A.Q.M.G., 1917.
    Major, 1918.
    Despatches (3).
    O.B.E.

PORTAL, C. F. A.   ... F 06–12
    Lieut.-Col.   Lieut., R.E., 1914. Despatch Rider.
    R.A.F.
    Major, 1918.
    Lieut.-Col., 1918, A. and S.
    Despatches (3).
    M.C. D.S.O. and Bar.

PORTER, C. P. G.   ... D 77–81   (Lieut., Cameronians, 84–90. Pemb. Coll.,
    Capt.   Cambridge. S. African War.)
    Capt., Norfolk Regt.
    Retired, 1917.

PORTMAN, G. M. B.   ... B 04–08
    Capt.   Capt., London Regt., P.O. Rifles, 1916.
    Prisoner of War.
    Interned in Holland, 1918.

POTT, R. B.   ...   ... I 75–77   (Stock Exchange. Imperial Yeomanry,
    Lieut.-Col., T.D.   S. African War. Capt., W. Kent Yeomanry.)
    Lieut.-Col., West Kent Yeomanry.

POTTER, A. G. ... ... I 04–09
    Capt.   Capt., R. West Surrey Regt., 4th Bn., 1916.
                                  Staff Capt., 1918.
                                  Despatches.

POTTER, K. B. ... I 11–15
    Lieut.   Lieut., R.F.A., 1917.
                                    H.Q., 20th Division.
                                    Staff Lieut., 1918.
                                    Despatches.
                                    M.C.

POTTER, R. B. ... ... I 12–18
    2nd Lieut.   2nd Lieut., R.F.A., 1919.

POTTER, R. W. ... ... I 00–06
    Major   Major, R. West Surrey Regt., 4th Bn., 1916.

POULTER, D. R. COLL. 84–88
    Capt.   (R.A., 1890. Capt., R.G.A., 1899. Retired,
                                    1907.)
                                    Capt., R.G.A. Reserve of Officers.
                                    Ordnance Dept.

POWELL, H. I. ... ... E 05–10
    Capt.   Capt., Northumberland Fusiliers, 1915.
                                    Wounded (2).

✠ POWELL, H. O. ... ... E 02–06
    2nd Lieut.   2nd Lieut., 4th Dragoon Guards.
                                    Killed, Oct. 31st, 1914, *first Battle of Ypres.*

POWELL, J. J. ... ... F 01–06
    Major   (Oxford and Bucks L.I., 1913.)
                                    Capt., Oxford and Bucks L.I., 1915.
                                    Comm. Coy. of Cadets, R.M. Coll., 1918.
                                    Acting Major, 1919.
                                    Wounded.   *Despatches.*

POWELL, R. A. ... ... D 02–07
    Capt.   Capt., Hampshire Regt., 1915.

✠ POWELL, R. C. ff. ... K 06–09
    2nd Lieut.   2nd Lieut., Highland L.I.
                                    Killed, September 14th, 1914, *Battle of the Aisne.*

PREST, C. E. ... ... F 11–16
    Lieut.   2nd Lieut., R.F.A., 1917.
                                      Lieut., 1918.
                                    Wounded.

PRICE, B. G., D.S.O. ... D 85–88   (Ch. Ch. Oxford. R. Fusiliers, 1892. Capt.,
   Brig.-Gen.   1899. S. African War.)
                                   Lieut.-Col., Royal Fusiliers.
                                   Temp. Brigadier-General, 1916.
                                   Brevet Col., 1917.
                                   Despatches (5).
                                   C.M.G. C.B. Order SS. Maurizio e Lazzaro.

PRICE, H. H. ... COLL. 12–17
   2nd Lieut.   2nd Lieut., R.F.C.
                                   R.A.F., 1918.

PRICE, H. R. ... ... D 02–07
   Lieut.   Lieut., R.B., 5th Bn., 1917.
                                   Acting Capt., 1916, 2nd Bn.
                                   Wounded.   *Despatches.*
                                   M.C.

PRINGLE, Rev. J. C. COLL. 86–91
                                   Gunner, R.F.A., 211th Battery, 1918.

✠ PRINGLE, R. S. ... ... A 99–04   (R.W. Surrey Regt., 1906.)
   Lieut.   Lieut., R.W. Surrey Regt.
                                   Killed September 15th, 1914, *Battle of the Aisne.*

PRIOUX, J. M. J. F. G. COLL. 14–16
                                   Pte., Field Artillery, Belgian Army
                                   Maréchal de logis, 1919.
                                   Louvain University.
                                   Despatches.

PROCTOR, G. ... ... B 91–96   (Ch. Ch., Oxford. Schoolmaster.)
   Lieut.   Lieut., R.F.A.

PROCTOR, L. J. ... ... B 93–96   (Pte., Canadian Engineers.)
   2nd Lieut.   2nd Lieut., R.F.A., 1918.
                                   Wounded.

PROPERT, W. A.... ... E 81–85   (Trin. Coll., Cambridge. Physician.)
                                   Physician Anglo-American Hospital, Wimereux,
                                     1915.

PROWSE, G. W. T. ... B 78–82   (D.C.L.I., 1885. Major, 1905. Retired.)
   Lieut.-Col.   Lieut.-Col. (unattached).
                                   G.S.O.$_2$. Press Censor, War Office.

PUGH, A. J. ... ... I 85–88
   Lieut.-Col.   Lieut.-Col., Comm. Calcutta Light Horse, 3rd Bn.

PUGH, R. A. C. ... ... I 93–97
                                     Sergt., Calcutta Light Horse.

PULLING, C. R. D. ... D 07–12
   Lieut.
         2nd Lieut., K.R.R.C., 5th Bn.
         Lieut., 1917.
         War Office.

PULTENEY, K. ... ... B 82–87
   2nd Lieut.
         (Ch. Ch., Oxford.)
         T.F.R., 2nd Lieut., Hampshire R.H.A., 1914.

PURDEY, J. A. ... ... B 05–08
   Capt.
         Capt., 12th Lancers, 1917.
         War Office.

PURDEY, T. D. ... ... B 10–15
   Lieut.
         2nd Lieut., Arg. and Suth. Highlanders.
         Lieut., R.A.F.
         Acting Capt., 1918, Administration.

PURDON, D. J. ... ... A   –18
         Gentleman Cadet, R.M. College.

✠ PURDON, G. H. ... A 10–15
   2nd Lieut.
         2nd Lieut., K.R.R.C.
         Killed July 22nd, 1916, *Pozières Ridge, Battle
          of Somme.*

PURDON, S. F. ... ... A 08–13
   Capt.
         Capt., R.B.
         War Office.
         Wounded (2).   *Despatches.*
         Relinquished commission, ill-health from
          wounds, 1919.

PYE, D. W. ... COLL. 11–16
         2nd Lieut., R.G.A., 1917.

PYM, A. R. ... ... B 05–07
   Lieut.
         Lieut., Irish Guards, 1916.
         Acting Capt., Household Brigade, Cadet Bn.,
          1918.
         Despatches.

✠ PYM, C. J. ... ... B 06–10
   Lieut.
         Lieut., Irish Guards, 2nd Bn.
         Died March 26th, 1917, *of wounds received*
          March 24th, *near Albert.*

QUILTER, E. G. C. ... c 12–16
   Lieut.

R.A.F., 2nd Lieut.
Lieut., A., 1918.
Prisoner of War.
Repatriated December, 1918.

QUIN, R. S. W. R.   H 02–04
   WYNDHAM-
   Capt.

(12th Lancers, 1907.)
Capt., 12th Lancers, 1916.
A.D.C., 1919.
Wounded.   *Despatches.*
M.C.

✠ RADCLIFFE, D. ...   ... K 07–09
   Capt.

Lieut., Royal Fusiliers.
Capt., 1915.
Killed, March 18th, 1916, *near Loos.*

RADCLIFFE, SIR P. P. DE B. B 87–91
   Major-Gen.

(R.A., 1893. Capt., 1900. S. African War.)
Temp. Brigadier-General, 1915.
Bt. Col., 1917.
Director of Military Operations, War Office,
   1918.
Major-General.
Despatches (5).
D.S.O.   C.B.   K.C.M.G.   Officier Légion
   d'Honneur.   Order Corona d'Italia.   Order
   of Leopold.   American D.S.M.

RAE, G. B. L. ...   ... G 00–05
   Major

(Liverpool Stock Exchange.)
Major, The King's Liverpool Regt., 10th Bn.,
   1917.
D.S.O.

RAMSAY, HON. C. F. M.   c 98–02
   Lieut.

(Ball. Coll., Oxford.)
Lieut., Northumberland Hussars.
Posted to Northumberland Fusiliers, 9th Bn.
Despatches.
M.C. and Bar.

RAMSAY, W. A. ...   ... B 10–15
   Lieut.

2nd Lieut., Oxford and Bucks L.I.
Lieut., 1917, att. T.M.B.
Prisoner of War, 1918.
Repatriated, Dec., 1918.

175

RAMSDEN, B. V. ... I 99–03 (Yorkshire Regt., 1905. Served with W.A.F.F.,
Capt. 1910–1915.)
Capt., Yorkshire Regt., 1914.
Brigade-Major, H.Q., 1918.

RAMSDEN, V. B. ... I 02–05 (S. Wales Borderers, 1908. Capt., 1913.)
(Lieut.-Col.) Capt., S. Wales Borderers.
Bt. Major G.S.O.,₃ 1915. Brigade-Major, 1916.
Temp. Lieut.-Col., Comm. Highland L.I., 15th
Bn., 1917.
Wounded. (2) *Despatches.* (2)
M.C. D.S.O. and Bar.

RANDALL, J. G. ... I 03–08 (R.W. Fusiliers, 1910.)
BRUXNER- Capt., R. Welsh Fusiliers, 1914.
Capt. W.A.F.F., Nigeria Regt., 1914.

RANDALL, W. G. ... D 02–05
BRUXNER- Lieut., K.A.R., 1917.
Lieut. Relinquished Commission, 1919.

RANDOLPH, C. F. ... C 74–79 (Lancs. Fusiliers, 1881. Capt., 1889. Retired,
Major 1902.)
Major, Lancashire Fusiliers, Comm. Depot.

RANDOLPH, H. C. F. ... C 12–14
Lieut. 2nd Lieut., R.F.A., 1917.
Lieut., 1918.

RANNIE, J. A. M. ... C 09–14
Lieut. Lieut., R.E., Monmouthshire Engineers, No. 2
Railway Coy.

RATTRAY, T. A. ... I 03–07
Capt. Capt., W. Somerset Yeomanry.
Posted to Somerset L.I., December 12th, 1916.
Acting Major, 1919.
Wounded. *Despatches.*
M.C.

RAYDEN, W. ... ... B 75–75 (W.I. Regt., 1885. Lieut., E. Kent Regt.,
Major 1889. Barrister.)
Major, Adjt. Infantry Base Depot.
Retired, 1918.

✠ RAYNOR, H. A. L. COLL. 12–17
2nd Lieut. 2nd Lieut., R.B.
Died, June 7th, 1918, *of wounds received May
22nd,* 1918.

176

READ, A. H. ... ... I 93–98 (Stock Exchange.)
    Lieut.   Lieut., R.A.F., Administrative Branch, 1918;
                                           unemployed list, 1919.

READ, J. ... ... B 12–15
    Capt.   2nd Lieut., 16th Bengal Lancers, I.A.
                                           Capt., 1918.

READ, J. H. ... ... H 14–18
                                           Cadet, O.C. Bn., 1918.

REDFERN, A. S. ... E 09–14
    Major   Capt., R. West Surrey Regt., 1917.
                                           R.A.F., Major, A., 1918.

REEVES, R. M. E. ... F 99–01 (Linc. Coll., Oxford.)
    Capt.   Capt., Leicester Regt.

✠ REID, G. E. H. ... ... F 01–05
    Lieut.   Lieut., K.A.R., 4th Uganda Bn.
                                           Killed, March 9th, 1915, *near Nairobi*.

REID, T. L. G. ... ... I 13–17
                                           Cadet, R.F.A.

REISS, A. E. J. ... ... I 84–88 (Merchant, Manchester.)
    Lieut.-Col.   Major, Cheshire Regt.
                                           Staff Capt., War Office.
                                           Lieut.-Col., Assistant Controller Aircraft Supply,
                                             1918.
                                           Despatches.
                                           O.B.E.

RENDALL, A. B. ... A 04–08
    Lieut.   R.A.F., Lieut., T.

RENTON, R. H., LINDSEY- F 01–06
    Major.   Major, London Regt., Queen Victoria's Rifles.
                                           Despatches (3).
                                           D.S.O., Croix de Guerre.

REYNOLDS, A. B. ... D 93–98 (New Coll., Oxford. 12th Lancers, 1900.
    Lieut.-Col.   Lieut., 1902. S. African War.)
                                           Major, 12th Lancers, 1914.
                                           Lieut.-Col., Northumberland Hussars, 1917.
                                           Despatches.
                                           D.S.O.

REYNOLDS, E. B. COLL. 06–12
    Capt.   Capt., Middlesex Regt., 8th Bn., 1916.
                                           G.H.Q., Great Britain.
                                           G.S.O.$_3$.
                                           Wounded (2).

REYNOLDS, G. F. ... D 98–04 (New Coll., Oxford. 9th Lancers, 1907.)
Major   Capt., 9th Lancers, 1914.
                            G.S.O.₃, 1917.
                            Brigade-Major, G.S.O.₂, 1918.
                            Major, 1918.
                            Wounded (2).   *Despatches* (2).
                            M.C.

REYNOLDS, G. N. ... D 94–98 (Oriel Coll., Oxford. Lieut., 21st Lancers,
Capt.   1902. Capt., 1912.)
                            Capt. and Adjt., 21st, att. 9th Lancers.
                            Prisoner of War. Interned, Holland.
                            Repatriated Dec., 1918.
                            Superintendent, Remount Service, 1919.
                            Wounded.
                            M.C.

REYNOLDS, P. K. B. COLL. 09–14
Lieut.   Lieut., R.F.A., 2nd W. Riding Battery, 1916.
                            Wounded (2).

RHODES, H. V. ... ... C 87–90 (Notts and Derby Regt., 1898. S. African
Major   War. Capt., 1905.)
                            Major, Notts and Derby Regt.
                            R.T.O.
                            Retired.
                            Despatches.
                            C.B.E.

RHODES, J. E. ... ... H 83–86 (K.R.R.C., 1889. Capt., 1898. Lieut.-Col.,
Lieut.-Col.   1908.)
                            Lieut.-Col., Hampshire Regt., Isle of Wight
                            Rifles.

RICARDO, A. ST. Q., D.S.O. G 81–84 (Inniskilling Fusiliers, 1888. Capt., 1897.
Brig.-Gen.   S. African War. Retired, 1904.)
                            Lieut.-Col., R. Inniskilling Fusiliers.
                            Temp. Brig.-Gen., Q.M.G.'s Staff.   Brevet
                                Lieut.-Col., 1918.
                            Despatches (7).
                            C.M.G., C.B.E.

RICARDO, H. G. ... C 73–77 (R.F.A., 1879. Capt., 1887.)
Lieut.-Col.   Temp. Lieut.-Col., R.F.A.
                            Retired, 1918.
                            Despatches (2).
                            D.S.O.

178

RICH, C. E. F. ...   ... D 84–88   (Lincolnshire Regt., 1891.   S. African War.
  Major   Major, 1904.   Retired.)
                             Hon. Major, Lincolnshire Regt.
                             A.P.M.
                             Despatches (3).
                             D.S.O.

RICHARDS, C. H.   ... B 86–90   (Oxford L.I., 1894.   Capt., 1900.   A.P.D.)
  Col.   Temp. Col., A.P.D.   Staff Paymaster, 1916.
                             Chief Paymaster, 1917.

RICHARDS, F. H.   ... I 04–09   (R.F.A., 1910.)
  Major   Lieut., R.F.A., 1914, A.D.C.
                             Capt., 1916.
                             Acting Major, 1917.
                             Major, School of Instruction, 1918.
                             Wounded (3).   *Despatches.*
                             D.S.O.

RICHARDS, H. M.   ... B 82–87   (R.W. Fusiliers, 1889.   Capt., 1897.   Retired
  Major   1905.)
                             Major, R. Welsh Fusiliers, 1914.

RICHARDSON, A. S.   ... K 09–14
  2nd Lieut.   Pte., R.A.M.C.
                             2nd Lieut., M.G.C., 1917.
                             Wounded.

RICHMOND, G. H. J.   ... A 12–17
  2nd Lieut.   2nd Lieut., R.F.A., 1917.

RICKETTS, E. W. C.   ... G 97–02   (I.A., 1905.)
  Major   Capt., 23rd Sikhs Pioneers, 1913.
                             Major, 1919.

RICKETTS, H. C.   ... I 79–83   (R. Irish Fusiliers, 1886.   Capt., I.A., 15th
  Lieut.-Col.   Lancers, 1897.   Major, 1904.)
                             Lieut.-Col., I.A., 15th Lancers.
                             Despatches.

RICKETTS, P. E., M.V.O.   G 81–86   Devon Regt., 1888.   Lieut., 1890, I.A., 18th
  Col.   Lancers.   Capt., 1899.)
                             Lieut.-Col., Comm. Welsh Regt., 10th Bn., 1916.
                             Col. Commandant, Sch. of Instruction, 1917.
                             Comm. Group of Labour Corps.
                             Wounded.   *Despatches.*
                             D.S.O.

RICKETTS, R. L. ... G 86–91   (I.A., 10th Lancers, 1892. Capt., 1901. Major,
   Brevet Col.   1910.)
                                                Lieut.-Col., I.A., 10th Lancers, 1916.
                                                D.A.A.G.
                                              G.S.O.$_1$, 1917. Brevet Col.
                                              Despatches (2).

RICKMAN, A. P. W. ... I 87–90
   Capt.   Capt., R. Berkshire Regt.
                                              Gen. List, 1917.
                                              Special Appt.
                                              Despatches (2).
                                              O.B.E.

RICKMAN, A. W. ... I 88–90   (Northumberland Fusiliers, 1897. Capt., 1901.
   Lieut.-Col.   S. African War. Retired, 1909.)
                                            Major, Northumberland Fusiliers, 3rd Bn.
                                            Comm. E. Lancs. Regt., 11th Bn.
                                            Lieut.-Col., 1918.
                                            Wounded (2).   *Despatches* (2).
                                            D.S.O. and Bar.

RICKMAN, G. E. ... I 83–85   (R.W. Fusiliers, 1890. Capt., 1899. S. African
   Major   War. Retired, 1905.)
                                            Major, R. Welsh Fusiliers, Depot.

RIDDELL, R. HUTTON ... E 95–98   (S. Staffs. Regt.)
   Lieut.   Lieut., R. Horse Guards, 1915.
                                            Reserve Regt. Cavalry, 1918.

RIGBY, T. ... ... C 11–15
   Lieut.   2nd Lieut., R.F.A., 1915.
                                            Lieut., 1917.
                                            M.C.

RIGDEN, W. P. ... ... A 90–93   (Solicitor.)
   Hon. Lieut.-Col.,   Major, R.F.A. Home Counties Brigade.
                                            O.B.E. T.D.

RISLEY, C. G. ... ... D 95–98   (R.F.A., 1901. Lieut., 1904. I.A., 18th Lancers,
   Major   Capt., 1910.)
                                            Major, R.F.A., 1916.
                                            Acting Lieut.-Col., 1918.
                                            Despatches.
                                            D.S.O.

✠ RITCHIE, HON. H. ... E 90–94
   Lieut.-Col.   Lieut.-Col., Cameronians (Scottish Rifles.)
                                            Wounded.   *Despatches* (2).
                                            D.S.O. and Bar.
                                            Died of Wounds, Oct. 28th, 1918, *Awoingt.*

RITCHIE, HON. P. C. T.   G 13–17
  2nd Lieut.   2nd Lieut., Suffolk Regt., Garrison Bn., 1918.

RITCHIE, R. K.   ...   H 85–89   (Tea Planting, Ceylon.)
  Capt.   Lieut., R. Fusiliers.
                                    Acting Capt., Labour Corps, 1917.

ROBERTS, G. E.   ...   C 97–01   (New Coll., Oxford.)
  Lieut.   Lieut., R. Welsh Fusiliers, 1917.

ROBERTS, W. ST. C. H.   COLL. 07–12
  Lieut.   2nd Lieut., R.F.A.
                                      Lieut., 1918.
                                      Wounded.
                                      M.C.

ROBERTSON, HON.   ...   A 87–90   (Ch. Ch., Oxford. Barrister. Lieut., Gloucester
  R. B. F.   Yeomanry. S. African War. Capt., 21st
  Capt.   Lancers, 1901. Retired, 1911.)
                                      Capt., 21st Lancers.
                                      Prisoner of War.
                                      Exchanged home, 1917.
                                      War Office.
                                      Wounded.

ROBERTSON, R. J. H.   A 12–17
  TINDAL   2nd Lieut., R.G.A.

ROBINSON, W. M.   ...   B 95–98
  Capt.   Capt., R. Dublin Fusiliers, 1915.

ROGERS, T. M. ...   ...   G 04–08
  Major   Lieut., Intelligence Corps.
                                        R.A.F., Capt.
                                        Major, Aircraft Production, 1918.
                                        Despatches.
                                        O.B.E.

ROLLAND, J. F. ...   ...   F 00–05
  Lieut.   Lieut., E. Riding Yeomanry, Comm. Brigade
                                        Signal Troop.
                                        Relinquished Commission, 1918.
                                        Wounded.   *Despatches.*

ROLLASON, M. H.   ...   A 13–17
  2nd Lieut.   2nd Lieut., R.F.A., 1918.
                                        Wounded.

RONALD, N. B. ... ... A 08–12   (Magd. Coll., Oxford.)
Lieut.   Lieut., Liverpool Regt.
    Lieut., Grenadier Guards, 1916.
    Acting Capt., Household Brigade, O.C. Bn.
       till 1919.
    Wounded.

ROOKE, J. W. ... ... C 00–04
Capt.   Capt., R. Wilts Yeomanry.
    Capt., R.A.S.C., 1917.

ROOPER, J. R. ... ... F 03–06
Capt.   Capt., Denbighshire Yeomanry.
    Invalided, 1916.

✠ ROPER, G. ... ... E 12–16   2nd Lieut., R.F.A., 1917.
    Wounded.
    Drowned in England, while on leave from front.

ROSEVEARE, H. L. ... I 16–18
    Naval Cadet, Keyham.

ROSEVEARE, R. V. H. COLL. 10–15
Lieut.   Lieut., R.F.A.
    Ministry of Munitions.
    Wounded.
    M.C.

ROSEVEARE, W. L. ... K 09–13
Capt.   R.E., 1914.
    Capt., 1917.
    Acting Major, 1918.
    Wounded.   *Despatches.*
    M.C.

ROSTRON, P. S. ... F 92–97   (R.F.A., 1900. Lieut., 1903. S. African War.)
Major   Major, R.H.A.
    Relinquished Commission, ill-health, 1919.
    Despatches.
    C.B.E.

ROUND, C. J. ... ... H 98–04   (Exeter Coll., Oxford.)
Capt.   Lieut., Essex Yeomanry.
    Acting Capt., 1918.

✠ ROWLEY, C. P. ... ... C 91–96   (Magd. Coll., Oxford. R.G.A., 1901. Lieut.,
Major   1902.)
    Major, R.G.A.
    Killed accidentally in England, Oct., 1916.

ROYDEN, SIR T., BART. ... F 85–90
    Director of Transports, Admiralty.

✠ Ruddock, H. M.　　...　h 08–13　(Canada.)
　　　　　　　　　　　　　　　　　　Lce.-Corpl., 2nd Canadian Div., 28th N.W.
　　　　　　　　　　　　　　　　　　　　Brigade.
　　　　　　　　　　　　　　　　　　Killed, Sept. 15th, 1916, *near Courcelette.*

Ruffer, M. E. ...　　...　c 04–08
　　Capt.　　　　　　　　　　　　　Lieut., R.G.A.
　　　　　　　　　　　　　　　　　　Acting Capt. and Adjt., 1918.

Russell, F. D. ...　　...　i 86–89　(I.A., 1895, 1st Lancers, Capt., 1902.　S. African
　　Bt. Col.　　　　　　　　　　　　　War.)
　　　　　　　　　　　　　　　　　　Lieut.-Col., 1st Lancers, I.A., 1916.
　　　　　　　　　　　　　　　　　　A.Q.M.G., 1916.
　　　　　　　　　　　　　　　　　　Bt. Col., 1919.
　　　　　　　　　　　　　　　　　　Despatches (2).

Russell, J. W.　　　coll. 06–12
　　Capt.　　　　　　　　　　　　　Lieut., R.F.A., 1915.
　　　　　　　　　　　　　　　　　　Acting Capt., R.G.A., 1918.

✠ Russell, L. C. B.　　...　f 08–12
　　Capt.　　　　　　　　　　　　　Capt., R.B., 3rd, att. 12th Bn.
　　　　　　　　　　　　　　　　　　Killed Oct. 7th, 1916, *between Gueudecourt and
　　　　　　　　　　　　　　　　　　　Le Transloi.*

Russell, P. N. ...　　...　g 90–94　(Barrister.　2nd Lieut., Imperial Yeomanry
　　Major　　　　　　　　　　　　　　S. African War.)
　　　　　　　　　　　　　　　　　　Major, K.R.R.C.
　　　　　　　　　　　　　　　　　　Wounded (2).
　　　　　　　　　　　　　　　　　　M.C.

Russell, P. W. H.　　...　b 10–14
　　Capt.　　　　　　　　　　　　　2nd Lieut., R.F.A., 1915.
　　　　　　　　　　　　　　　　　　Lieut., 1917.
　　　　　　　　　　　　　　　　　　Acting Capt., 1918.

Ryan, C. M., d.s.o.　　...　g 81–84　(Jesus Coll., Camb.　Dublin Fusiliers, 1888.
　　Brig.-Gen.　　　　　　　　　　　　R.A.S.C., 1890.　Major, 1901.　S. African
　　　　　　　　　　　　　　　　　　　War.)
　　　　　　　　　　　　　　　　　　Col., R.A.S.C., 1914.
　　　　　　　　　　　　　　　　　　Brigadier-General, Director of Supplies, 1918.
　　　　　　　　　　　　　　　　　　Despatches (2).
　　　　　　　　　　　　　　　　　　C.M.G.　C.B.E.　Officier Légion d'Honneur.

Rycroft, N. E. O.　　...　h 00–04
　　　　　　　　　　　　　　　　　　Cyclist, 20th Light Division.

Ryder, C. F.　　...　　...　d 04–08
　　Lieut.　　　　　　　　　　　　　2nd Lieut., Yorkshire Hussars.
　　　　　　　　　　　　　　　　　　1st Dragoon Guards.
　　　　　　　　　　　　　　　　　　Lieut., 13th Hussars, 1917.
　　　　　　　　　　　　　　　　　　Att. 14th Hussars, 1918.

ST. JOHN, HON. R. T. ...	B 96–00	(Durham L.I., Lieut., 1905.)	

ST. JOHN, HON. R. T. ...   B 96–00   (Durham L.I., Lieut., 1905.)
Lieut.-Col.   Capt., Durham L.I., 1914.
Major, 1917.
Acting Lieut.-Col., att. Lincolnshire Regt., 8th Bn.

ST. JOHN, W. HARRIS ...   I 91–94   (R.W. Fusiliers, 1898. S. African War. Capt., 1906. Major, 1910.)
Major   Major, R. Welsh Fusiliers.
1916, G.S.O.$_3$, Brigade-Major.
1917, G.S.O.$_2$.
Wounded.   *Despatches.*
D.S.O.

SALMON, REV. T.   ...   C 87–92   (Magd. Coll., Oxford. Vicar of Stoneham.)
C.F.   Chaplain to Forces till 1918.

SALMONSON, H. S.   ...   K 07–12   (Scottish Rifles, Lieut., 1913.)
CRITCHLEY-   Lieut., Cameronians (Scottish Rifles).
Lieut.   Assistant Staff Officer to Col. Comm. Manchester District.
Invalided, 1918, ill-health, contracted on Active Service.

✠ SANDEMAN, S. R.   ...   G 01–06
Capt.   Capt., R.G.A., 2nd London Brigade.
Wounded.
Killed, May, 1915, *St. Julien, near Ypres.*

SANDERS, J. H. ...   ...   F 96–99   (Sidney Sussex Coll., Camb.)
Lieut.   Lieut., Lovat Scouts, 2nd Bn.
Lieut., M.G.C. Cavalry, 1916.

✠ SAVORY, M. J. ...   ...   I 08–12
Capt.   Capt., Duke of Wellington's W. Riding Regt.
Wounded.
Killed, Feb. 3rd, 1917, *Sailly Saillisel.*

SAWBRIDGE, B. F.   ...   A 97–02   (Univ. Coll., Oxford.)
Capt.   Lieut., London Rifle Brigade, 1917.
Capt. Officer in Charge Anti-Gas School.
Wounded (2).

SAYER, A. C.   ...   ...   B 00–05
Major, Sussex Yeomanry.
Major, R. Sussex Regt., 16th Bn., 1918.
Despatches (2).
M.C. D.S.O.

✠ SCHUSTER, C. J. C.   ...   E 11–17
2nd Lieut.   2nd Lieut., R.B., 5th, att. 1st Bn.
Killed, Aug. 10th, 1918, *La Bohème, near Robecq.*

SCHUSTER, F. V.	COLL. 98–04	
Capt.		Capt. and Adjt., Highland Cyclist Corps.
		Staff Capt., 1918.
		Despatches (2).

SCHWABE, A. G. T. ... H 10–13
Lieut.
2nd Lieut., R.F.A., 1915.
Lieut., 1917.

SCHWERDT, G. F. COLL. 05–10
Capt.
Capt. and Adjt., Hampshire Carabiniers.
Late Temp. Major, Hampshire Regt., 15th Bn.

SCLATER, A. L. ... ... G 87–89
Lieut.
(Ranching, S. Rhodesia. S. African War.)
Lieut., R.A.S.C., 1918.

SCOBELL, S. J. P. ... H 92–94
Bt. Lieut.-Col.
(Norfolk Regt. Lieut., 1900. Capt., 1906.)
Major, Norfolk Regt., 1915.
Brigade-Major, 1914–16. G.S.O., 1916.
G.S.O.$_1$, 1917.
Brevet Lieut.-Col., 1918.
Despatches (7).
D.S.O. C.M.G.

SCOONES, P. ... COLL. 87–93
Lieut.
(New Coll., Oxford. Eton College Staff.)
Lieut., R. Defence Corps, 1916.

✠ SCOTT, B. J. H. ... F 08–10
2nd Lieut.
2nd Lieut., S. Staffordshire Regt.
Despatches.
Killed, Oct. 23rd, 1914, *Pilkem, First Battle of Ypres.*

SCOTT, HON. D. ... H″91–93
Capt.
(Lieut., R. W. Fusiliers, 1901. S. African War.
Capt., R.N. Devon Yeomanry. Retired,
1901. T.F.R.)
Capt., Labour Corps, Agricultural Coy.
Lieut., Tank Corps, 1916.
Capt., Tank Corps, 1918.

SCOTT, I. B. W. ... D 08–10
Major
Lieut., R.F.A. G.S.O.$_3$.
Capt., 1918. G.S.O.$_2$.
Temp. Major, 1918. G.H.Q., Great Britain.

SCOTT, HON. M. ... H 92–94
Capt.
Capt. Assistant Military Landing Officer, 1915.
Despatches.
O.B.E.

SCOTT, HON. O. ... ... H 89–93
Lieut.
Lieut., R.A.S.C., Mechanical Transport.

SCRIVENER, P. S.   ...   K 12–15
    Lieut.
            2nd Lieut., Worcestershire Yeomanry.
            Lieut., 1917.

SEATON, LORD   ...   ...   E 69–72
    Major
            (R. Irish Rifles, 1878. Major, 1886. Kandahar.
                  S. African War.)
            Hon. Major, Gen. List.
            Assistant Military Landing Officer till 1917.

SEBASTIAN, E. G.   ...   C 06–11
    Capt.
            (Univ. Coll., Oxford.)
            2nd Lieut., E. Kent Regt., 1914.
            Lieut., 1915.
            Capt., 1917.
            D.A.A.G., 1918. A.D.C., 1919.
            D.S.O.

SEBASTIAN, G. N. B.   ...   C 97–00
    Capt.
            (St. George's Hospital.)
            Lieut., R.A.M.C., 1914.
            Capt., 1915.
            Wounded.
            Relinquished Comm., 1917.

✠ SEBASTIAN, S. R.   ...   C 00–03
    Lieut.-Col.
            (Univ. Coll., Oxford. Barrister.)
            2nd Lieut., Hampshire Regt.
            Att. Oxford and Bucks L.I., 5th Bn.
            Lieut., 1915.
            Capt. and Adjt., 1916.
            Lieut.-Col., 1917.
            Despatches (2).
            M.C.
            Died, March 27th, 1918, at Rouen, of wounds
               received at Cugny, March 23rd.

SELBY, C. W. P.   ...   G 11–15
    Lieut.
            Lieut., R. West Kent Regt., 1917.
            R.A.F.
            Prisoner of War.
            ### Exchanged Home, 1917.
            Wounded.

✠ SELBY, G. P.   ...   ...   G 04–08
    Capt.
            Capt., R.A.M.C.
            Wounded.
            Killed, Sept. 25th, 1916, Mouquet Farm, Battle
               of the Somme.

SELBY, P. R.   ...   ...   F 87–92
    Capt.
            (New Coll., Oxford. Lloyds.)
            2nd Lieut., Royal Marines.
            Capt., 1917.

SERGEANT, G. O. H. ...	G 12–15	
Lieut.		2nd Lieut., Hampshire Regt., 1916.
		Lieut., 1918.
		Wounded.
		M.C.

SERGEANT, T. W. ... G 13–18
2nd Lieut.
2nd Lieut., K.R.R.C.

SERGENT, V. L. B. COLL. 00–05
Lieut.
2nd Lieut., R.A.S.C.
Lieut., 1918.
Wounded.

✠ SEWELL, H. E. ... COLL. 88–94
Major
(New Coll., Oxford. R.A., 1900. Lieut., 1902).
Major, R.G.A.
Died in France, June 4th, 1918, *Neuville St. Vaast.*

SEYMER, V. KER ... H 80–83
Capt.
Capt. Train Conducting Officer.

SEYMOUR, C. E. ... H 96–01
(Magd. Coll., Oxford. Stock Exchange.)
Lieut., Scots Greys. 2nd Dragoons.
A.D.C.
Capt., 1918.
Despatches (2).
Chevalier Légion d'Honneur.

SEYMOUR, C. H. ... H 00–04
Capt.
2nd Lieut., Norfolk Regt.
Capt., Scots Guards, 1917.
A.D.C.
R.A., Special Reserve.
Wounded (2).
M.C.

SEYMOUR, J. W. CULME- C 91–93
Capt.
Lieut., R.N.V.R.
Att. R.A.F. Wireless operations in France.
Capt., R.A.F., Administrative Branch, 1918.

SHADWELL, L. J. ... G 75–78
Lieut.-Col.
(E. Surrey Regt., 1882. Lieut., Suffolk Regt.
Capt., 1889. D.A.A.G., India, 1895. Lancs.
Fusiliers, Major, 1904. Lieut.-Col., 1907.
Staff Officer, S. Africa, 1907–15.)
Assistant to Major-Gen. in charge of Administration, Southern Command, 1915.
Director of Labour, Southern Command, 1916.

SHADWELL, W. N. LUCAS   c 96–99   (Vice-Consul, Paris.)
    Capt.   2nd Lieut.   Interpreter.
                    Temp. Capt., Gen. List.
                    Wounded.
                    D.S.O.   Chevalier, Star of Roumania.

SHAW, R. C.   ...   ...   H 12–17
    2nd Lieut.   2nd Lieut., Hampshire Regt.

SHEDDEN, REV. R. G.   ...   I 96–01
    C.F.   Chaplain to Forces, R. Fusiliers, 1st Bn.

SHEEPSHANKS, T. H.   COLL. 08–13
    Capt.   Lieut., Norfolk Regt.
                    Capt., Suffolk Regt., 11th Bn., 1915.

✠ SHEEPSHANKS, W.   COLL. 04–09
    2nd Lieut.   2nd Lieut., K.R.R.C., 6th, att. 2nd Bn.
                    Killed, July 10th, 1917, *Nieuport.*

SHELLEY, J. F. ...   ...   D 98–03
    Capt.   Capt., R. 1st Devon Yeomanry.

SHENNAN, K. G. W.   ...   D 07–12
    Lieut.   2nd Lieut., R. Horse Guards, 1915.
                    Lieut., 1917.
                    Guards M.G.C.
                    Relinquished Commission, 1919.

SHEPHARD, J. W.   ...   H 01–05   (New Coll., Oxford.   Barrister.)
    Capt.   Capt., R.A.S.C., 1916.
                    Relinquished Commission, 1919, ill-health.
                    Despatches.
                    M.C.   Croix de Guerre.

SHERBROOKE, C. A.   ...   G 96–00
    Lieut.   Lieut., Coldstream Guards.

SHERINGHAM, C. J. DE B.   E 97–02   (Cameron Highlanders, of Canada.)
    Lieut.-Col.   Capt., Cameron Highlanders.
                    A.D.C.   Brigade-Major, 1917.
                    Temp. Lieut.-Col., Gen. List.
                    Somerset L.I., 8th Bn.
                    Wounded.   *Despatches* (3).
                    M.C.   D.S.O.

SHEWAN, R. E.   COLL. 80–85   (Lieut., R.E., 1885.   Major, 1903.)
    TOMLIN MONEY-   Major, R.A., 1st Welsh Brigade.
    Major   1917, Dep. Assistant Director of Railways.
                    C.B.E.

SHIRLEY, R. D. ...   ... A 03–06
   Lieut.   Lieut., R.B.
                                  Training Reserve.

SHIRLEY, S. R. ...   ... A 98–02   (I.A., 1905.)
   Capt.   Capt., 54th Sikhs, I.A., 1914.
                                  Brigade-Major, 1915.
                                  G.S.O.$_2$, 1917.
                                  Despatches.
                                  M.C.

SHONE, T. A.   ...   ... K 08–12
   Capt.   Capt., Hampshire Regt., 1915.
                                  Att. H.Q., 41st Division.
                                  Wounded.   *Despatches.*

SHORT, H. G. R. BURGES   A 88–92   (Somerset L.I., 1898. Capt., 1906. S. African
   Major   War.)
                                  Major, Somerset L.I., 1915.
                                  Temp. Lieut.-Col., D.C.L.I., 7th Bn., 1916.
                                  Wounded, and Prisoner of War, 1918.
                                  Repatriated, 1919.
                                  Despatches.
                                  D.S.O.

✠ SHORT, W. A.   ...   ... E 84–88   (R.F.A., 1891. Capt., 1900.)
   Lieut.-Col.   Lieut.-Col., R.F.A.
                                  Despatches (3).
                                  C.M.G.
                                  Killed, June 21st, 1917, *Armentières.*

SHUTTLEWORTH, C. E.   D 87–90   (Capt., Durham L.I. Sergt., Ceylon M.I.
   Capt.   S. African War.)
                                  Capt., R.A.S.C., 1914.

SHUTTLEWORTH, P. P. ...   D 87–90   (Univ. Coll., Oxford. With Lord Strathcona's
   Lieut.   Horse, S. African War.)
                                  Lieut., S. Nottinghamshire Hussars.
                                  Retired, 1918.

SICH, G. W.   ...   ... H 11–17
   2nd Lieut.   2nd Lieut., Grenadier Guards.
                                  Wounded.

SICH, J. W.   ...   ... H 14–15
                                  Cadet, Household Brigade O.C.B.
                                  2nd Lieut., Grenadier Guards, S.R.

✠ SIDGWICK, A. H.   COLL. 95–01   (Ball. Coll., Oxford. Fellow of Univ. Coll.)
   Capt.   Capt. and Adjt., R.G.A.
                                  Killed, Sept. 16th, 1917, *near Ypres.*

189

SILVER, S. W. H.   ... B 98–00   (Suffolk Regt., 1905. Served with K.A.R.,
    Capt.   1909–14.)
                                            Capt., Suffolk Regt., 1914.
                                            R.T.O., 1918.

✠ SIMONDS, C. H.   ... A 10–14
    Lieut.   2nd Lieut., R.E.
                                            Lieut., 1917.
                                            Wounded.   *Despatches.*
                                            M.C. Croix de Guerre. Chevalier, La Couronne.
                                          Died of Wounds, April 29th, 1918, *near Ypres.*

SIMONDS, G. T.   COLL 94–00   (New Coll., Oxford.)
    Lieut.   Lieut., Berkshire Regt.
                                            Brigade M.G. Officer.
                                            Relinquished Commission.

✠ SIMONDS, J. DE L.   COLL. 97–01   (R.G.A., 1903.)
    Major   Major, R.G.A.
                                              R.A.F., 1st Wing.
                                            D.S.O.
                                            Killed, April 22nd, 1917, *Mazingarbe.*

SIMONDS, R. H.   ... A 66–71   (Ch. Ch., Oxford. Barrister.)
    Col.   Col. Secretary Dorset T.F. Association.
                                            Despatches.
                                            O.B.E.

SIMPSON, A. A. LE M.   COLL. 11–16
    Lieut.   2nd Lieut., K.R.R.C., 6th Bn. 1917.
                                            Lieut., 1918.

SIMPSON, P. O. ...   COLL. 13–17
    2nd Lieut.   2nd Lieut., R.F.A., 1918.

SINGER, C. M. ...   COLL. 13–18
                                            Cadet, R.E.

✠ SINGLE, F. A. ...   ... A 01–06
    Capt.   Capt., Acting Major, 2nd Dragoon Guards.
                                            Wounded.
                                            M.C.
                                            Killed, March 30th, 1918, *Le Hamel, near
                                                  Amiens.*

SINGLE, J.   ...   COLL. 13–18
                                            Cadet, R.F.A.

✠ SKAIFE, A. F. ...   ... B 96–01   (Middlesex Regt., 1902. Lieut., 1904.)
    Capt.   Capt., Middlesex Regt., 1st Bn.
                                            Killed, Nov. 1st, 1914, *La Boutillerie, near
                                                Armentières.*

SKAIFE, E. O. ... ... B 97–02   (R. Welsh Fusiliers, 1903.)
Major
     Capt., R. Welsh Fusiliers, 1912.
     Prisoner of War.
     Interned in Holland, 1918.
     Repatriated, 1918.
     Major, G.S.O.$_1$, 1918.
     Wounded.   *Despatches* (2).

SKENE, P. G. M. ... D 94–95   (Ch. Ch., Oxford.   Black Watch, 1902.
Lieut.-Col.
        Capt., 1914.)
     Capt., Black Watch (Royal Highlanders), 1914.
     Major, 1917.
     Lieut.-Col.
     Ministry of Munitions, G.S.O.$_1$, 1918.
     Wounded (2).   *Despatches.*
     O.B.E.   Croix de Guerre.

SKINNER, W. M. ROSS ... K 13–17
2nd Lieut.   2nd Lieut., R.B., 1919.

SLADE, J. G., M.D. ...   (Clare Coll., Cambridge.   St. Bartholomew's
        Hospital.)
Capt.   Capt., R.A.M.C.

SLADEN, J. M. ... COLL. 09–15
Capt.   2nd Lieut., K.R.R.C., 2nd Bn., 1915.
     Lieut., 1917.
     Capt., 1919.
     Wounded.

SLEE, F. E. ... ... I 72–78   (New Coll., Oxford.   Barrister.)
Lieut.   Sub-Lieut., R.N.V.R., 1915.
     Lieut., R.G.A., 1916.
     1st A.A. Mobile Brigade, 1916.

SLEE, P. H. ... ... I 74–78   (R.F.A., 1881. Major, 1899. S. African War.
Brevet Col.
        Brevet Lieut.-Col., 1907.   Retired, 1912.)
     Brevet Col., R.F.A.
     Despatches (2).
     C.M.G.

SLEE, R. A. ... ... I 78–81   (Capt., Middlesex Regt.   S. African War.
Major
        Retired, 1914.)
     Major, Middlesex Regt., Sp. Res. Bn.
     Despatches.

SLINGSBY, F. H. COLL. 08–13
Lieut.   Lieut., S. Staffordshire Regt.
     M.G.C. Infantry till February, 1918.

191

SMITH, A. C. ... ... I 92–97 (Ch. Ch., Oxford. Barrister.)
    Capt.   Lieut., R.F.A.
                                        Capt., 1916.
                                        Despatches (3).
                                        M.C.

SMITH, A. C. H. PARKER... E 98–00 (King's Coll., Camb.)
    Capt.   Capt., Arg. and Suth. Highlanders, 1915.
                                        1st Class Instructor, Command Depot, 1918.

SMITH, A. C. S., M.D. ... D 03–08
    Lieut.   Lieut., R.A.M.C.
                                          2nd Lieut., R.F.A.
                                        Lieut., Staff Lieut., 1918.
                                        Despatches (2).
                                        M.C.

✠ SMITH, A. G. ... COLL. 04–09
    Capt.   Capt., N. Lancashire Regt.
                                          Wounded, and Prisoner of War.
                                        M.C.
                                        Died of wounds April 18th, 1918, *Givenchy*.

SMITH, D. C. STEWART ... G 08–12
    Lieut.   2nd Lieut., Royal Fusiliers, 1914.
                                          Lieut., Royal Highlanders, 1915.
                                        Prisoner of War, 1918.
                                        Wounded.
                                        Repatriated Dec., 1918.

✠ SMITH, E. C. ... ... D 97–03 (R. Fusiliers, 1905.)
    Lieut.   Lieut., Royal Fusiliers.
                                          Wounded.
                                      Killed Aug. 23rd, 1914, *Nemy, near Mons*.

SMITH, G. E., C.M.G. ... I 82–86 (R.E., 1888. Capt., 1899. S. African War.)
    Brig.-Gen.   Lieut.-Col., R.E., 1915, H.Q. Staff.
                                        Brig.-General, Assistant Director of Works,
                                            1917.
                                        Despatches (3).
                                        D.S.O.

SMITH, G. F. DARWALL, A 89–92 (New Coll., Oxford. St. George's, Hospital.)
   M.B.   Surgeon, County of London War Hospital.

SMITH, G. H. G. COLL. 01–08
    Major   Major, R.E.
                                          D.A.D.P.S., Batum.
                                        M.C.

SMITH, REV. G. VERNON   D 93–98
C.F.
Chaplain to Forces.
Officier, Greek Order of the Redeemer.
M.C.

✠ SMITH, G. W.   ...   COLL. 94–99
Capt.
Capt., R.B.
Killed July 10th, 1916, *near Pozieres.*

SMITH, L. P. DENRACHE   C 07–12
2nd Lieut.
2nd Lieut., (Black Watch (Royal Highlanders.)
Lieut., 1918.
Wounded.

✠ SMITH, J. H.   ...   COLL. 89–95
HATTERSLEY-
Lce.-Cpl.
(Lincoln Coll., Oxford.)
Lce.-Cpl., Norfolk Regt.
Died Oct. 7th, 1915, *of wounds received Battle
of Loos,* Sept. 25th.

SMITH, N. C.   ...   COLL. 83–90
2nd Lieut.
(New Coll. Winchester Coll. Headmaster
Sherborne.)
2nd Lieut., Dorset Vol. Regt.
Retired, 1917.

✠ SMITH, P.   ...   ...   H 08–12
Lieut.
Lieut., R.E.
Att. R.A.F.
Despatches.
Killed April 28th, 1917, *Avesnes-le-Comte.*

SMITH, T. C.   ...   ...   E 92–95
Capt.
(Exeter Coll., Oxford.)
Capt., Bucks Yeomanry.
2nd Mounted Division, Egypt.
Assistant Embarkation Staff Officer.

SMITH, T. P. C.   ...   B 85–88
Lieut.-Col.
(W. Kent Regt., 1892. Capt., 1902. Major, 1909.
Lieut.-Col., R.W. Kent Regt. Retired, 1911.)
Assistant Director Ordnance Service, 1914.

✠ SMITH, V. HERBERT   ...   B 05–13
2nd Lieut.
2nd Lieut., R.B.
Killed March 21st, 1915, *Neuve Chapelle, near
Armentières.*

✠ SMITH, W. A.   ...   ...   G 99–04
2nd Lieut.
2nd Lieut., Gloucestershire Hussars.
Killed April 26th, 1916, *Katia, Sinai Peninsula.*

✠ SMITH, W. B. PARKER   E 99–04
Lieut.
(King's Coll., Camb.)
Lieut., Scottish Horse.
Died Sept. 11th, 1914, *at Malta, of wounds
received Suvla Bay,* Sept 2nd.

✠ SMITHERS, E. H. K. ... K 09–14
　　Lieut.　　　　　　　　　　　Lieut., Manchester Regt.
　　　　　　　　　　　　　　　　Wounded
　　　　　　　　　　　　　　　　Killed July 10th, 1916, *Trône Wood.*

SMYTH, G. M. ...　...　C 06–10
　　Capt.　　　　　　　　　　　Capt., N. Lancashire Regt.
　　　　　　　　　　　　　　　　R.A.F., Capt., A.
　　　　　　　　　　　　　　　　Wounded.

SNOW, E. G. ...　...　H 76–78　(N. Staffs Regt., 1882. Major, 1899. Lieut.-Col.,
　　Lieut.-Col.　　　　　　　　　　Devon Regt., 1910.　Retired, 1912.)
　　　　　　　　　　　　　　　　Lieut.-Col., Devonshire Regt.
　　　　　　　　　　　　　　　　Resigned Command, 1915.　Staff Lieut.
　　　　　　　　　　　　　　　　Censor's Office, 1916.

SNOW, G. R. S. ...　COLL. 10–15
　　Lieut.　　　　　　　　　　　2nd Lieut., R.F.A., 1916.
　　　　　　　　　　　　　　　　Lieut., 1918.

SNOW, R. M. ...　...　C 80–82　(Devon Regt., Militia, 1887.　Capt., 1899.
　　Capt.　　　　　　　　　　　　Retired, 1901.)
　　　　　　　　　　　　　　　　Capt., Devonshire Regt., 1914.

SOAMES, C. T. ...　...　A 08–12
　　Capt.　　　　　　　　　　　2nd Lieut., K.A.R.
　　　　　　　　　　　　　　　　Capt., 1918.
　　　　　　　　　　　　　　　　Relinquished Commission, 1919.
　　　　　　　　　　　　　　　　Despatches.

SOLLY, R. V. ...　...　C 79–81
　　Capt.　　　　　　　　　　　Capt., R.A.M.C., 4th Southern.

SOLOMON, P. H. ...　I 08–11
　　Capt.　　　　　　　　　　　Lieut., R.F.A.
　　　　　　　　　　　　　　　　Capt., 1917.
　　　　　　　　　　　　　　　　Acting Major, 1918.
　　　　　　　　　　　　　　　　Wounded.　　　*Despatches.*

SOMERVILLE, D. H. S. ...　I 03–08　(S. Wales Borderers, 1909.)
　　Capt.　　　　　　　　　　　Capt., S. Wales Borderers, 1915.
　　　　　　　　　　　　　　　　Prisoner of War, May, 1918.
　　　　　　　　　　　　　　　　Repatriated, Dec., 1918.
　　　　　　　　　　　　　　　　Wounded.　　　*Despatches.*
　　　　　　　　　　　　　　　　M.C. and Bar.

SOMERVILLE, J. A. C. ...　G 07–11　(I.A., 1913.)
　　MAY-　　　　　　　　　　　Lieut., 11th Bengal Lancers, I.A.
　　　　Capt.　　　　　　　　　Capt., 1917.

SOWERBY, R. T. R. ...　H 12–17
　　Sub-Lieut.　　　　　　　　Sub-Lieut., R.N.V.R.

SPARROW, A. A.   ... A 05–10   (R. Berks Regt., 1911.)
    HANBURY-   Capt., R. Berkshire Regt., 1915.
        Lieut -Col.   Acting Lieut.-Col., 1916.   G.S.O.$_3$.
                                Lieut.-Col., London Regt., 3rd Bn., 1917.
                                Lieut.-Col., Wiltshire Regt., 4th Bn., 1919.
                                Wounded (3).   *Despatches* (3).
                                M.C.   D.S.O. and Bar.

✠ SPENCE, C. B. ...   ... F 01–06
        Lieut.   Lieut., R.F.A.
                                R.A.F.
                                Despatches.
                                Killed, May 9th, 1915, *near Bethune.*

✠ SPENCER, G.   ...   ... D 00–03
        Lieut.   Lieut., London Regt., 20th Bn.
                                Att. R.B.
                                Died of Wounds, Dec. 4th, 1917, *Tincourt.*

SPENDER, R. E. S.   ... E 91–96   (New Coll., Oxford.)
        Lieut.   Capt., R. Irish Rifles, 17th Bn.
                                Lieut., R.A.S.C., 1918.

SPENDER, W. B.   ... E 89–93   (R.G.A., 1897.   Capt., 1902.   Retired, 1913.)
    Bt. Lieut.-Col.   Brevet Lieut.-Col., R.G.A., 1916.
                                G.S.O.$_1$, 36th (Ulster) Division.
                                Despatches (3).
                                M.C.   D.S.O.

SPOTTISWOODE, A.   ... C 05–10
        Capt.   Capt., Middlesex Regt., 16th Bn., 1915.
                                Att. R. Fusiliers, 20th Bn.
                                M.C. and Bar.

✠ SPOTTISWOODE, J.   ... G 88–92   (K.R.R.C., 1894.   Printer.)
        Capt.   Capt., K.R.R.C., 2nd Bn.
                                Killed, Oct. 31st, 1914, *Gheluvelt, First Battle of
                                    Ypres.*

SPRAGVE, W. N.   ... A 92–94
        Capt.   Capt., No. 5 Advanced Remount Depot, 1915.

SPRANGER, F. J.   ... B 87–91   (Magd. Coll., Oxford.   Barrister.)
        Major   Major, R.A. Ordnance Dept.
                                Dep. Assistant Director Ordnance Dept.
                                O.B.E.

✠ SPROAT, G. M. ...   COLL. 06–12
        Lieut.   Lieut., Manchester Regt.
                                Killed, July 1st, 1915, *Montauban.*

195

✠ Sprot, J. W. L. ... D 99–02 (Black Watch, 1906.)
Capt., Black Watch (Royal Highlanders.)
Wounded.
Missing, believed killed, Nov. 11*th*, 1914.

Spurling, Rev. H. W. COLL. 87–92

Pte., Hampshire Regt.

✠ Stable, L. L. ... ... B 99–04
Capt.
Lieut., R. Welsh Fusiliers.
Capt., 1914.
Killed, Oct. 26th, 1914, *between Fromelles and Armentières.*

Stable, R. H. ... ... A 07–11 (I.A., 1914.)
Major
Capt., 122nd Rajput Infantry, I.A., 1917.
Acting Major, 1917.
Wounded (2).
D.S.O.

Stable, W. N. ... ... B 01–07
Capt.
Capt., Montgomeryshire Yeomanry.
Posted to R. Welsh Fusiliers, 25th Bn., till 1919.
Despatches (2).   *Despatches.*
M.C.

Stables, F. H. A. ... D 13–15
2nd Lieut.
2nd Lieut., 115th Gurkha Rifles, I.A., 1918.

✠ Stables, J. Howard ... D 08–13
Lieut.
Pte., Hampshire Regt., 6th Bn., 1914.
Lieut., 1/5th, att. 1/8th, Gurkha Rifles, I.A.
Wounded.
Died of Wounds, Feb., 1917, *Sanna-i-yat.*

✠ Stack, E. H. B. ... C 99–02 (I.A., 1905.)
Capt.
Capt., 8th Gurkha Rifles.
Killed, Oct. 29th–30th, 1914, *Festubert.*

Stainer, J. F. R. COLL. 79–85 (Magd. Coll., Oxford. Barrister.)
2nd Lieut.
2nd Lieut., E. Surrey Regt.
Relinqu'shed Commission.

Stainton, J. A. COLL. 01–07
Capt.
Capt. and Adjt., Arg. and Suth. Highlanders, 1916.
Wounded.

Stainton, W. A. ... C 10–11
Lieut.
Lieut., Grenadier Guards.
Relinquished Commission.

196

STANSFELD, T. W., D.S.O.   E 91–95   (Yorkshire Regt., 1897.   Capt., R. Warwickshire
    Brig.-Gen.   Regt., 1902.   S. African War.)
                                        Major, Yorkshire Regt., 1914.
                                        Brevet Lieut.-Col., 1916.   Brevet Col., 1919.
                                        Brigadier-General, 1917.
                                        Wounded.   Despatches (5).
                                        C.M.G.   Croix de Guerre.   Officier Légion
                                            d'Honneur.

STEAD, A. E. W.   ...   F 09–10
    2nd Lieut.   2nd Lieut., W. Yorkshire Regt.
                                        Relinquished Commission.

STEER, REV. C.   ...   C 94–99
    C.F.   R.A.M.C., with S. African Infantry.
                                        Capt. and Chaplain to Forces.   S. African F.F.
                                            to R.F.A.
                                        Prisoner of War, 1918, France.
                                        Despatches.
                                        M.C.
                                        Repatriated, Nov., 1918.

STEPHENS, E. E. BYNG-   I 90–96   (With Imperial Yeomanry, S. African War.)
    Capt.   Capt.   A.D.C. to General Altham, 1914.
                                        Unattached List, T.F.
                                        Winchester Coll., O.T.C.

STEPHENS, F. G. BYNG-   H 99–05
    Capt.   Capt., R.B., 1915.
                                        A.D.C., H.Q. 5th Division.

STEPHENS, G. E. BYNG-   I 88–94   (R.B., 1897.   Capt., 1902.   S. African War.
    Major   Retired, 1914.)
                                        Major, R.B.   Reserve of Officers, 1914.
                                        G.S.O.   D.A.A.G.
                                        District Remount Officer, 1918.
                                        Despatches.
                                        Italian Medal.

STEPHENS, G. R.   ...   A 87–89   (Lancaster Regt., 1895.   Capt., 1900.   S. African
    Major   War.   Major, 1909.   Retired, 1911.)
                                        Lieut., R.N.V.R.   Motor Boats till 1915.
                                        Draft Conducting Officer till 1919.

STEPHENS, SIR R. BYNG-   C 82–86   (R.B., 1890.   Capt., 1897.   Major, 1905.)
    Lieut.-Gen.   Lieut.-Col., R.B., 1914.
                                        Temp. Brigadier-General, 1915.
                                        Major-General, 5th Infantry Division, 1917.
                                        Lieut.-General, Xth Corps, 1918.
                                        Despatches (6).
                                        K.C.B.   C.M.G.   C.B.   Croix de Guerre.   Comm.
                                            SS. Maurizio e Lazzaro.   Comm. Légion
                                            d'Honneur.

197

| STEPHENSON, J. E. | COLL. 07–12 | |
| Capt. | | Capt., Somerset L.I. |

STEVENS, A. L. B. ... K 07–12
    Capt.

Lieut., R. West Surrey Regt.
Att. Munster Fusiliers.
Capt., 1918.
Wounded (2).   *Despatches.*

STEVENS, F. G.   COLL. 92–97
    2nd Lieut.

(New Coll., Oxford. Colonial Office.)
2nd Lieut., R.G.A.
Acting Major, 1918.
Wounded.

STEVENS, J. A. R.   ... K 06–10
    WESTON
    Capt.

Lieut., Dorset Regt.
Capt., 1918.
Staff Lieut.
Wounded.

STEVENS, L. M. ...   ... B 93–98
    Bt. Lieut.-Col.

(Worcester Regt., 1899. S. African War. Capt.,
    1903.)
Major, Worcestershire Regt.
Brevet Lieut.-Col., Manchester Regt., 23rd Bn.,
    1916; Lancs. Fusiliers, 18th Bn.
Temp. Brigadier-General, 1918.
Comm. Sch. of Musketry.
Despatches (3).
D.S.O.

STEVENS, R. A. MOORE– ... H 68–73
    Major

(Ch. Ch., Oxford. Capt., 2nd Devon Militia,
    1883. Lieut.-Col., Devonshire Regt., 3rd
    Bn. Retired, 1904.)
Major. Draft Conducting Officer.

STEVENS, T. E. A.   ... H 08–14
    Capt.

2nd Lieut., Berkshire Yeomanry.
Lieut., 1916.
Capt., 1918.

STEWARD, N. O. W.   COLL. 13–18

Cadet, R.G.A.

✠ STEWART, J. A. L.   ... I 06–11
    Lieut.

2nd Lieut., R.B., 1st Bn.
Lieut., 1915.
Killed, May 13th, 1915, *near Ypres.*

STEWART, W. E. L.,   ... I 87–90
    D.S.O.
    Major

(Welsh Regt., 1895. Capt., 1902. S. African
    War.)
Major, Pembrokeshire Yeomanry.
Relinquished Commission.

STILL, J. ... ... A 93–97   (Tea Planting, Ceylon.)
     Lieut.   Lieut., E. Yorkshire Regt., Pioneer Bn.
     Prisoner of War, Dardanelles, 1915, Kara Hissar
         Camp.
     Wounded.
     Repatriated, 1918.

STILLMAN, R. C. B.   COLL. 04–10   (R.F.A., 1911.)
     Capt.   Capt., R.F.A., 1916.

STILWELL, J. G.   ... D 08–13
     Capt.   Capt., Hampshire Regt.
     Prisoner of War, 1916, Relief of Kut, Kara
         Hissar Camp.
     Wounded.
     Repatriated, 1918.

STISTED. J. L. H.   ... B 10–13
     Postal Censorship Dept., War Office.

STOBART, ST. C. E. M.   G 99–03
     Capt.   Lieut., Gen. List. W.A.F.F.
     Capt., Nigeria Regt.
     G.S.O.$_3$.
     Despatches (2).
     Relinquished Commission, 1918.

STOKES, H. F. SCOTT   COLL. 09–14
     Lieut.   Lieut., Hampshire Regt., 1917.
     M.C.

STONE, W. G. ...   ... G 08–11
     Capt.   2nd Lieut., N. Lancashire Regt., 1914.
     Capt., 1917.
     Serving with K.A.R.
     Wounded.

STOPFORD, C. M.   ... B 88–91
     Capt.   Capt., Queen's Westminster Rifles.
     Staff Capt., London District.

STOPFORD, W. J.   ... I 10–14
     Lieut.   2nd Lieut., R.F.A., 1915.
     Lieut., 1917.
     Acting Capt. and Adjt.
     M.C.

STOW, J. L. ...   COLL. 93–98   (Exeter Coll., Oxford. Schoolmaster.)
     Lieut.   Lieut., K.R.R.C.
     Wounded.
     A.D.C., 1918.
     Relinquished Commission, 1919.

STOW, G. P. PHILIPSON- C 12–1
 2nd Lieut.   2nd Lieut., R.G.A.

STOW, H. M. PHILIPSON- F 94–99
                                         Cpl., R.A.S.C.
                                         Ministry of Munitions.

STOW, R. M. P.   ... I 07–11
 PHILIPSON-   Lieut., R. Lancaster Regt., 1917.

✠ STRANGWAYS, T. S. FOX- I 76–79   (R. Irish Rifles, 1884.   Soudan.   S. African
 Major   War.   Major, 1904.)
                                         Major, R. Irish Rifles.
                                         Comm. Depot.
                                         Died in England, March, 1917.

STRANGWAYS, V FOX- ... A 12–16
 Lieut.   2nd Lieut., unattached I.A., 1917.
                                         Lieut., 1918.
                                         Despatches.

✠ STRAUSS, B. L. ...   ... D 06–11
                                         Major, E. Kent Regt.
                                         Killed Dec. 1st, 1917, *Fins.*
                                         M.C.

STRUTT, E. J.   ...   ... A 97–01
 Capt.   Capt. and Adjt., Essex Regt.

STRUTT, G. M.   ...   ... A 94–98   (Oxford Yeomanry.   S. African War.)
 Capt.   Lieut., Essex Yeomanry.
                                         Capt., 1918.

STRUTT, G. ST. J.   ... A 02–07
 Capt.   Capt., Essex Regt.
                                         Att. Gloucestershire Regt.
                                         Wounded.
                                         Relinquished Commission, 1919.

✠ STRUTT, R. N. ...   ... A 99–04   (Trin. Coll., Oxford.)
 2nd Lieut.   2nd Lieut., Royal Scots.
                                         Wounded and Missing Sept., 1915.
                                         Died in German Hospital, Wervicq, Oct.15th, 1915.

STUART, A. MOODY-   ... C 13–17
 2nd Lieut.   2nd Lieut., R.F.A., 1918.

STUDD, B. C.   ...   ... A 06–10
 Sergt.   Sergt., Calcutta Light Horse.

STUDD, E.   ...   ... A 00–05
 2nd Lieut.   Capt., Calcutta Light Horse.
                                         Garrison Q.M., Fort William.
                                         2nd L'eut., I.A.

200

✠ STUDD, Rev. L. F. ... A 04–09
    Capt.
          Capt., London Regt., 12th Bn.
          Killed Feb. 14th, 1915, *near Ypres.*

✠ STURGES, E. E. ... H 02–03
    Pte.
          Private, K.O.Y.L.I.
          Killed Sept. 25th, 1916, *Guendecourt.*

STURT, G. C. N. ... H 97–01
    Capt.
          (Ch. Ch., Oxford.)
          Capt., Worcestershire Regt., 1916.
          Wounded.

✠ SUFFOLK AND BERKSHIRE, H 91–94
    EARL OF
    Major
          Major, R.F.A.
          Despatches.
          Killed May 22nd, 1917, *Mesopotamia.*

SUMNER, B. H. ... COLL. 07–13
    Capt.
          Lieut., K.R.R.C.
          Wounded (2).
          Capt., 1917, employed at War Office.

SUMNER, C. R. B. ... E 09–13
    Pte.
          Private, Hampshire Regt.

✠ SUTTHERY, D. M. ... F 09–14
    Lieut.
          2nd Lieut., Arg. and Suth. Highlanders.
          Lieut., 1916.
          Wounded (3).
          Died May 19th, 1917, *in London of wounds
             received* April 28th.

SUTTON, G. F. S. ... K 05–08
    2nd Lieut.
          Private, Queen's Westminster Rifles.
          2nd Lieut., K.R.R.C, 5th Bn., 1918.
          Wounded (2).
          M.C.

SWAINSON, E. A. ... G 82–86
    Formerly SMITH
    Capt.
          Capt., R.A.M.C.

SYLVESTER, C. K. ... D 98–03
    Capt.
          Capt., R.A.M.C.

✠ SYNGE, F. P. H. ... A 02–07
    Capt.
          Acting Capt., Irish Guards.
          Killed July 29th, 1917, *Elverdinghe.*
          Wounded (2).   *Despatches.*
          M.C.

TALBOT, Rev. E. K.　　　　E 91–96　(Ch. Ch., Oxford.　Mirfield.)
　C.F.　　　　　　　　　　　　　　Chaplain to Forces.
　　　　　　　　　　　　　　　　Acting Senior Chaplain, 1918.
　　　　　　　　　　　　　　　　M.C.

✠ TALBOT, G. W. L.　...　H 04–10　(Ch. Ch., Oxford.)
　Lieut.　　　　　　　　　　　Lieut., R.B.
　　　　　　　　　　　　　　　　Killed July 30th, 1915, *Zouave Wood, near
　　　　　　　　　　　　　　　　　Hooge.*

TAMWORTH, VISCOUNT　...　D 07–12
　　　　　　　　　　　　　　　　British Red Cross Society.

TAPP, A. G.　...　　...　C 10–13
　Capt.　　　　　　　　　　　Capt., R.F.A.
　　　　　　　　　　　　　　　　Staff Capt.
　　　　　　　　　　　　　　　　M.C., Croix de Guerre, O.B.E.

TATE, G. A.　...　　...　H 02–04
　Sub-Lieut.　　　　　　　　Sub-Lieut., R.N.V.R.
　　　　　　　　　　　　　　　　Relinquished Commission, 1916.

TATE, G. V.　...　　...　H 03–09
　Capt.　　　　　　　　　　　Lieut., Middlesex Regt.
　　　　　　　　　　　　　　　　Capt., 1917.
　　　　　　　　　　　　　　　　M.C.

✠ TATE, W. L.　...　　...　D 04–05
　　　　　　　　　　　　　　　　Lieut., Royal Fusiliers.
　　　　　　　　　　　　　　　　Wounded.
　　　　　　　　　　　　　　　　Killed March 13th, 1915, *near St. Eloi.*

✠ TATHAM, J. S.　...　　...　E 03–07
　2nd Lieut.　　　　　　　　2nd Lieut., K.R.R.C.
　　　　　　　　　　　　　　　　Att. R. Lancaster Regt., 6th Bn.
　　　　　　　　　　　　　　　　Wounded.
　　　　　　　　　　　　　　　　Killed Feb. 9th, 1917, *Mesopotamia, Tigris Line.*

TATHAM, P. R.　...　　...　K 12–16
　　　　　　　　　　　　　　　　2nd Lieut., I.A., 23rd Cavalry.

TATHAM, R. P.　...　　...　E 98–01　(Solicitor.)
　2nd Lieut.　　　　　　　　2nd Lieut., R.A.S.C., 1917.

TAVERNER, E. S.　...　...　K 07–11
　Lieut.　　　　　　　　　　　Lieut., Warwickshire Regt., 1917.
　　　　　　　　　　　　　　　　Att. Oxf. and Bucks L.I., 8th Bn.

TAVERNER, L. M.　　...　F 80–84
　Capt.　　　　　　　　　　　Capt., N.Z. Territorial Force.

✠ TAYLER, J. G.　...　COLL. 06–11
　2nd Lieut.　　　　　　　　2nd Lieut., Leicestershire Regt.
　　　　　　　　　　　　　　　　Killed May 16th, 1915, *Richebourg L'Avoué.*

TAYLOR, C. M. ... A 99–04
Capt.   Capt. and Adjt., E. Africa Mounted Rifles.

TAYLOR, E. M. ... COLL. 87–91   (21st Hussars, 1893. Lieut., I.A., 1895. Capt.,
Lieut.-Col.   1902.)
                                Lieut.-Col., 22nd Sam Browne's Cavalry, 1914.
                                G.S.O.₁, 1916, A.Q.M.G.

✠ TAYLOR, H. H. ... ... E 89
                                Capt., Chinese Labour Bn.

TEALE, Rev. K. W. P., E 90–   (Emmanuel Coll., Camb.)
C.F.   Chaplain to Forces, 1917.
                                Relinquished Commission, 1918.

TEALE, M. A. ... ... E 81–85
Lieut.   Lieut., R.A.M.C.
                                Relinquished Commission, 1918.

TEALE, T. P., F.R.S. COMM. 44–49
                                Lieut.-Col., R.A.M.C., 2nd Northern General
                                Hospital.

TEESDALE, H. ... ... G 99–03   (Oriel Coll., Oxford.)
Lieut.   2nd Lieut., Inns of Court O.T.C.
                                Lieut., 1918.
                                R.A.F., Lieut., T.

TEESDALE, J. H. ... D 85–91   (Solicitor at Shanghai.)
Capt.   Acting Capt., Chinese Labour Corps.

TEESDALE, K. J. M. ... G 84–90   (Magd. Coll., Oxford.)
                                British Red Cross with Croix Rouge Française.
                                Ministry of National Service.

✠ TENNANT, Hon. E. W. F 11–14
Lieut.   Lieut., Grenadier Guards.
                                Killed Sept. 22nd, 1915, *Guillemont.*

✠ TENNANT, G. C. S. ... K 11–16
2nd Lieut.   2nd Lieut., Welsh Guards.
                                Killed Sept. 3rd, 1917, *Langemarck, 3rd Battle
                                of Ypres.*

TERRY, W. E. C. ... I 01–01   (Oxf. and Bucks L.I., 1917.)
Major   Capt., Oxf. and Bucks L.I., 1915
                                Staff Capt., 1914.
                                G.S.O.₃, 1915.
                                Temp. Major, D.A.Q.M.G., 1918.
                                Wounded.

203

TETLEY, F. C. ...   ... K 11–15
    Lieut.

        Lieut., R.F.A., 1917.
        Wounded.
        R.G.A. Anti-Aircraft.

THACKWELL, O. M. R. COLL. 74–78
    Brig.-Gen.

        (R.E., 1880.   Major, 1899.   Tirah Exp.   Col.,
           1910.)
        Brig.-General.
        7th (Meerut) Divisional Area.
        Retired, 1917.

THESIGER, Hon. E. R.... B 87–89
    Lieut.-Col.

        (Major, Surrey Yeomanry, 1904.   S. African
           War.)
        Capt., R. Horse Guards.
        Staff Capt.
        Acting Lieut.-Col., R. West Surrey Regt.
        Lieut.-Col., R. West Kent Regt. 10th Bn.,
           1918.
        Wounded (2).   *Despatches* (2).
        D.S.O.

✠ THESIGER, Hon. F. I. ... G 10–14

        2nd Lieut., R.F.A.
        Wounded.   *Despatches* (2).
        Killed May, 1917, *near Tekrit, Mesopotamia.*

THESIGER, Hon. P. M. ... B 83–87
    Capt.

        (Solicitor.)
        Lieut., W. Kent Mounted Rifles, 1914–1915.
        R.A.F., T., till 1918, Egypt.
        Capt., E. Kent Yeomanry, 1918, France.
        Relinquished Commission, 1919.
        Despatches.

✠ THICKNESSE, F. W.   COLL. 99–04
    Major

        (R.G.A., 1906.   Hong Kong, 1907–1915.)
        Major, R.G.A.
        Comm. 122nd Heavy Battery, 1915–1917.
        Despatches (2).
        D.S.O.
        Killed Oct. 19th, 1917, *near Zonnebeke.*

✠ THOMAS, H. V. F.   ... I 11–15
    Capt.

        2nd Lieut., Royal Scots, 3rd Bn.
        Lieut., 1917.
        Acting Capt., 11th Bn., 1918.
        Wounded.
        Killed, Oct. 22nd, 1918, *Vichte, in Flanders.*
        M.C.

✠ Thomas, J. G. ...   COLL. 07–12   (Univ. Coll., Oxford.)
      Brandon-   2nd Lieut., Inniskilling Fusiliers.
        2nd Lieut.   *Despatches.*
                                         Died at Boulogne, Nov. 17th, 1914, *of wounds received at Armentières.*

Thompson, A. G.   ... D 09–12
        Capt.   Capt., S. Lancashire Regt., 1916.
                                  M.C.

Thompson, G. K   ... A 07–12
        Lieut.   Capt., Yorkshire Regt.
                                Lieut., Irish Guards.
                                Wounded.
                                M.C. and Bar.

Thompson, G. L.   ... I 11–16
        Lieut.   2nd Lieut., R.F.A.
                                Lieut., 1918.

Thompson, G. M.   ... B 92–96
     .   Major   Major, R. West Surrey Regt., 1916.
                                Employed Ministry of Munitions.

Thompson, J. E. S.   ... A 12–15
        2nd Lieut.   Pte., London Regt., 19th Bn.
                                2nd Lieut., Grenadier Guards, 1918.
                                Relinquished Commission, 1919.
                                Wounded.

Thompson, O. S.   ... K 06–10
                                R.N. Surgeon, Naval Brigade.

✠ Thompson, P. ...   ... B 11–16
        Capt.   Capt., R.A.F.
                                Killed, March 23rd, 1918, *Prouville, near Le Quéant.*

Thompson, P. G.   ... H 07–12
                                Capt., R. West Kent Regt.
                                Prisoner of War, April, 1917.
                                Repatriated from Turkey, 1918.

✠ Thompson, R. H.   ... F 97–02   (Trin. Coll., Oxford. Barrister.)
        Vaughan-   Capt., Royal Fusiliers.
        Capt.   *Despatches.*
                                Killed, Sept. 26th, 1916, *Thiepval.*

Thompson, V. F. P.   ... B 04–07
        Lieut.   Lieut., R.F.A., 1917.
                                Ministry of Nat. Service.

Thompson, W. G. M.   ... F 13–17
        2nd Lieut.   2nd Lieut., 18th Bengal Lancers, I.A.

THOMSON, B. H. H.   ... E 88–91   (Probate Registry.)
Red Cross Ambulance, France, 1914.

THOMSON, SIR GRAEME-... F 89–94   (New Coll., Oxford. Admiralty.)
Director-General of Naval Transport.
K.C.B.   Orders: La Couronne, Rising Sun,
Corona d'Italia.

THOMSON, H. G.   ... E 92–94   (Land Agent.)
Major   Major, R.F.A., 5th Hampshire Battery.
Wounded.
D.S.O.

THOMSON, SIR W.   ...   (Ball. Coll., Oxford.)
MITCHELL   Hon. Lieut., R.N.V.R.
Blockade Director.
C.B.E. K.B.E. Chevalier Légion d'Honneur.

THORBURN, S. K.   ... I 08–10
Capt.   2nd Lieut., R.F.A., 1914.
Capt. and Adjt., 1917.
Temp. Major, G.S.O.$_2$, 1918.
Wounded.   *Despatches* (2).
M.C.

THORNEWILL, J. M. H. ... B 01–06
Lieut.   Lieut., R.F.A., N. Midland Brigade.
Asst. Instructor, Artillery Training School.
Acting Capt., 1917.

✠ THORNTON, G. ST. L.   ... A 94–99   (R.F.A. S. African War.)
Lieut.-Col.   Major, R.F.A., 1914.
Lieut.-Col., 1916.
Invalided, 1917.
Wounded (2).   *Despatches* (2).
Died, Feb. 4th, 1918, *from effects of Active
Service.*
D.S.O.

THORNTON, W. H.   ... C 99–04   (Trin. Coll., Oxford.)
Major   Capt., R.F.A., West Riding Brigade.
Major, 1916.
M.C.

THOROLD, G. F.   ... D 12–16
2nd Lieut.   2nd Lieut., R.F.A., 1917.
Wounded.

THOROLD, W. G. P.   ... K 06–11
Capt.   Capt., Berkshire Yeomanry.
Brigade Signalling Officer, 1917.

THRESHER, J. H. ... G 84–86   (R.B., 1892.   Capt., 1899.   Retired, 1909.)
    Brevet Lieut.-Col.   Brevet Lieut.-Col., R.B.
                               Camp Commandant, H.Q.
                               Despatches.
                               M.V.O., Croix de Guerre. Officier Légion
                                 d'Honneur, La Couronne.

THRING, T. M. ...   ... E 13–17
    2nd Lieut.   2nd Lieut., P.A. Somerset L.I.

TIDY, H. L., M.D.   ... B 91–96   (New Coll., Oxford.)
    Major   Hon. Major, R.A.M.C., 1918, late Netley Hosp.

✠ TILLARD, P. A. ...   ... C 95–00   (Magd. Coll., Oxford.)
    Lieut.   Lieut., Shropshire Yeomanry.
                               Att. E. Surrey Regt.
                               Killed Nov., 1916.

TIRARD, N. S. ...   ... E 06–09
    Lieut.   Lieut., R.A.M.C.

TOLLEMACHE, Hon. D. P. I 97–01   (7th Hussars, 1902. Lieut., 1906.)
    Brevet Major   Capt., 7th Hussars, 1916.
                               G.S.O.,₃ 1914.
                               Brigade-Major, 1915.
                               Acting Lieut.-Col., Northamptonshire Regt.,
                                 1st Bn., 1916–17.
                               Brevet Major.
                               Prisoner of war.
                               Repatriated, 1918.
                               D.S.O.

TOLLEMACHE, L. D'O. COLL. 05–10
    2nd Lieut.   2nd Lieut., Bradfield College O.T.C.

TOMKINSON, C.   ... D 06–12
    Capt.   Temp. Capt., Volunteer Force, B.E. Africa.
                               Despatches.

TOMKINSON, G. S.   ... D 95–00   (King's Coll., Cambridge.)
    Major   Capt. and Adjt., Worcestershire Regt.
                               Serving with R.E.
                               Major, 1918.
                               Acting Lieut.-Col., 1918, G.H.Q. Defences.
                               Major, Forward Light Railway Training School.
                               Wounded (3).
                               M.C. O.B.E.

TOMKINSON, H. ...   COLL. 87–92
    Major   Major, Worcestershire Yeomanry.
                               Staff Capt.
                               Despatches (2).

TOMPSON, H. W. ... G 84–87   (Hampshire Regt., 1892. Capt., 1899. Brevet
Col.   Major, 1900. S. African War. Retired,
                                       1909.)
                                 Major, Hampshire Regt., 1914.
                                 Colonel.
                                 Dep. Director, Remounts.
                                 Despatches (3).
                                 C.M.G.

TOMPSON, R. H. D., D.S.O.   I 93–97   (Merton Coll., Oxford. R.F.A., 1900. Lieut.,
Brevet Lieut.-Col.   1902.)
                                 Lieut.-Col., R.F.A., 1917.
                                 A.Q.M.G., 1918. Director of Railway Transport.
                                 Wounded.   *Despatches* (6).

TOOGOOD, C., D.S.O. ... C 84–87   (Border Regt., 1890. Lieut., 1892. Capt.,
Lieut.-Col.   Manchester Regt., 1900. S. African War.)
                                 Major, Lincolnshire Regt., 1912.
                                 Prisoner of War.
                                 Exchanged home, 1918.
                                 Lieut.-Col., 1919.
                                 Wounded.   *Despatches.*

TOPPIN, J. F. T. ... F 13–18
                                 Cadet, Household Brigade, O.C.B., 1918.

TORKINGTON, O. M. ... C 93–96   (Cameronians, 1899. Lieut., 1900. Capt., 1908.
Lieut.-Col.   S. African War.)
                                 Major, Cameronians (Scottish Rifles), 1915.
                                 G.S.O.$_3$, 1915. D.A.Q.M.G.
                                 Temp. Lieut.-Col., Norfolk Regt., 4th Bn.,
                                 1917.
                                 Despatches.
                                 D.S.O.

✠ TOTTIE, E. H. ... ... A 09–13
2nd Lieut.   2nd Lieut., Northumberland Fusiliers.
                                 Died Sept. 22nd, 1914, *of wounds received, Battle*

                                      of the Aisne.

TOTTIE, F. B. ... ... A 06–11
Capt.   Lieut., K.R.R.C.
                                 Gen. List, Staff Lieut.
                                 Capt., 1918.
                                 Despatches.
                                 Croix de Guerre.

TOWNE, R. T. ... ... I 11–16
Pte.   Private, R.A.S.C.
                                 52nd Remount Depot.

Toye, E. G. ... ... c 02–05
Major
Lieut., D.C.L.I.
Capt., R.A.F., Photographic Officer.
Major, R.A.F., S.O.$_2$, 1918.
Despatches (3).

Toye, J. F. ... coll. 96–02
Lieut.
(Trin. Coll., Camb.)
Lieut., Gen. List, Interpreter. Retired, 1918.
Temp. Lieut., R.N.V.R., 1918.

✠ Toynbee, G. P. R. coll. 98–02
Capt.
(R.B., 1905.)
Capt., R.B.
Killed Nov. 15th, 1914, *St. Ives, Ploegsteert
Wood, near Armentières.*

Toynbee, J. W. H. ... d 09–14
Lieut.
Lieut., E. Kent Regt.
M.G.C. Infantry.
Acting Major, 1918.
Despatches.
M.C. and Bar. Croix de Guerre.

Toynbee, R. L. ... e 98–00
Capt.
(Lincolnshire Regt., 1905.)
Capt., Lincolnshire Regt., 1914.
Army Signal Coy.
Despatches.
Retired, 1915.
M.C.

Toynbee, R. V.... ... d 10–16
2nd Lieut.
2 d Lieut., R.B., 1917.
Wounded.

Trasenster, W. A. ... g 03–09
Capt.
(Trin. Coll., Cambridge. R. Fusiliers, 1912.)
Lieut., Royal Fusiliers, 1914.
Capt., 1915.
Acting Major, 1917.
Despatches (2).
M.C.

Trask, C. S. L. ... d 07–12
Capt.
Lieut., H.Q. Staff, 1916.
Capt., 1917.
Staff Lieut., L.O.C.
Despatches.

Treatt, B. D. C. coll. 04–09
Major
(R.F.A., 1910.)
Capt., R.H.A., 1916. Staff Capt., H.Q.
Major, Instructor in Gunnery, 1918.
Wounded. Despatches.
M.C.

209   P

TREE, R. L. ... ... B 11–16
    Ensign

Automobiles Americains, Section Militaire, 1916.
Ensign, U.S. Naval Force.
Naval Station, L'Abervrach, France.
Released from active duty, Dec., 1918.

TRENCH, G. F. ... H 73–77
    CHENEVIX-, C.I.E.
    Lieut.-Col.

(R. Scots, 1879. Major, 1899. Lieut.-Col., 1905.
    Consul Gen., Ispahan.)
Lieut.-Col., retired, I.A.
1914, British Red Cross, Motor Ambulance.
    France.
1915, Military Attaché, Cairo; Base Com-
    mandant, British Adriatic Mission.
1916, Special Officer, Selection of Pilots, R.A.F.
1917, War Office, Demobilization.
Orders: Corona d'Italia, White Eagle.

TRENCH, R. CHENEVIX- ... H 12–16
    2nd Lieut.

2nd Lieut., K.R.R.C., 1st Bn.

TRENCH, R. H. ... ... B 88–92
    CHENEVIX-
    Major

(Lieut., I.A., 1898.)
Major, I.A., Supernumerary List.
O.B.E.

TREVILIAN, M. F. CELY- E 95–98
    Major

(Magd. Coll., Oxford.)
Major, W. Somerset Yeomanry.
Retired, 1916.

TREVOR, H. E. ... ... A 84–87
    Brig.-Gen.

(Yorkshire Regt., 1892. Capt., 1899.)
Lieut.-Col., K.O.Y.L.I., 2nd Bn.
Temp. Brigadier-General, 1917.
Despatches (5).
D.S.O. C.M.G.

TRIBE, W. H. ... COLL. 96–01
    Capt.

(Trin. Coll., Oxford.)
Capt., R. Sussex Regt.

✠ TRITTON, A. G. ... D 95–99
    Capt.

(Coldstream Guards, 1900. Lieut., 1903.
    S. African War.)
Capt., Coldstream Guards.
Despatches (2).
Killed, Dec. 26th, 1914, *near Béthune*.

TRITTON, C. H. ... D 88–93
    Major

(New Coll., Oxford.)
Major, R.A.S.C.
Despatches.
O.B.E.

✠ TROUTON, D. G. ... B 07–11
   Lieut.

Lieut., R.F.A.
Acting Capt.
Wounded (2).   *Despatches.*
Killed, Oct. 13th, 1917, *near Ypres.*

✠ TROUTON, E. A. ... B 05–09
   Lieut.

Lieut., Inniskilling Fusiliers.
Missing, presumed killed, July 1st, 1916, *Thiepval.*

✠ TROUTON, F. T. ... B 05–09
   Major

Capt., Cameronians (Scottish Rifles).
Major, 1915.
Killed, Oct. 13th, 1915, *near Ypres.*

✠ TUDOR, P. B. ... COLL. 11–16
   2nd Lieut.

2nd Lieut., R.F.A.
Died of Small-pox, Basra, Oct. 9th, 1918.

TUFNELL, G. M. ... H 81–84
   Lieut.-Col.

(Essex Regt., 1887. Capt., 1898. S. African
   War. Major, 1907.)
Lieut.-Col., Essex Regt., 1915.
Comm. Cadet Bn.
Wounded.   *Despatches.*
Relinquished Comm., 1919.

TUKE, A. W. ... ... H 10–15
   Lieut.

2nd Lieut., Cameronians (Scottish Rifles).
Lieut., 1918.

TURNBULL, R. C. ... A 93–96
   Capt.

(With Brabant's Horse, S. African War.)
Capt., 8th Mounted Rifles, S. Africa.

TURNBULL, S. K. ... A 89–94
   Major

(Arg. and Suth. Highlanders, 1900.)
Major, Arg. and Suth. Highlanders, 1914.

TURNBULL, W. J. U. ... A 99–01
   Lieut.

Lieut., S. Provinces Mounted Rifles, Madras.

TURNER, A. G. ... ... I 93–97
   Lieut.-Col.

(R.E., 1900. S. African War. Lieut., 1903.)
Major, R.E., 1916.
Lieut.-Col., Assistant Director of Works.
L.O.C., Palestine.
Wounded.   *Despatches* (2).
D.S.O.   Croix de Guerre.

TURNER, A. M. ... ... G 92–97
   Major

(1st D.G., 1900. S. African War.)
Major, 1st Dragoon Guards, 1914.
Brigade-Major, 1915.
G.S.O.$_2$, 1917.
Despatches (2).
D.S.O.

211

TURNER, E. V. ...   ... I 86–90   (R.E., 1892.   S. African War.   Capt., 1903.
        Bt. Col.   Bt. Major.   Director of Posts and Telegraphs,
                                                Soudan.)
                                                Bt. Col., R.E.
                                                Temp. Col., Dep. Director Army Signals, 1916.
                                                Dep. Signal Officer in Chief, 1918.
                                                Despatches (6).
                                                D.S.O.   C.M.G.   Order of Savoia.

TURNER, F. C. ...   COLL. 79–84   (Northumberland Fusiliers, 1887.   Capt., 1897.
        Lieut.-Col.   S. African War.   Major, 1903.)
                                                Lieut.-Col., Northumberland Fusiliers, 1914.
                                                D.A.Q.M.G.
                                                Despatches.
                                                Retired.

TURNER, R. B. ...   ... I 92–95   (Temp. Lieut., R.E.   S. African War.)
        Lieut.-Col.   Lieut.-Col. and A.Q.M.G., advanced G.H.Q.,
                                                East Africa E.F.
                                                Despatches.
                                                D.S.O.   C.M.G.

TWEDDELL, J. R. M.   ... F 94–98   (Clare Coll., Cambridge.)
        Lieut.   Lieut., R. Defence Corps.
                                                Capt., R.A.F., Administrative Branch.

TWEMLOW, F. R., D.S.O.   G 66–71   (Ch. Ch., Oxford.   Major, N. Staffs Regt.
        Major   S. African War.)
                                                Lieut.-Col., N. Staffordshire Regt.
                                                Major, T.F.R.

✠ TYACKE, E. H. ...   ... C 10–14
        Lieut.   Lieut., Border Regt.
                                                M.G.C.
                                                Wounded (2).
                                                Killed, May 28th, 1918, *Montigny sur Vesle,
                                                near Rheims.*

TYNDALE, H. E. G.   COLL. 00–06   (Winchester College Staff.)
        Lieut.   Lieut., K.R.R.C.
                                                War Office, Intelligence Dept.
                                                Unattached List, T.F.   O.T.C.
                                                Wounded.   *Despatches.*
                                                M.B.E.

TYSER, H.   ...   ... A 82–85   (Jesus Coll., Cambridge.   Lloyds.)
        Capt.   Capt., S. Lancashire Regt.
                                                Staff Lieut.
                                                Special Appointment, 1917.

UDAL, A. U. ... ... A 92–97   (R.A.S.C. Capt., 1904. S. African War.)
    Major   Major, R.A.S.C., 1914.

ULLMAN, R. B. ...   COLL. 07–13
    Capt.   Lieut., R.F.A., 8th London Brigade.
                               Acting Capt., 1918.
                               Wounded (2).
                               M.C.

UNDERHILL, S. W. F. COLL. 04–09
                               Surgeon, R.N.

UPCOTT, J. D. ...   ... E 05–09
    Capt.   Lieut., Devonshire Regt.
                               Capt., 1916.
                               Wounded (2).
                               Employed at Admiralty.

UPPERTON, S. ...   ... G 81–84   (S. Lancs. Regt., 1887. Capt., 1894. S. African
    Major   War. Major, 1904. Retired, 1905.)
                                   Major, S. Lancashire Regt., Comm. Depot.

URMSTON, E. A. B. ... A 11–15
    Lieut.   2nd Lieut., Queen's Westminster Rifles.
                               Lieut, 1917, T.M.B.

URWICK, R. H. ...   A 89–94   (Trin. Coll., Camb.)
    Capt.   Capt., R.A.M.C.
                               Relinquished Commission Feb., 1919.

USHER, T. C. ...   ... I 94–98   (R.F.A., 1900. Lieut., 1902.)
    Capt.   Capt., R.F.A.
                               Staff Capt.
                               Acting Major, 1919.
                               Despatches (2).

UTTERTON, Rev. E. E. S., H 89–95   (New Coll., Oxford.)
    C.F.   Chaplain to Forces, 1918.

UTTERTON, F. LE C. ... H 95–99   (Land agent.)
    Lieut.   Lieut., York and Lancaster Regt., Hallamshire
                                   Bn., 1917.
                               Wounded.

VALENTINE, F. C. O. ... I 11–16
    Lieut.   2nd Lieut., R.F.A.
                               Lieut., 1918.
                               Wounded.

VANDELEUR, T. P. ... A 91–93
    Capt.   Capt., R.F.A.
                               Labour Corps.

VAUGHAN, E. J. F. ... D 89–92   (Lieut., Devonshire Regt., 1898. Capt., Man-
   Brevet Col.   chester Regt., 1901. S. African War.
                                 Egyptian Army, 1902.)
                      Brevet Lieut.-Col., Devonshire Regt., 1917.
                      D.A.Q.M.G., 1917.
                      Temp. Brig.-General, 1918.
                      Brevet Colonel, 1919.
                      Despatches (4).
                      D.S.O. C.M.G.

VENNING, J. ... ... F 93–98   (New Coll., Oxford. Solicitor.)
   Capt.   Capt. and Adjt., London Regt., 1st Bn., Royal
                      Fusiliers.
                      Acting Major, 6th Bn.
                      Wounded.   *Despatches.*
                      M.C.

VERNON, G. R. ... ... B 12–17
   2nd Lieut.   2nd Lieut., Inland Waterways and Docks
                      Section, 1917.

VERNON, H. A. ... ... H 07–11   (New Coll., Oxford.)
   Capt.   Capt., R. Irish Fusiliers.
                      Instructor, Imp. Sch. of Instruction, Cairo,
                      1918.

VERNON, J. E. ... ... H 02–06   (R. Dublin Fusiliers, 1908.)
   Capt.   Capt., R. Dublin Fusiliers, 1917.
                      Wounded, and Prisoner of War, 1914.
                      Exchanged home, 1915.
                      Att. R.A.F., 1917, 1918.
                      Adjutant, Royal Dublin Fusiliers, Depot.

VERRALL, P. J., M.B.   COLL. 96–02   (Trin. Coll., Camb.)
                      Lieut., R.A.M.C.
                      Relinquished Commission.

VILLIERS, E. F., D.S.O.   B 89–92   (Sussex Regt., 1895. S. African War. Capt.,
    Major   1904.)
                      Temp. Lieut.-Col., R. Sussex Regt., 2nd Bn.,
                      1915.
                      Wounded.   *Despatches* (5).
                      C.M.G.

✠ VILLIERS, W. E. ... ... C 10–15
   Capt.   Capt., K.R.R.C.
                      Killed Nov. 10th, 1917, *Wiltje, near Ypres.*

VLASTO, M. ... ... C 02–04
                      Surgeon, R.N.
                      Malta Hospital.

WAIT, H. G. K.   ... B 84–87   (R.E., 1889. Capt., 1900.)
    Lieut.-Col.   Lieut.-Col., R.E., 1917.
                                  Deputy Director of Works.
                                  D.S.O.

WAIT, H. W. K.   ... B 78–83   (Trin. Coll., Oxford.)
    Major   Major, R.G.A.
                                  Comm. Bristol Heavy Brigade.

WAKE, D.   ...   ... F 90–94   (Ch. Ch., Oxford.)
    Capt.   Capt., R.B., 1916.
                                  Special Appointment.

WALL, G. R. P.   ... A 11–16
    Lieut.   2nd Lieut., R.F.A.
                                  Lieut., 1918.
                                  M.C.

WALLACE, C. L. W.   ... D 88–91   (R. Irish Rifles, 1899. Lieut., 1900.)
    Lieut.-Col.   Lieut.-Col., R. West Kent Regt.
                                  Retired, 1918.

WALLACE, C. W.   ... B 98–02   (I.A., 1905.)
    Capt.   Capt., 22nd Punjabis, I.A., 1913.
                                  Prisoner of War (Kut), 1916.

WALLACE, J. S. ...   ... H 13–17
    2nd Lieut.   2nd Lieut., R.F.A., 1919.

✠ WALLACE, R.   ...   ... B 00–03
    Capt.   Capt., E. Yorkshire Regt.
                                  Brigade M.G. Officer.
                                  Died of wounds, May 6th, 1915, *Boulogne*.

WALLACE, R. W. A.   ... K 13–16
    2nd Lieut.   2nd Lieut., I.A., Kumaon Rifles, 1918.

WALLACE, W. J. L.   COLL. 90–96   (Ball. Coll., Oxford. Schoolmaster.)
    Lieut.   Capt., Oxf. and Bucks L.I.
                                  Relinquished Commission, ill health, 1918.

WALLOP, G. V. ...   ... K 11–16
    Lieut.   2nd Lieut., 2nd Life Guards.
                                  Lieut., Guards, M.G. Regt., 1918.

WALWYN, F. J., D.S.O.   F 89–91   (R. Welsh Fusiliers, 1896. Capt., 1904.)
    Major   Major, R. Welsh Fusiliers, 1915.
                                  Brigade-Major, 1916.
                                  G.S.O.$_2$, 1917.
                                  Wounded.   *Despatches.*

WARBURTON, G. A. ... B 80–82 (Norfolk Regt., 1888. Capt., 1900. Durham
    Major L.I. S. African War.)
    Major, Durham L.I., 1917.
    Att. Dorsetshire Regt.

WARD, A. C. ... ... F 09–13
    Lieut. 2nd Lieut., R.F.A., Home Counties Brigade.
    Lieut., 1917.
    Acting Capt., R.A., 1918.

WARD, B. R. ... ... B 76–80 (R.E., 1882. Major, 1899. Lieut.-Col., 1906.)
    Col. Col., R.E., 1911.
    Chief Engineer, 1917.
    Wounded.   *Despatches.*
    C.M.G.

WARD, E. F. ... ... G 83–86 (K.R.R.C., 1892. Capt., 1900. S. African
    Lieut.-Col. War. Retired as Major, 1907.
    Capt., Temp. Lieut.-Col., K.R.R.C.
    Officer, Coy. of Cadets, R.M. Coll., till 1918.
    Retired as Lieut.-Col., 1919.
    Wounded.   *Despatches* (2).
    D.S.O.

WARD, H. C. S. ... I 92–95 (Lieut., I.A., 1900.)
    Brevet Lieut.-Col. Major, Temp. Lieut.-Col., 2nd Lancers, I.A.,
    1915.
    G.S.O.$_2$, 1916.
    G.S.O.$_1$, 1917.

✠ WARE, F. H. ... ... A 86–91 (Trin. Coll., Camb. Solicitor.)
    Capt. Capt., London Regt., Kensington Bn.
    Wounded.
    Killed, July 1st, 1916, *Hébuterne.*

✠ WARE, J. W. ... COLL. 10–14
    2nd Lieut. 2nd Lieut., R.E.
    Died as Prisoner of War July 11th, 1916,
    Vermelles.

WARNER, B. A. ... ... B 02–05
    Lieut. Lieut., London R.B.
    Assistant District Commissioner, Uganda.

WARNER, C. F. A. COLL. 08–14
    Capt. Capt., Royal Fusiliers.
    Att. London Regt., P.O. Rifles.
    Wounded.

WARRACK, G. D. H. ... B 13–18
    Cadet, R.F.A., 1918.

WARRAND, K. C. C. ... I 15–16 Gentleman Cadet, R.M. College.

WARREN, R. G. ... ... B 98–02 Ch. Ch., Oxford.
Major Major, London Regt., Queen Victoria's Rifles.
Officer, Cadet Bn.
D.A.Q.M.G., 1918.

WARRY, B. A. ... ... A 79–83 (Essex Regt., 1885. Capt., 1895. S. African
Major War. Retired, 1904.)
Temp. Major, 1914.
Assistant Director R.T., Aldershot Command.

WARRY, R. A. ... ... E 00–05
Lieut. Lieut., K.R.R.C.

WARWICK, H. B. ... G 90–94 (Trin. Coll., Camb. Northumberland Fusiliers,
Brevet Lieut.-Col. 1898. Capt., 1901. S. African War.
Retired, 1913.)
Major, Northumberland Fusiliers, 1915.
Lieut.-Col., Comm. Depot.
Wounded. Despatches (2).

✠ WATERS, G. T. ... COLL. 86–92 (New Coll., Oxford. Schoolmaster.)
Lieut. Capt., Suffolk Regt.
Lieut., Training Reserve.
Died of wounds March 29th, 1918, *Wimereux.*

WATNEY, F. D. ... ... F 83–88 (Solicitor.)
Lieut.-Col. Lieut.-Col., R.W. Surrey Regt., 4th Bn.
Despatches (3).
C.B.E. T.D.

WATNEY, R. D. ... D 05–08
Capt. Capt., R. West Kent Regt., 1914.
Commandant Rest Camp.

WATSON, Hon. A. G. ... C 90–94 (W.S.)
Lieut. Lieut., Royal Scots, 1916.

WATSON, A. W. H. ... H 05–09 (Trin. Coll., Camb.)
Capt. Capt. and Adjt., K.R.R.C.
Gen. List, Brigade-Major, 1918.
Despatches (2).
M.C. D.S.O.

WATSON, Hon. D. K. ... C 91–95 (Solicitor.)
Capt. Capt., Devonshire Regt.
Cyclist Bn.

217

WATSON, H. W. M.	...	F 95–99	(K.R.R.C., 1900. Lieut., 1901. S. African
Brevet Lieut.-Col.			War.)

WATSON, H. W. M.   ... F 95–99   (K.R.R.C., 1900.   Lieut., 1901.   S. African
Brevet Lieut.-Col.   War.)
                Major, K.R.R.C., 1915.
                G.S.O.$_3$, 1915.   Brigade-Major, 1915.
                Lieut.-Col., Comm. Bn. W. Surrey Regt.
                Temp. Brig.-General, 1918.
                Comm. Senior Officers' School, Aldershot, 1918.
                Wounded (2).   *Despatches* (2).
                D.S.O. and Bar.   C.M.G.

WATSON, J.   ...   ... C 96–99   (Merton Coll., Oxford.   Solicitor.)
Major   Capt., R.F.A., 2nd Northumberland Brigade.
                Major, 1916.

✠ WATSON, R. W.   ... I 07–11   (King's Coll., Camb.)
Lieut.   Lieut., K.R.R.C.
                Killed July 30th, 1915, *Hooge.*

WATT, R. P.   ...   ... B 11–16
Lieut.   2nd Lieut., 5th Lancers.
                Lieut., 1918.

WATT, S. A.   ...   ... I 90–94
Capt.   Capt., S. Irish Horse.

WATTS, H. L.   ...   ... I 97–02   (New Coll., Oxford.)
· Lieut.   Lieut., London Regt., 11th Bn.
                Staff Lieut., 1917.

✠ WAVELL, A. J. B.   ... B 95–98   (Welsh Regt., 1903.   S. African War.)
Capt.   Capt., Welsh Regt.
                Att. Arab Rifles, E.A. Force.
                M.C.
                Killed Sept. 1st, 1916, *Mevele Ndogo, E. Africa.*

WAVELL, A. P. ...   COLL. 96–00   (Black Watch, 1901.   S. African War.   Lieut.,
Lieut.-Col.   1904.)
                Lieut.-Col., Black Watch (Royal Highlanders)
                  1917.
                G.S.O.$_3$.   Brigade-Major, 1914.   G.S.O.$_1$, 1916.
                A.A. and Q.M.G., 1916.
                Temp. Brig.-General, 1918.
                Despatches (2).
                M.C.   C.M.G.   Order S. Stanislas.

WEATHERBY, E. M.   ... H 84–89
2nd Lieut.   2nd Lieut., Bucks Vol. Regt.

WEATHERBY, F.   ... H 98–03   (Magd. Coll., Oxford.)
Capt.   Capt. and Adjt., Oxford Yeomanry.
                Wounded.
                M.C.

WEATHERBY, J. T.   ... II 89–96   (Magd. Coll., Oxford.   Oxford and Bucks L.I.,
    Lieut.-Col.   Capt., 1905.   Somaliland Expedition.)
                                     Major, Temp. Lieut.-Col., Oxford and Bucks
                                     L.I., 1916.

G.S.O.$_3$,1912. Brigade-Major,1914. G.S.O.$_1$,1915.
War Office, 1916–1917.
Lieut.-Colonel.   Assistant Military Secretary,
    G.H.Q., 1918.
Despatches (5).
D.S.O.

WEATHERBY, R. C.   ... II 94–98   (Artist.)
    Lieut.   Lieut., Essex Yeomanry.
Relinquished Commission, ill-health, 1918.
Wounded.

✠ WEATHERBY, T.   ... II 07–13
    Capt.   Capt., Duke of Wellington's W. Riding Regt.,
                                     1915.
Died in England on service, May 8th, 1915.

WEBB, H. LUMLEY   ... C 75–78   (Solicitor.   Major, Middlesex Rifle Vol.)
    Lieut.-Col.   Lieut.-Col., London Regt., Kensington Bn.
T.F.R.

✠ WEBB, T. H. B.   ... K 12–16
    2nd Lieut.   2nd Lieut., Welsh Guards.
Killed, Dec. 1st, 1917, *Gouzeaucourt.*

WEBSTER, F.   ... K 05–09

                                     Gunner, R.F.A.

WEDD, R. P.   ...   ... D 96–99   (E. Kent Regt., 1901.   S. African War.)
    Major   Major, E. Kent Regt.
Training Reserve, 29th Bn.
Relinquished Commission, 1919, ill-health.
Wounded.

WEECH, W. N.   ...   COLL. 91–97   (New Coll., Oxford.   Headmaster, Sedbergh
    Bt. Major   School.)
Capt., O.T.C., Sedbergh School.
Brevet Major.

WEGG, W. H. J.   ... E 90–93   (Caius Coll., Cambridge.   Barrister.)
    2nd Lieut.   2nd Lieut., R.G.A., 1918.

WELCH, R. H.   ...   ... A 94–97
    Capt.   Capt., R. Marines, 1916.

✠ WELLESLEY, E. G. ... A 09–14
   2nd Lieut.
                            2nd Lieut., Yorkshire Regt.
                            Killed, Dec. 21st, 1915, *La Houssoie, near*
                                    Armentières.

WELLS, H. B. ... ... E 04–09 (O.U.B.C.)
   Lieut.
                            Lieut., R.F.A., 6th London Brigade.
                            War Office.
                            M.B.E.

WELLS, L. COLLINGS- ... E 02–06
   Lieut.
                            Lieut., K.A.R., 1st Central Africa Bn.
                            Wounded.

WELSFORD, G. M. ... I 09–15
   Lieut.
                            Lieut., K.R.R.C., 5th Bn., 1916.
                            Att. R.E. for Army Signal Service, 1918.
                            Wounded.

WELLS, J. L. ... ... A 14–18
                            Cadet, Household Brigade O.C.B.

✠ WERE, REV. C. N. ... B 95–00
   C.F.
                            Chaplain to Forces.
                            Died on Active Service, Jan. 8th, 1918, *near*
                                      Bailleul.

WERE, H. D. ... ... E 90–93 (Settled in New Zealand.)
   Lieut.
                            Lieut., R.F.A., 1917.
                            M.C.

WEST, Hon. B. G. ... E 86–90 (Ch. Ch., Oxford.)
   SACKVILLE-
   Lieut.
                            Lieut., R.N.V.R.

WEST, Hon. Sir C. J. ... E 84–88 (K.R.R.C., 1889. S. African War. Major, 1905.)
   SACKVILLE-
   Major-Gen.
                            Col., Temp. Brigadier-General, 1917.
                            Major-General.
                            Acting British Representative, Supreme War
                                      Council, Versailles.
                            Wounded (2).   *Despatches* (5).
                            C. M. G.   K. B. E.   Commandeur Légion
                                      d'Honneur.

✠ WEYMOUTH, VISCOUNT ... K 09–12
   2nd Lieut.
                            2nd Lieut., Scots Greys.
                            Killed, Sept. 12th, 1916, *Hulluch.*

WHATELY, F. B. ... A 97–02 (Ch. Ch., Oxford.)
   Lieut.
                            2nd Lieut., K.R.R.C., 6th Bn.
                            Lieut., 1917.   Adjt., Vol. Bn.

WHINERAY, R. W. ... B 12–17
   2nd Lieut.
                            2nd Lieut., R.F.A., 6c Reserve Brigade, 1918.

WHITCOMBE, D. M. P. ... D 03–09

Surgeon, R.N.

WHITCOMBE, P. S. ... B 07–10
Capt.

2nd Lieut., R.A.S.C., 1914.
Capt., 1917.
Dep. Assistant Director Transport, July to
Oct., 1918.

WHITE, A. F. KEBLE- ... A 05–11
Capt.

Capt., Suffolk Regt.
R.A.F., Acting Capt., T., 1918.

WHITE, L. A. ... ... F 92–96
Capt.

(Journalist.)
Capt., Middlesex Regt., 7th Bn.

WHITE, S. B., M.B. ... B 02–05
Lieut.

Lieut., R.A.M.C.

WHITEHEAD, G. R. B. ... E 10–11

Lieut., R.A.S.C., 1917.

WHITEHEAD, T. C. ... D 03–08
2nd Lieut.

Corpl., H.A.C.
2nd Lieut., 1917.

WHITING, H. N. ... C 09–10
Lieut.

2nd Lieut., Somerset L.I.
Lieut., 1917.

WHITTAKER, A. ... ... E 86–89

Private, R.A.S.C.
Expeditionary Force, N. Russia, 1918.

WICKHAM, A. K. ... F 10–15
Lieut.

Lieut., London Regt., 7th Bn.
M.G.C., 1917.
Wounded (2).

WICKHAM, D. H. ... H 10–14
Lieut.

2nd Lieut., Connaught Rangers, 1914.
Lieut., 1916.
Acting Capt., 1917, 5th Bn.
h.p., ill health owing to wounds, 1919.
Wounded.   *Despatches.*

WICKHAM, R. ... ... E 00–04
Capt.

Lieut., R.N.A.S.
Capt., R.A.F.

WICKS, C. L. ... ... A 06–12
Capt.

Lieut., Oxf. and Bucks L.I.
Capt., 1918.

221

WIDDRINGTON, B. F. ... E 87–89   (K.R.R.C., 1894. Capt., 1901. S. African War.)
Brig.-Gen.   Lieut.-Col. K.R.R.C., 4th Bn., 1914.
Temp. Brig.-Gen., 1916.
81st Infantry Brigade.
Relinquished Command, 1919.
Wounded.   *Despatches* (5).
D.S.O. C.M.G. Greek Order of The Redeemer.

✠ WIGGETT, A. J. ... ... C 10–14
2nd Lieut.
    2nd Lieut., K.R.R.C.
Wounded, and prisoner, March 3rd, 1916.
Died in German Hospital, Ayette, March 15th,
1916.

WIGHTWICK, H. E. ... I 06–09
Capt.
    Capt., Cameronians.
W. African F.F., Sierra Leone Bn., 1916.

WIGRAM, C., C.S.I., C.V.O. II 86–91   (R.A., 1893. Lieut., 1896. Capt., Bengal
Lieut.-Col.   Lancers, I.A., 1902. S. African War.)
Lieut.-Col.
Equerry and Assistant Secretary to H.M.
C.B.

WIGRAM, C. C. ... F 96–98   (Somerset L.I., 1901. Lieut., 1904. S. African
Major   War. W. African F.F.)
R.A.F., Major, A., 1918.

WIGRAM, G. M. ... I 85–86   (Highland L.I., 1889. Ceylon Mounted Infantry
Major   in S. African War.)
Major, K.R.R.C.
Major, Labour Corps, 1918.
Despatches.

WIGRAM, K. ... ... H 88–94   (2nd Gurkha Rifles, 1896. Capt., 1906. Tirah
Brig.-Gen.   Exp., Tibet Exp.)
1914, Major, G.S.O.$_3$, G.S.O.$_2$, India.
1915, Brevet Lieut.-Col., G.S.O.$_2$, G.S.O.$_1$,
France.
Brig.-Gen., Gen. Staff. Head of Operations,
B Section.
1918, Brig.-Gen., Air Staff. R.A.F., France,
Brevet Col.
Director of Staff Duties, India, 1919.
Despatches (5).
D.S.O., C.B., C.B.E., Chevalier Légion d'Hon-
neur, Croix de Guerre, Commandeur La
Couronne.

✠ WILBERFORCE, W. R. S.   E 07–11
    Capt.

Lieut., K.R.R.C.
Capt., R.A.F.
Instructor, Central Flying School.
Killed flying June 2nd, 1918.

WILKINSON, E. A. G. ... D 89–94
    Surgeon Lieut.-Commander

(Univ. Coll., Oxford.)
Staff Surgeon, R.N.
H.M.S. *Revenge.*
O.B.E.

✠ WILKINSON, J. R. M. ... F 01–05
    Lieut.

Lieut., Middlesex Regt.
Killed Aug. 23rd, 1914, *at Oburg, in retreat
    from Mons.*

WILKINSON, W. H. J. COLL. 86–93
    Capt.

(Univ. Coll., Oxford. I.C.S.)
Capt., Intelligence Corps, 1st Army.
Staff Capt., G.S.O.$_3$.
Relinquished Commission, 1919.
Despatches (3).
Croix de Guerre. Chevalier Légion d'Honneur.
    Order Leopold.

WILLES, H. W. H.   ... E 00–03
    Lieut.

(Ch. Ch., Oxford.)
2nd Lieut., Oxford and Bucks L.I.
Lieut., 1918.
Wounded.

WILLIAMS, A. H. K.   COLL. 09–14
    Capt.

Lieut., Berks Yeomanry.
39th Central India Horse.
Acting Capt., 1918.

✠ WILLIAMS, C. M.   ... G 99–04
    Capt.

Lieut. and Adjt., R.G.A.
Capt., 1917.
Killed April, 1918, *Guivry.*

WILLIAMS, Rev. D. H. A. E 04–09
    Naval Chaplain

Chaplain, R.N., H.M.S. *Conqueror.*
To R.A.F.

WILLIAMS, E. S.   ... K 13–16
    Lieut.

R.A.F., Lieut., A.

WILLIAMS, E. S. B.   ... I 06–10
    Capt.

(R.B., 1911.)
Capt., R.B., 1915.
Att. R.E., Army Signal Service.
G.S.O.$_3$, 1916.
Brigade-Major.
Wounded (2).   *Despatches.*
Chevalier Légion d'Honneur.

WILLIAMS, F. G. M. ... D 01–05
   Capt.
                                   Lieut., R.F.C., Salonica.
                                   R.A.F., Capt., T.

WILLIAMS, G. W. MONIER- E 94–99 (Univ. Coll., Oxford.)
   Major
                                   Major, Central London Rangers.
                                   Chemical Adviser on Staff, 5th Army.
                                   Sec. for Service with R.E.
                                   Despatches (3).
                                   M.C. O.B.E.

WILLIAMS, Sir H. B., D.S.O. I 79–83 (R.E., 1895. Major, 1902. S. African War.
   Major-Gen.
                                       Col., 1912.)
                                   Temp. Brigadier-General, 1915.
                                   Major-General, 37th Division, 1917.
                                   Despatches (8).
                                   C.B. K.C.B. Croix de Guerre. Commandeur
                                         Légion d'Honneur and La Couronne.

WILLIAMS, H. D. ... B 67–72 (Staffordshire Regt., 1880. Lieut.-Col., 1895.
   Col.
                                       Col., 1900. Retired, 1902.)
                                   Col., N. Staffordshire Regt.
                                   In charge of Records, T.F., Preston.

WILLIAMS, L. MONIER- G 08–12
   Lieut.
                                     Lieut., R.A., E. Anglian Brigade.
                                   2nd Lieut., I.A., unattached.
                                   Lieut., 3rd Gurkha Rifles, 1916.
                                   Acting Capt. and Adjt., 1917.

WILLIAMS, P. ... ... F 98–03 (Trin. Coll., Cambridge.)
   Lieut.
                                     Lieut., Home Counties Divisional Engineers.

WILLIAMS, P. V. ... E 11–14
   Lieut.
                                       2nd Lieut., R.F.A., 1916.
                                   Lieut., 1917, R.H.A., 10th Res. Brigade.
                                   Despatches.

WILLIAMS, R. F. ... F 04–08
   GARNON-
                                     2nd Lieut., Royal Fusiliers, 1916.
                                   Lieut., 1917.
                                   Acting Capt. and Adjt., 1918.
                                   Wounded.   *Despatches.*

WILLIAMS, R. T. ... E 99–04 (Univ. Coll., Oxford.)
   MONIER-
    Major
                                     Capt., E. Kent Regt.
                                   Staff Capt., G.H.Q.
                                   Temp. Major, Gen. List, D.A.A.G., 1919.
                                   Despatches (3).
                                   O.B.E.

WILLIAMS, W. D'E. ... B 00–03   (Yorkshire L.I., 1906.)
  Bt. Major   Capt., Yorkshire L.I., 1914.
G.S.O. Staff Capt.
Dep. Assistant Military Secretary.
Dep. Assistant Director of Labour.
D.A.A.G., 1918. Bt. Major.
Wounded.   *Despatches* (4).
Chevalier Légion d'Honneur.

WILLOUGHBY, G. ST. M.   F 95–96

Major, Hampshire Regt.
Retired, 1916.

WILLOUGHBY, M. E.,   ... E 78–80   (Lieut., Bengal Staff Corps, 1885. Major, I.A.,
  C.M.G.   1902.)
  Brig.-Gen.   Col., I.A., 1914.
Brigadier-General, Comm. 2nd Lancers, I.A.
D.A.Q.M.G., 1916.
Despatches (4).
C.B. Order St. Anne.

WILLS, F. N. H.   ... B 01–06
  Lieut.   Lieut., R. North Devon Yeomanry.
M.G.C.

WILLSON, L. F. WYNNE COLL. 91–98   (W.I. Regt., 1901. S. African War.)
  Major   Major, Gloucester Regt.
Officer, Cadet Wing.
Despatches.

WILSON, A. J. ...   ... B 11–16
  Lieut.   2nd Lieut., R.W. Kent Regt., 1916.
Lieut., 1917.
Att. E. Kent Regt., 2nd Bn.
M.C. Croix de Guerre.

WILSON, A. M. P.   COLL. 11–15
  Lieut.   Lieut., R.F.A., 1917.

WILSON, A. T. ...   ... D 13–17
  2nd Lieut.   2nd Lieut., Arg. and Suth. Highlanders, 1919.

✠ WILSON, C. BLAIR   ... I 0 8–13
  Major   Capt., R. Canadian Highlanders.
Major, 1916.
Killed, Sept. 15th, 1916, *Courcelette.*

WILSON, H. C. B.   ... D 88–93   (New Coll., Oxford. Yorkshire L.I.)
  Major   Major, Yorkshire L.I., 1914.
Acting Lieut.-Col., York and Lancaster Regt.,
  4th Bn.
Wounded.   *Despatches.*

✠ WILSON, J. N. ...　　... H 05–09
    Lieut.

Lieut., Acting Capt., Black Watch (R. High-
    landers).
Killed, July 4th, 1917, *Poperinghe.*

WILSON, J. N. H.　　... K 09–13
    Lieut.

2nd Lieut., R.F.A., 1915.
Lieut., 1917.
Wounded.　　　*Despatches* (2).

WILSON, J. P. ...　　... H 11–12
    Lieut.

(To Malvern College.)
2nd Lieut., R.F.A., 1916.
Lieut., 1918.
M.C.

WILSON, J. S. ...　　COLL. 03–08
    Capt.

(New Coll., Oxford.)
Capt., K.R.R.C.
War Office.
Staff Lieut., H.Q.
Wounded (2).
Order Corona d'Italia.

WILSON, M. F. F.　　... D 99–01
    Lieut.-Commander

(R.N.)
Lieut.-Commander.
H.M.S. *Calypso*, 1918.
Wounded.
D.S.O.

WILSON, M. J. H.　　... H 12–16
    2nd Lieut.

2nd Lieut., Cameron Highlanders.
Wounded.

✠ WILSON, P. J. C.　　... H 08–14

Lieut., Cameron Highlanders, 1st Bn.
Killed, May 9th, 1915, *Richebourg L'Avoué.*

WILSON, P. LEA　　... B 00–06
    Capt.

Capt., R. Irish Regt.

WILSON, R. P.　　... I 08–12
    Lieut.

2nd Lieut., R. West Kent Regt.
Lieut., 1917.

WILSON, T. N. F.　　... E 09–13
    Capt.

2nd Lieut., K.R.R.C., 1914.
Capt., 1917.
With M.G.C., 1918.
Capt. and Adjt., K.R.R.C., 1st Bn., 1919.
Despatches.
D.S.O.　M.C.

226

✠ WINGATE, M. R. ... I 07–12   (2nd Lieut., R.E., 1912.)
     Bt. Major   Lieut., R.E., 1914.
                           Capt., 1915. Staff Capt.
                           (Staff Officer to Engineer-in-Chief, D.A.A.G.)
                           26th Field Coy., 1917.
                           Brevet Major, 1918.
                           Despatches (4).
                           Killed, March 21st, 1918, *near Lagnicourt.*
                           M.C. D.S.O. Croix de Guerre.

WINKWORTH, W. W. ... c 10–14
     Lieut.   2nd Lieut., R.F.A.
                           Lieut., 1918.
                           M.C.

WINLAW, W. W. ... A 88–91   (Engineer.)
     Capt.   Capt., R.A.S.C.
                           Dep. Assistant Director M.T.
                           Despatches (2).

WINTER, C. E. ... A 07–12   (2nd Lieut., R.B., 1913.)
     formerly PURDON   Capt., and Adjt., R.B., 1916.
     Capt.   M.C.

WINTER, REV. E. E. ... G 99–03   (Trin. Coll., Cambridge.)
     C.F.   Chaplain to Forces, 1916.

WINTOUR, U. F., c.m.g.   c 91–94
                           Director of Contracts, War Office, 1914.
                           C.B. Officier Légion d'Honneur. Order
                                 Leopold.

✠ WINWOOD, T. R. O. ... F 98–99
     Capt.   Capt., R.F.A.
                           Killed, April 28th, 1917, *Salonica.*

WISELY, G. L. K. ... c 07–11   (R.F.A., 1913.)
     Capt.   Lieut., R.F.A., 1915.
                           Capt., 1917.
                           Acting Major, 1918.
                           Despatches.
                           M.C.

WISEMAN, SIR W. G. E.,   F 98–00
     BART.
        Lieut.-Col.   Capt., Duke of Cornwall's L.I., 1915.
                           War Office.
                           Temp. Lieut.-Col. till 1919.
                           Despatches.
                           C.B.

WODEHOUSE, E. ... B 07–12 (R. Welsh Fusiliers, 1913.)
Capt. Lieut., R. Welsh Fusiliers, 1914.
Capt., 1916.
Prisoner of War.
Interned in Holland, 1918.
Repatriated, 1918.
Wounded.

WOLMER, VISCOUNT ... F 00–03
Capt. Capt., Hampshire Regt., 3rd Bn., 1914.

WOOD, A. H. ... ... A 82–84 (K.R.R.C., 1887.)
Major Major, R. Sussex Regt.

✠ WOOD, C. HARALD ... I 09–14
2nd Lieut. 2nd Lieut., K.R.R.C., 9th Bn., 1915.
Died, Aug. 25th, 1916, *of wounds received Aug.
24th, Delville Wood.*

WOOD, H. L. ... ... B 92–97 (Oxford L.I., 1898. Capt., 1905. S. African War.),
Major Major, Oxford and Bucks L.I., 1915.
Brigade-Major, 1915.
G.S.O.$_2$, 1916.
Temp. Lieut.-Col., 1917.
Wounded.

WOODCOCK, W. J. ... G 92–96 (Lancs. Fusiliers, 1898. S. African War. Capt.
Bt. Lieut.-Col. 1901. Retired, 1913.)
Lieut.-Colonel, Lancashire Fusiliers.
Employed Manchester Regt., 7th Bn.
Temp. Brigadier-General, 1918.
Wounded. *Despatches.*
D.S.O. Chevalier Légion d'Honneur. Croix de
Guerre.

✠ WOODHOUSE, REV. D. C. I 97–02
C.F. Chaplain to Forces.
Died in Hospital, Oct. 6th, 1916, *result of
exposure in trench duties.*

WOODHOUSE, R. ... B 68–72 (Trin. Coll., Cambridge. S. African War.)
Major Major, Essex Yeomanry.
T.F.R.

✠ WOODHOUSE, R. C. ... H 06–11
Lieut. Lieut., R.H.A., Warwickshire.
Killed, Aug. 14th, 1915, *Zillebeke.*

WOODMAN, W. J. ... A 85–89 (Colonial Medical Service, Hong-Kong.)
Capt. Capt., R.A.M.C., Constantinople, 1918.

228

WOODS, G. C. ... COLL. 97–03 (Pemb. Coll., Cambridge.)
Lieut. Lieut., R.G.A., 1917.

WOOSNAM, M. ... ... F 05–10 (Trin. Coll., Cambridge.)
Lieut. Lieut., Montgomeryshire Yeomanry, 1916.
Acting Capt., 1918.

✠ WORDSWORTH, O. B. COLL. 99–06
2nd Lieut. 2nd Lieut., M.G.C., 21st Coy.
Killed, April 2nd, 1917, *Henin sur Cojeul.*

WORDSWORTH, R. J. ... C 01–06
Major Major, Notts and Derby Regt., 8th Bn., 1915.
Staff Capt.
D.A.Q.M.G., 1918.
Despatches (2).
D.S.O.

✠ WORSLEY, E. G. ... A 98–03 (Magd. Coll., Oxford.)
2nd Lieut. 2nd Lieut., Grenadier Guards.
Killed Sept. 17th, 1916, *Corbie.*

✠ WORSLEY, J. F. ... A 02–07
Lieut., Grenadier Guards.
Killed Nov. 27th, 1917, *Fontaine Notre Dame,
near Cambrai.*

WORTHAM, O. O. ... E 90–90
Capt. Capt., Army Ordnance Corps.
Assistant Inspector, Ordnance Dept.
Temp. Major, 1918.

WORTHINGTON, L. J. ... E 05–08
Major Major, Derbyshire Yeomanry.
Comm. Notts and Derby Mounted Brigade
Signal Troop.
R.E., 20th Corps, Signal Coy., Egypt.
Wounded.
Order of Nile.

WREFORD, J. M. R. ... D 12–16
Lieut. 2nd Lieut., Irish Guards.
Lieut., 1918.
Wounded.

WREY, W. A. B. ... F 98–01
Capt. Capt., R.E.

WRIGHT, E. H. D 09–12
FAULCONER- Capt., Suffolk Regt., 1917.
Instructor, M.G., R.M. College.

229

✠ WRIGHT, E. I. ...   ... G 98–04   (New Coll., Oxford.)
     Capt.   Capt., Oxford and Bucks L.I.
                                        G.S.O.₃. Brigade-Major.
   Killed May 11th, 1918, *Barly.*
   Despatches (2).
   M.C.

WRIGHT, F. L.   ... G 07–11   (W. Yorkshire Regt., 1913.)
     Capt.   Capt., W. Yorkshire Regt., 1916.
   G.S.O.₃.
   Wounded.   *Despatches.*
   h.p., ill-health, 1918.

WRIGHT, G. L. ...   ... G 96–01   (Univ. Coll., Oxford.)
     Capt.   Lieut., R.F.A., N. Midland Brigade.
   Capt., 1917.
   M.C.

WRIGHT, J. A. CECIL   ... A 00–04
     Major   Hon. Major, R.A.S.C.
   R.A.F., Acting Capt., A.

WRIGHT, M. N.   ... C 90–93   (Yorkshire Yeomanry.)
     Major   Major, Remount Service, T.F.R.

WRIGHT, P. L. .   ... G 05–09
     Capt.   Capt. and Adjt., Oxford and Bucks L.I., 1917
   Acting Major, 1918.
   Despatches (2).
   M.C.   D.S.O.

WRIGHT, P. L. M.   ... F 12–17
     Lieut.   2nd Lieut., R.F.A., 1918.
   Lieut., 1919.

WRIGHT, R. M.   COLL. 03–09

   Capt., Coldstream Guards.
   Acting Major, Guards, M.G. Regt., 1917.
   Wounded (2).   *Despatches.*
   M.C. and Bar.

WYATT, G. N. ...   ... I 90–93   (R.F.A., 1897. Tirah Exp. Capt., 1904.)
     Lieut.-Col.   Lieut.-Col., R.F.A., 1917.
   Chief Instructor, R.M. Academy.

✠ WYATT, G. W. P.   ... D 09–15
     Lieut.   Lieut., E. Kent Regt.
   Killed Sept. 15th, 1916, *near Guillemont, Battle*
      of Somme.

✠ WYATT, H. G. P. ... D 04–09
    2nd Lieut.
2nd Lieut., Sussex Yeomanry.
Died in Hospital, Alexandria, Nov. 12th, 1915.

WYATT, O. E. P. ... D 11–16
    Lieut.
2nd Lieut., R.F.A., 1918.
Lieut., 1919.
M.C.

WYATT, R. J. P. ... G 06–11
    Capt.
    Brevet Major
Capt., Duke of Wellington's W. Riding Regt.,
    1915.
Gen. List. G.S.O.$_3$.
Despatches (3).
M.C. and Bar.

WYATT, W. ... ... D 11–16
    Lieut.
2nd Lieut., 21st Lancers.
Lieut., 1918.

WYLD, J. W. G. ... A 10–13
    Capt.
Lieut., Oxford and Bucks L.I., 1914.
Staff Capt., G.S.O.$_3$, 1916.
Capt., Brigade-Major, 1917.
G.S.O.$_2$, 1918.
Despatches (4).
M.C. and Bar. D.S.O.

✠ WYLIE, C. H. M.   COLL. 82–87
    DOUGHTY-, C.M.G.
(R. W. Fusiliers.   Capt., 1896.   Soudan.
    S. African War.)
Lieut.-Col., R. Welsh Fusiliers.
𝖁.𝕮. C.B.
Killed April 26th, 1915, *Sedd-ul-Bahr.*

YATES, H. W. M.   ... I 97–00
    Brevet Major
(Lancs. Fusiliers, 1903.   Lieut., Royal Irish
    Fusiliers, 1908.   Capt., 1913.)
Capt., Royal Irish Fusiliers.
Staff Capt., A.A.Q.M.G.
D.A.A.G., 1916.
Despatches.

YATES, J. M. ST. J.   ... I 92–97
    Lieut.
(Trin. Coll., Camb.   Barrister.)
Lieut., Lancashire Fusiliers.

YATES, O. ST. J. L.   ... K 13–17
    Pte.
Pte., Hampshire Regt.

✠ YEATHERD, M. L. ... F 97–01   (7th Hussars, 1903.)
   Capt.   Capt., 12th Lancers.
                             Killed April 11th, 1917, *Wancourt, Arras.*

✠ YEATHERD, R. G. H. ... F 04–08   (Ch. Ch., Oxford.)
   Lieut.   Lieut., 2nd Dragoon Guards.
                            Wounded (2).   *Despatches.*
                            Killed Sept., 15th, 1916, *Guinchy, Battle of
                               the Somme.*

✠ YEATMAN, H. F. ... C 93–98   (Ch. Ch., Oxford.)
   Capt.   Capt., Dorset Yeomanry.
                           Killed Jan., 1918.

   YEATMAN, L. L. ... C 93–98   (Ch. Ch., Oxford.)
   Lieut.   Lieut., Dorset Yeomanry, July 17th.
                           Acting Capt., Adjt.

✠ YEATMAN, M. E. ... G 97–01   (S.W. Borderers, 1903.)
   Capt.   Capt., S. Wales Borderers.
                           Killed Sept., 15th, 1914, *Battle of the Aisne.*

   YORKE, H. R. ... ... D 88–91   (Black Watch, 1896. Munster Fusiliers, Lieut.,
   Capt.   1900.)
                            Capt., Munster Fusiliers.
                            Comm. Depot Dorset Regt.

   YORSTOUN, M. A. ... F 10–14
   CARTHEW-
   Lieut.   2nd Lieut., Black Watch (Royal Highlanders),
                               1916.
                           Lieut., 1917. A.D.C.
                           M.B.E.·

   YOUNG, L. E. ... ... I 05–10
                           Lieut., I.A.R.O., 38th Dogras.

   YOUNG, W. W. ... ... I 03–07
   Capt.   2nd Lieut., R.B.
                           Capt., 1917.

                           Prisoner of War.
                           Interned in Holland.
                           Repatriated, 1919.
                           Wounded.   *Despatches.*

✠ YOUNGER, C. F. ... F 99–04   (New Coll., Oxford.)
   Lieut.   Lieut., Lothian and Border Yeomanry.
                            Died March 21st, 1917, *Aveluy, near Albert,
                               of wounds received* March 20th.

   YOUNGER, H. J.... ... I 12–16
                           2nd Lieut., Highland L.I., 1917.

YOUNGER, J. ... ... F 93–99 (New Coll., Oxford.)
    Lieut.-Col.   Major, Fife and Forfar Yeomanry.
                                           Posted to Black Watch, 14th Bn.
                                           Lieut.-Col., 1918.
                                           Wounded.   *Despatches (2).*
                                           T.D.

YOUNGER, J. A. C. ... F 84–87 (Reserve of Officers.)
    Major   Major, R.G.A., 1914.

YOUNGER, J. W. H. B. I 11–16
    Lieut.   2nd Lieut., R.G.A.
                                             Lieut., 1918.

YOUNGER, W. J. ... c 81–86 (Trin. Coll., Camb.)
    Lieut.-Col.   Lieut.-Col., Royal Scots.
                                           Relinquished Commission.

ADDENDUM.

Foster, M. R. ... ... A 07–11
                                         2nd Lieut., I.A.R.O.
                                           T. Capt., 1918, N.W.F.F.

LIST OF QUIRISTERS.

BENNETT, D. J.   ... 96–02 Australian Contingent.

BENNETT, G. W.   ... 06–10 Signalling Bombardier, R.F.A.

BENNETT, H. T.   ... 09–13 Corporal, Argyll and Sutherland Highlanders.

BENNETT, J. H.   ... 88–93 Co.-Col.-Sergt., R.B.
                                   Wounded.
                                   D.C.M.

BREWER, H. G.   ... 04–08 Private.

CATER, F. L.   ...   ... 98–99 2nd Lieut., A.S.C.

CHAMBERS, P. R.   ... 11–16 Pioneer, R.E. Signal Service.

✠ CLIFT, T. V.   ...   ... 01–06 Private, 1/15th London Regt.   Civil Service Rifles.
                                   Killed at Verbranden Molan, Nov. 16th, 1916.

CONDUIT, F. C. ...   ... 02–04 R.G.A.

CONDUIT, E. W.   ... 93–97 Lieut., 229th Overseas Batt. (Canada).

CONDUIT, G. W.   ... 01–06 Capt., Mounted Gun Section.

CROFT, E. A.   ...   ... 96–01 Lieut., 340th Battery, R.G.A.

CROFT, H. G.   ...   ... 96–00 2nd Lieut., 6th Loyal North Lancs.

DAVIDGE, A. J.   ... 04–11 Sapper, R.E.

DAVIDGE, H. F.   ... 01–07 Sergeant, Hampshire Regt., 15th Bn.

DAVIDGE, H. L.   ... 97–03 Sapper, R.E.

DAVIDGE, R. G.   ... 10–15 Pilot Sergeant, R.A.F.

DOWN, A.   ...   ... 06–11 Private, Hampshire Regt., 6th Bn.

GARDINER, C. A.   ... 02–08 Corporal, R.A.M.C.

GOLDING, F. W.	...	97–02	Sergeant, Bedford Regt. *Missing.*
✠ JOHNSON, F.	...	07–10	Private, M.G.C. *Killed in France* Jan. 29th, 1918.
LONGBOTTOM, G. G.	...	04–10	1st A.M., R.A.F.
LONGBOTTOM, H. H.	...	02–07	2nd A.M., R.A.F.
MARTIN, R. J. ...	...	10–15	Private, Berkshire Regt.
MAY, F. A.	...	02–09	L.-Corporal, R.E.
MAY, H. A.	...	09–15	R.A.F.
McCARTHY, H. G.	...	03–08	8th Cavalry Brigade, M.G.C.
MOSS, E. J.	...	91–96	Private, Hampshire Regt.
MUNDEN, W. J.	...	05–11	City of London Rough Riders.
PAVEY, A. E. ...	...	96–02	Private, R.A.M.C.
PEARCE, C.	...	90–96	R.G.A.
PENDERED, G. S.	...	93–98	Private, London Regt.
✠ POWELL, A.	...	97–02	Private, 2/22nd London Regt., C.M.G.C. *Killed* July 29th, 1916, *Vimy Ridge.*
PRITCHARD, A. J.	...	02–09	Capt., Pioneer Bn. *Wounded.*
ROBERTS, A. E.	...	03–09	R.A.F.
SAUNDERS, C. ...	...	09–13	Private, Hampshire Regt., 4th Bn.
SEARGENT, W. H.	...	80–87	Sergeant, Hampshire Regt., 4th Bn.
SPARKS, V. R. ...	...	07–13	Private, Hampshire Regt., 4th Bn.
SPIRE, D. A.	...	11–14	Sergeant, 51st Hampshire Regt.
SPRINGETT, H. ...	...	08–12	Private, 2nd Life Guards.
TAYLOR, E. D. ...	...	09–14	Private, Argyll and Sutherland Highlanders.
TAYLOR, F.	...	10–16	Private, 2/1st Q.O.W.H.

✠ TILBURY, A. ... ... 96–03 Capt., Heavy Trench Mortar Battery, 58th Div.
Killed at Bullecourt, June 8th, 1917.

TILBURY, ED. ... ... 91–98 Major, G.H.Q. Staff, 2nd Echelon.

TILBURY, ERNEST ... 98–05 Asst. Paymaster, R.N.R.

TONG, A. E. ... ... 96–01 Private, Hampshire Regt.
Wounded.

TRAVIS, R. W. ... ... 98–03 2nd Lieut., Royal Warwickshire Regt.
Wounded.

TUERSLEY, A. J. ... 86–92 Bombardier, R.H.A.

✠ WILSON, D. O. ... ... 07–11 2nd Lieut., Royal Irish Fusiliers.
Killed on the Somme.

✠ YOUNG, L. ... ... 08–14 Lieut., R.A.F.
Killed Oct. 4th, 1918, *Cambrai East.*

APPENDIX.

Prayers in use at Winchester College.

MAY, 1916.

1.—A Prayer for Wykehamists and Friends on Service.

ALMIGHTY God, the Refuge of all that put their trust in Thee, we beseech Thee to protect and bless all those who have gone forth from this School, and from our own homes and families, to serve their King and Country. Thou knowest the places where they are, and the trials and dangers which beset them. In all their perils bring to the heart of each, O Lord, the comfort of Thy presence, and the assurance of Thy unchanging love and power. Give them Thy grace at all times to discern and do their duty; and grant that in dangers often, in watchings often, in weariness often, they may serve Thee with a quiet mind; through Jesus Christ, our Lord.

2.—A Prayer in Remembrance of our Fallen.

O MERCIFUL God, with whom do live the spirits of them that depart hence in the Lord, we desire to remember those with whom in Thee we still have fellowship, whose lives on earth were knit with ours, and whose deaths have brought us nearer to the Death of Thy dear Son. We bless Thy Holy Name for the example of their sacrifice, and commend their souls to Thy most loving mercy, in sure and certain hope of the Resurrection to eternal life; through our Redeemer, Jesus Christ.

3.—A Prayer for our Prisoners, Wounded, and Sick.

O GOD of Mercy, and Giver of all Comfort, we commend to Thy Fatherly care our prisoners, our wounded, and our sick; that Thou wouldest give them patience to endure all trials that they are called upon to bear. And may Thy Holy Spirit, the Comforter, abide with them; that in weakness or in loneliness, in pain of body or distress of mind, they may feel Thy presence and renew their hope in Thee. O let the sorrowful sighing of the prisoners come before Thee, and preserve Thou those that are appointed to die. Hear us, O Father, for His sake who Himself hath borne our griefs and carried our sorrows, our Saviour, Jesus Christ.

237

4.—A Prayer for Grace that we may be made worthy of Victory.

O ETERNAL Father, who hast called us to be citizens of this Realm and Empire, and hast given us such helps as we have beyond so many others, enable us, we beseech Thee, even here and now to do our Country service. Make plain to us Thy teaching in this time of trial; give us understanding minds and daily remembrance of our calling. Help us to seek out the evil in our own lives, and so manfully to fight against it, that we may in all ways help the lives of others, and with ready will prepare ourselves for Thy Divine purpose. O Thou who hast made us members one of another, help us all to bear and to forbear; and so support our ignorance by Thy wisdom, our weakness by Thy strength, that we may be found worthy in Thine own good time to receive Thy blessing of Victory and Peace; through Jesus Christ, our Lord.

Lightning Source UK Ltd.
Milton Keynes UK
UKOW04f1829220814

237400UK00001B/13/A

9 781843 424239